MW01127769

Uncommon Bible Studies

Topical Bibles Studies on Subjects
Not Commonly Found in Church

BY

Daniel E. Loeb

Dwell with Prudence Publishing © 2005

Uncommon Bible Studies
Topical Bible studies on subjects not commonly found in church
By Daniel E. Loeb

Copyright © 2005 by Daniel E. Loeb
Published by Dwell with Prudence Publishing
Dwellwithprudence.com

ISBN: 1-4116-5882-5

Printed and Distributed by Lulu Press

Table of Contents

Preface

This book consists of uncommon bible studies on a variety of topics that are not normally taught in churches. I did not become a Christian until I was an adult. I did not grow up going to church, which allows me to view the Bible differently than many Christians that did grow up going to a church. By not growing up in a church I did not receive any of the enculturated beliefs taught by many churches. Whenever I have a question about Christianity I go to the Bible for the answers.

The Bible studies in this book are the result of some of my quests for answers. Many of these topics focus on concerns I had shortly after becoming and Christian, and others are matters of doctrine that I have been researching for several years.

There is a large difference between the concept of what a Christian is that you are enculturated to believe in modern day society, and what the Bible teaches a Christian should be. Many modern day Christians dress up in their finest clothes and go to church every Sunday. While at church they worship a triune godhead different from the God in the Bible. Many modern day Christians confuse the attitudes of Christ with the attitudes of Gandhi.

There is also a tendency to confuse Christianity with Political Correctness. Modern churches are beginning to allow female and homosexual pastors to teach in their churches, not because the Bible has changed, but because the culture has. Some modern churches are driven by politically correctness instead of Biblical teaching. Just being a good person doesn't make you a Christian. Many people that grew up in churches don't know the first thing about being a Christian.

Some people don't read the Bible and teach unbiblical doctrines like, *"God loves you for who you are, and when you die you will go to Heaven no matter what."* Others when confronted with scripture will make statements like, *"that's not my God, my God is a loving God that loves everybody and would never condemn anyone to hell."* The problem with these people is that their God is a figment of their imaginations, and not the God of the scriptures.

Some modern churches practice speaking in tongues and being slain in the spirit. People prophecy things in direct contradiction to the Bible and say that their teachings come from the Holy Spirit and therefore are true. If you challenge these people with scripture they say that you are blaspheming the work of the Holy Spirit, and committing the only unforgivable sin.

The only way to truly be a Christian is to follow Christ, and the example set forth in the Bible. Christians cannot allow the changes in culture and society to redefine what a Christian is supposed to be. God doesn't care what changes have taken place in our culture, or who has what rights now. God cares that we obey His commandments, and the teachings set forth in the Bible.

The Topical Bible studies contained in this book were written as apart of my own quest to determine what the scriptures teach on these different topics. These topics are made available to you so that you can benefit from my research. This book is not meant to be read in order from cover to cover, but to allow you to read whatever chapter is relevant to your Christian walk at that time in your life. You may not agree with my interpretations of the included scriptures, but having all of the verses together may help you to gain a better understanding of the material. The goal of all Christians is to serve God, my hope is that through these Bible studies you may know or serve God better.

The Door

In this Bible study we will be discussing some of the most important verses in the Bible, because they have to do with saving your soul. All Bible verses in this chapter are taken from the New American Standard version of the Bible.

(NASB) Luke 13:23-28 And someone said to him," Lord, are there just a few who are being saved?" And He said to them, 24 "Strive to enter through the narrow door; for many, will seek to enter but will not be able. 25 "Once the head of the house gets up and shuts the door, and you begin to stand outside and knock on the door saying, "Lord, open up to us!' Then He will answer and say to you, 'I do not know where you are from.' 26 Then you will begin to say, 'We ate and drank in Your presence, and You taught in our streets'; 27 and He will say,' I tell you, I do not know where you are from; DEPART FROM ME, ALL YOU EVIL DOERS.' 28 "In that place there will be weeping and gnashing of teeth when you see Abraham and Isaac and Jacob and all the prophets in the kingdom of God, but yourselves being thrown out.

(NASB) Matt 25:10-13 "And while they were going away to make the purchase, the bridegroom came, and those who were ready went in with him to the wedding feast; and the door was shut. 11 "Later the other virgins also came , saying, Lord, Lord, open up for us.' 12 But he answered ,'Truly I say to you, I do not know you.' 13 "Be on the alert then, for you do not know the day nor the hour.

(NASB) Matt 7:21-24 "Not everyone who says to me, 'Lord,Lord,' will enter the kingdom of heaven, but he who does the will of My Father who is in heaven will enter. 22 "Many will say to me on that day,'Lord,Lord, did we not prophesy in Your name, and in Your name cast out demons, and in Your name perform many miracles?' 23 "And then I will declare to them,' I never knew you; DEPART FROM ME, YOU WHO PRACTICE LAWLESSNESS,'

The above verses state that there will be a time when it will be to late to enter the kingdom of heaven. The way to enter heaven is to do the will of the Father who is in heaven, and by hearing the words of Jesus and acting upon them.

(NASB) Luke 11:7 and from inside he answers and says, 'Do not bother me; the door has already been shut and my children and I are in bed; I cannot get up and give you anything.

(NASB) Proverbs 1:24,25,27,28,29 "Because I called and you refused, I stretch out my hand and no one paid attention; 25 And you neglected all my counsel And did not want my reproof; 27 When your dread comes on you like a storm And calamity comes like a whirlwind, When distress and anguish come upon you. 28 "They will call on me, but I will not answer; They will seek me diligently but they will not find me, 29 Because they hated knowledge and did not choose to fear the Lord.

(NASB) Amos 8:10-12 "Then I will turn your festivals into mourning And all your songs into lamentation; And I will bring sackcloth on everyone's loins And baldness on every head. And I will make it like a time of mourning for an only son, And the end of it will be a bitter day.11 "Behold, days are coming," declares the Lord God, "When I will send a famine on the land, Not a famine for bread or thirst for water, But rather for hearing the words of the LORD. 12 "People will stagger from sea to sea And from the north even the east; They will go to and fro to seek the word of the LORD, But they will not find it.

The above verses also state that there will be a time when the door will be closed and it will be to late. They also state why the door will be shut to them, because they did not hear and heed the words of God when they had the chance.

(NASB) James 5:8-9 You too be patient; strengthen your hearts,for the coming of the Lord is near. 9 Do not complain, brethren, against one another, so that you yourselves may not be judged; behold, the Judge is standing right at the door

(NASB) Mark 13:29 Even so, you too, when you see these things happening, recognize that He is near, right at the door.

The previous verses state that you need to be prepared for the coming of the Lord, because He is right at the door.

(NASB) Luke 12:42-46 And the Lord said,"Who then is the faithful and sensible steward, whom his master will put in charge of his servants, to give them their rations at the proper time? 43 "Blessed is that slave whom his master finds him so doing when he comes. 44 "Truly I say to you that he will put him in charge of all his possessions. 45 "But if that slave says in his heart,'My master will be along time in coming,' and begins to beat the slaves, both men and women, and to eat and drink and get drunk; 46 the master of that slave will come on a day when he does not expect him and at an hour he does not know, and will cut him to pieces, and assign him a place with the unbelievers.

(NASB) Matt 7:16-20 "You will know them by their fruits. Grapes are not gathered from thorn bushes nor figs from thistles, are they? 17 So every good tree bears good fruit, but the bad tree bears bad fruit. 18 "A good tree cannot produce bad fruit, nor can a bad tree produce good fruit. 19 "Every tree that does not bear good fruit is cut down and thrown into the fire 20 "So then, you will know them by there fruits.

(NASB) Matt 3:10 "The axe is already at the root of the tree; therefore every tree that does not bear good fruit is cut down and thrown into the fire.

The above verses show that you need to be prepared, because you don't know when the Lord is coming. You need to make sure you are bearing good fruit, and acting according to God's will so that you will not be cast out and thrown into the fire.

(NASB) Matt 3:2 "Repent for the kingdom of heaven is at hand."

(NASB) Romans 3:23 for all have sinned and fall short of the glory of God,

(NASB) Luke 13: 5 "I tell you, no, but unless you repent, you will all likewise perish."

The previous verses say you need to repent of your sins or you will likewise perish, and that the kingdom of heaven is at hand. This means you need to repent now. Time is running out. Romans 3:23 states that everyone has sinned and all need to repent.

(NASB) 2 Peter 3:9,13,14 The Lord is not slow about His promise, as some count slowness, but is patient toward you, not wishing for any to perish but for all to come to repentance. 13 But according to His promise we are looking for new heavens and a new earth, in which righteousness dwells. 14 Therefore, beloved, since you look for these things, be diligent to be found by Him in peace, spotless and blameless,

(NASB) Luke 15:7 "I tell you that in the same way, there will be more joy in heaven over one sinner who repents than over ninety-nine righteous persons who need no repentance.

The previous verses show how much God loves you. He is not being slow in coming, but patient with us giving everyone time to repent. We know from earlier verses in this study that there will be a time when it will be to late, but because of God's mercy He has given us time to repent; not wanting any to perish but for all to repent. Luke 15:7 tells us how overjoyed all the heavens are when a sinner repents.

(NASB) Luke 16:30-31 But he said, 'No, father Abraham, but if someone goes to them from the dead, they will repent!' 31 "But he said to him, 'If they do not listen to Moses and the Prophets, they will not be persuaded even if someone rises from the dead.'"

Luke 16:30-31 shows how reluctant sinners are to repent. They want a sign to call them to repentance; like someone rising from the dead. We all know that this sign was given through our Lord Jesus Christ who Himself was raised from the dead, and He spent His entire life calling sinners to repentance. Jesus' life is an example to us all that we need to carry on Jesus' work, calling sinners to repentance, and doing the will of our Father in heaven.

(NASB) James 5:19-20 My brethren, if any among you strays from the truth and one turns him back, 20 let him know that he who turns a sinner from the error of his way will save his soul from death and will cover a multitude of sins.

(NASB) Matt 28:19-20 "Go therefore and make disciples of all the nations, baptizing them in the name of the Father and the Son and the Holy Spirit, 20 teaching them to observe all that I commanded you; and lo, I am with you always, even to the end of the age."

(NASB) Romans 12:1-2 Therefore I urge you, brethren, by the mercies of God, to present your bodies a living and holy sacrifice, acceptable to God, which is your spiritual service of worship. 2 And do not be conformed to this world, but be transformed by the renewing of your mind, so that you may prove what the will of God is, that which is good and acceptable and perfect.

(NASB) Phil 2:3-5 Do nothing from selfishness or empty conceit, but with humility of mind regard one another as more important than yourselves; 4 do not merely look out for your own personal interests, but also for the interests of others. 5 Have this attitude in yourselves which was also in Christ Jesus,

The previous verses describe how we are to live, and how we are to serve God; by calling sinners to repentance, preaching to others, making them disciples also, obeying all His commands, renewing our minds, presenting our bodies as living sacrifices, and serving others with more concern for them than for ourselves.

(NASB) Luke 17:9-10 "He does not thank the slave because he did the things which were commanded does he?" 10 "So you too, when you do all the things which are commanded you, say, 'We are unworthy slaves; we have done only that which we ought to have done.'"

Luke 17:9-10 reminds us to always remain humble, because we are saved by God's grace, and not by our works. Obeying God's will and serving Him is not a way of earning our way into heaven, but in doing so we are following His commandments. Of course you cannot get into heaven if you do not obey His commandments, but you do not earn your way in by doing so. Remember Romans 3:23 states that we all fall short of the glory of God, and that while observing all of God's commands it is by God's grace that we are allowed to enter His kingdom. Following God's commands and living by Jesus' example is very important, as you will see in the following verses.

(NASB) Joshua 22:5 "Only be very careful to observe the commandment and law which Moses the servant of the Lord commanded you, to love the Lord your God and walk in all His ways and keep His commandments and hold fast to Him and serve Him with all your heart and with all your soul.

(NASB) 1 John 2:3,6 By this we know that we have come to know Him, if we keep his commandments. 6 the one who says he abides in Him ought himself to walk in the same manner as He walked.

(NASB) 1 John 3:16-18 We know love by this, that He laid down His life for us; and we ought to lay down our lives for the brethren. 17 But whoever has the world's goods, and sees his brother in need and closes his heart against him, how does the love of God abide in him? 18 Little children, let us not love with word or with tongue, but in deed and truth.

(NASB) James 2:17,20,24 Even so faith, if it has no works, is dead, being by itself. 20 But are you willing to recognize, you foolish fellow, that faith without works is useless? 24 You see that man is justified by works and not by faith alone.

(NASB) Gal 6:10 So then, while we have opportunity, let us do good to all people, and especially to those who are of the house hold of faith.

(NASB) Hebrews 6:10 For God is not unjust so as to forget your work and the love which you have shown toward His name, in having ministered and in still ministering to the saints.

(NASB) Hebrews 13:15-16 Through Him then, let us continually offer up a sacrifice of praise to God, that is, the fruit of lips that give thanks to His name.16 And do not neglect doing good and sharing, for with such sacrifices God is pleased.

You can see from the previous verses that you are justified and please God by works, deeds, obeying God's will and commandments, and by giving thanks to His name in everything that you do. You are saved by God's grace, but it is necessary and very important to take every opportunity to do good works as well.

(NASB) 1Peter 4:18 AND IF IT IS WITH DIFFICULTY THAT THE RIGHTEOUS IS SAVED, WHAT WILL BECOME OF THE GODLESS MAN AND THE SINNER?

(NASB) 1 Thess 4:6-8 and that no man transgress and defraud his brother in the matter because the Lord is the avenger in all these things, just as we also told you before and solemnly warned you. 7 for God has not called us for the purpose of impurity, but in sanctification. 8 So, he who does this is not rejecting man but the God who gives His Holy Spirit to you.

(NASB) Matt 22:11-14 But when the king came to look over the dinner guest, he saw a man there that was not dressed in wedding clothes, 12 and he said to him, 'Friend, how did you come in here without wedding clothes?' And the man was speechless. 13 "Then the king said to the servants, 'Bind him hand and foot, and thrown him into the outer darkness; in that place there will be weeping and gnashing of teeth,' 14 "For many are called, but few are chosen."

(NASB) Mat 25:42,45,46 for I was hungry, and you gave Me nothing to eat; I was thirsty, and you gave Me nothing to drink; 45 Then He will answer them, 'Truly I say to you, to the extent that you did not do it to Me,' 46 "These will go away into eternal punishment, but the righteous into eternal life."

(NASB) Rev 21:12 "Behold, I am coming quickly, and My reward is with Me, to render to every man according to what he has done.

(NASB) Rev 3:7,8.10,11 "And to the angel of the church in Philadelphia write: He who is holy, who is true, who has the key of David, who opens and no one will shut, and who shuts and know one opens says this: 8 'I know your deeds. Behold, I have put before you an open door which no one can shut, because you have a little power, and have kept My word, and have not denied My name. 10 'Because you have kept My word and My perseverance, I also will keep you from the hour of testing, that hour which is about to come upon the whole world, to test whose who dwell on the earth.11 'I am coming quickly; hold fast what you have, so that no one will take your crown.

The previous verses tell us that it is difficult even for the righteous to enter heaven, and that the Lord is a rewarder and an avenger. He is right at the door and is coming quickly, and will render unto everyone according to what they have done. Our God is a God of justice and mercy, and we are and will be held accountable for the things that we do and the things that we don't do while here on earth. We must take every opportunity to serve Him. We need to hold fast to His teachings and obey all of His commandments.

(NASB) John 10:9 I am the door; if anyone enters through Me, he will be saved, and will go in and out and find pasture.

(NASB) Rev 3:20-21 Behold, I stand at the door and knock; if anyone hears My voice and opens the door, I will come in to him and dine with him, and he with Me. 21 'He who overcomes, I will grant to him to sit down with Me on My throne, as I also overcame and sat down with My Father on His throne.

(NASB) Luke 11:9-10 "So I say to you, ask, and it will be given to you; seek, and you will find; knock , and it will be opened to you. 10 "For everyone who asks, receives; and he who seeks, finds; and to him who knocks, it will be opened.

The previous verses state that Jesus is the door; if you seek Him you will find Him. His gift is for everyone who follows Him and the example He set. It is not God's will that any should perish, and He is willing to share His throne with us even though we are unworthy of it. All that He asks is that we love Him and each other, believe in Him, and obey His commandments.

(NASB) Mark 16:15-16 And He said, "Go into all the world and preach the gospel to all creation. 16 "He who has believed and has been baptized shall be saved; but he who has disbelieved shall be condemned.

(NASB) Rev 22:17 The Spirit and the bride say, "Come." And let the one who hears say, "Come". And let the one who is thirsty come; let the one who wishes take the water of life without cost.

The previous verses tell us to peach to all creation, calling sinners to repentance, spreading the words of Christ and the commandments of God to all creation, which is our duty as Christians. All who believe and are baptized will be saved. Rev 22:17 is a call to all sinners, all who thirst for righteousness, and all who hear the words of Jesus, to follow Him and receive His gift of eternal life, and entrance into His kingdom without cost. Rev 22:17 also says for those who are His followers (Christians) to call for Jesus to come quickly so that we may live and dwell in the house of righteousness forever.

If you are not a Christian (a follower of Jesus), I urge you to repent and be baptized, follow Jesus and obey His commands. Do it now. Don't delay, for the kingdom of heaven is at hand. He is right at the door and coming quickly. Realize that once the door is shut it will be too late. Waste no time; repent from your sins and live your life for Jesus with a newness of mind worship Him in spirit and truth in everything you do loving God and serving others. Choose not to be locked out of the door and thrown into the fire with the unbelievers; but serve Him who gave you life in the first place, and offers you life eternal.

If you are a Christian I hope this Bible study reminds you to hold fast to what you have been commanded. Examine your hearts and the way you live, Rev.22: 17 says to say, "Come", are you confident in your heart that you are ready to say that. If Jesus were to come this hour would He catch you sleeping or are you prepared for His coming? Are you working diligently to be found by Him in peace, spotless and blameless? Do you bear good fruits? Have you been spreading the gospel, and loving your neighbor as yourself?

Do you feel that you live a righteous life and obey His commands to the point that you say, "COME!" If so hold fast to what you have and keep up your faith, because he is right at the door and coming quickly. He who made the promise is faithful, so you know He is coming quickly, and all He said will come to pass. If you are not yet in your heart confident enough to say, "COME!" remember that there is no time like the present. Start serving God in everything you do, offer prayers of thanksgiving, and devote your life to doing the will of our Father in heaven; so that when He comes you will be ready.

References

The Bride

You are invited to a wedding. Not a wedding like we have on earth, but the ultimate wedding between the bridegroom and the bride; Christ and His saints. This Bible study is on the bridegroom and the bride; the preparation for the wedding feast, and your salvation.

(NASB) Matt 22:2-3, 5, 7-14 "The kingdom of heaven may be compared to a king who gave a wedding feast for his son. 3 "And he sent out his slaves to call those who have been invited to the wedding feast, and they were unwilling to come. 5"But they paid no attention and went their way, one to his own farm, another to his business, 7 "But the king was enraged, and he sent his armies and destroyed those murderers and set their city on fire. 8 "Then he said to his slaves, 'The wedding is ready, but those who were invited were not worthy. 9 'Go therefore to the main highways, and as many as you find there, invite to the wedding feast.' 10 "Those slaves went out into the streets and gathered together all they found, both evil and good; and the wedding hall was filled with dinner guests. 11 "But when the king came to look over the dinner guest, he saw a man there that was not dressed in wedding clothes, 12 and he said to him, 'Friend , how did you come in here without wedding clothes?' And the man was speechless. 13 "Then the king said to the servants, 'Bind him hand and foot, and thrown him into the outer darkness; in that place there will be weeping and gnashing of teeth,'14 "For many are called, but few are chosen."

The above parable that Jesus spoke is important for us to understand. As you will learn in this Bible study the above verses have to do with Christ's return to earth, and the judgment of the people on the earth who in this parable are at the wedding feast. In the above verses a wedding guest was thrown out into outer darkness, which represents being cast into hell. In this Bible study I'm not going to explain why the weeping and gnashing of teeth represents hell, but I will include verses on why the wedding guest was thrown out, who the bridegroom is, and who the wedding guests are. The above verses speak about people who are invited to a wedding feast, but are too busy in their own lives to go. They miss their opportunity and in turn lose their salvation. These verses are a constant reminder for us to always put God first in our lives, and to be ready for His return.

(NASB) Ephesians 5:22-25, 27-33 Wives, be subject to your own husbands, as to the Lord. 23 For the husband is the head of the wife, as Christ is the head of the church, He Himself being the Savior of the body. 24 But as the church is subject to Christ, so also the wives ought to be to their husbands in everything. 25 Husbands, love your wives, just as Christ also loved the church and gave Himself up for her, 27 that He might present to Himself the church in all her glory, having no spot or wrinkle or any such thing; but that she would be holy and blameless. 28 So husband ought also to love their own wives as their own bodies. He who loves his own wife loves himself; 29 for no one ever hated his own flesh, but nourishes and cherishes it, just as Christ also does the church, 30 because we are members of His body. 31 FOR THIS REASON A MAN SHALL LEAVE HIS FATHER AND MOTHER AND SHALL BE JOINED TO HIS WIFE, AND THE TWO SHALL BECOME ONE FLESH. 32 This mystery is great; but I am speaking with reference to Christ and the church. 33 Nevertheless, each individual among you also is to love his own wife even as himself, and the wife must see to it that she respects her husband.

The above verses state that Christ is the Bridegroom, and the church is the Bride. They point out that we need to be subject to our God at all times, loving Him as we love our own flesh. It also says that as members of the church we our of Christ's body, and that we need to live holy lives so that we will be found spotless and blameless on the day of the wedding feast. In the following two sets of verses Jesus identifies Himself to be the Bridegroom.

(NASB) Matt. 9:15 And Jesus said to them,"The attendants of the bridegroom cannot mourn as long as the bridegroom is with them, can they? But the days will come when the bridegroom is taken away from them, and then they will fast.

(NASB) Mark 2:19-20 And Jesus said to them,"While the bridegroom is with them, the attendants of the bridegroom cannot fast, can they? So long as they have the bridegroom with them, they cannot fast. 20 "But the days will come when the bridegroom is taken away from them, and then they will fast in that day.

In the next set of verses John the Baptist identifies Christ as the Bridegroom.

(NASB) John 3:28-29 "You yourselves are my witnesses that I said,'I am not the Christ,'but'I have been sent before Him' 29 "He who has the bride is the bridegroom; but the friend of the bridegroom, who stands and hears him, rejoices greatly because of the bridegroom's voice. So this joy of mine has been made full.

In the next set of verses the Old Testament Prophet Isaiah identifies that our husband is our creator.

(NASB) Isa. 54:5-6 "For your husband is your Maker, Whose name is the Lord of hosts; And your Redeemer is the Holy One of Israel, Who is called the God of all the earth. 6 "For the Lord has called you, Like a wife forsaken and grieved in spirit, Even like a wife of one's youth when she is rejected," Says your God.

The next set of verses has to do with our need to be found spotless and blameless when the Bridegroom comes for us. That we need to be dressed in readiness, and keep our lamps lit; prepared for the day our Lord comes for us. Remember the parable at the beginning of this Bible study where a wedding guest is thrown out for not wearing the correct wedding clothes to the wedding? We need to always be living for the Lord, and prepared for is coming.

(NASB) Matt 25:6-13 "But at midnight there was a shout, 'Behold, the bridegroom! Come out to meet Him.' 7 "Then all those virgins rose and trimmed their lamps. 8 "The foolish said to the prudent, 'Give us some of your oil, for our lamps are going out.' 9 "But the prudent answered, 'No, there will not be enough for us and you too; go instead to the dealers and buy some for yourselves.' 10 "And while they were going away to make the purchase, the bridegroom came, and those who were ready went in with him to the wedding feast; and the door was shut. 11 "Later the other virgins also came , saying, Lord, Lord, open up for us.'12 But he answered ,'Truly I say to you, I do not know you.' 13 "Be on the alert then, for you do not know the day nor the hour.

(NASB) Luke 12:35-37 "Be dressed in readiness, and keep your lamps lit. 36 "Be like men who are waiting for their master when he returns from the wedding feast, so that they may immediately open the door to him when he knocks. 37 "Blessed are those slaves whom the master will find on the alert when he comes; truly I say to you, that he will gird himself to serve, and have them recline at the table, and will come up and wait on them.

(NASB) Jeremiah 2:32 "Can a virgin forget her ornaments, Or a bride her attire? Yet my people have forgotten Me Days without number.

The following verses describe the love, mercy, kindness, and compassion that the Lord will bestow on us (the bride). There will no longer be any danger, and we will be called God's people, and He will be our God. I find the following verses truly inspirational.

(NASB) Hosea 2:18-19 "In that day I will also make a covenant for them With the beasts of the field, The birds of the sky And the creeping things of the ground. And I will abolish the bow, the sword and war from the land, And make them lie down in safety. 19 I will betroth you to Me forever; Yes, I will betroth you to Me in righteousness and in justice, In loving kindness and in compassion,

(NASB) Hosea 2:23 "I will sow her for Myself in the land. I will also have compassion on her who had not obtained compassion, And I will say to those who were not My people,'You are My people!' And they will say,'You are my God!'"

(NASB) Sam. 62:5 For as a young man marries a virgin, So your sons will marry you; And as the bridegroom rejoices over the bride, So your God will rejoice over you.

The following verses describe the wedding feast of the Lamb (bridegroom), and also tell us what the right wedding clothes to wear; so that we don't end up in outer darkness like the guest in the beginning parable. The wedding garments are not actual clothes, but they represent righteous acts of the saints.

(NASB) Rev. 7-9 "Let us rejoice and be glad and give glory to Him, for the marriage of the Lamb has come and His bride has made herself ready." 8 It was given to her to clothe herself in fine linen, bright and clean; for the fine linen is the righteous acts of the saints. 9 Then he said to me,"Write, Blessed are those who are invited to the marriage supper of the Lamb.'" And he said to me, "These are true words of God."

The following verses state how we are to clothe ourselves in righteousness. God will cause righteousness to spring up among all nations. We need to remember two words that Jesus spoke; these words are, "Follow

Me". If we live our lives following Jesus each day we will live more righteous lives clothing ourselves in the appropriate wedding attire.

> **(NASB) Isa. 61:10-11 I will rejoice greatly in the Lord, My soul will exult in my God; For He has clothed me with garments of salvation, He has wrapped me with a robe of righteousness, As a bridegroom decks himself with a garland, And as a bride adorns herself with her jewels. 11 For as the earth brings forth its sprouts, And as a garden causes the things sown in it to spring up, So the Lord GOD will cause righteousness and praise To spring up before all nations.**

The next verses have to do with remaining humble, and watching our attitudes. I included these verses so that we will remember how to act at the feast we are so much looking forward to.

> **(NASB) Luke 14:7-11 And He began speaking a parable to the invited guests when He noticed how they had been picking out the places of honor at the table, saying to them, 8 "When you are invited by someone to a wedding feast, do not take the place of honor, for someone more distinguished than you may have been invited by him, 9 and he who invited you both will come and say to you, Give your place to this man, and then in disgrace you proceed to occupy the last place. 10 "But when you are invited, go and recline at the last place, so that when the one who has invited you comes, he may say to you,'Friend, move up higher'; then you will have honor in the sight of all who are at the table with you. 11 "For everyone who exalts himself will be humbled, and he who humbles himself will be exalted."**

The last two verses are an invitation to the wedding feast, and an offer of eternal life for all those who wish to follow Jesus. They have to do with the Bride (which is us) saying Come, eagerly awaiting our Lord's coming.

> **(NASB) Rev. 22:16-17 "I Jesus, have sent My angel to testify to you these things for the churches. I am the root and the descendant of David, the bright morning star." 17 The Spirit and the Bride say,"Come". And let the one who hears say,"Come." And let the one who is thirsty come; let the one who wishes take the water of life without cost.**

Are you ready to say COME? Have you been keeping your lamps lit so that you are prepared for when the Bridegroom comes? Are you wearing the correct wedding clothes? If not I urge you to start living your life for God. If you are a Christian and are prepared to say, "Come," that is wonderful! I rejoice over all of the wonderful Christians out there whom love and live for the Lord. Stay strong in the faith.

References

"Scripture taken from the NEW AMERICAN STANDARD BIBLE® (NASB), Copyright© 1960, 1962, 1963,1968,1971,1972, 1973,1975,1977, 1995 by The Lockman Foundation. Used by permission."

Overcoming Sin

Once you become a Christian you must spend the rest of your life living for God. Jesus has paid the price for our sins with His life, and now it is up to us to spend the rest of our lives following Him. We must overcome the sinful life we lived before we became Christians, and we must walk in God's ways so that we will be holy and blameless upon Jesus' return. In order to be found blameless we must first work at overcoming our sins.

(NIV) 1 John 1:6-9 If we claim to have fellowship with him yet walk in the darkness, we lie and do not live by the truth. 7 But if we walk in the light, as he is in the light, we have fellowship with one another, and the blood of Jesus, his Son, purifies us from all sin. 8 If we claim to be without sin, we deceive ourselves and the truth is not in us. 9 If we confess our sins, he is faithful and just and will forgive us our sins and purify us from all unrighteousness.

The above verses tell us that we must walk in the light and follow His ways. Of course we all fall short and sin, but we must try our best not to. If we do happen to sin we need to repent, and work to correct the error of our ways.

(NIV) 1 John 2:17 The world and its desires pass away, but the man who does the will of God lives forever.

The world is coming to an end. You don't know if you will die tomorrow, so NOW is the time to find out what God's will is, and to obey it. The next verses I we will go over have to do with how we as Christians are supposed to live.

(NIV) 1 Peter 2:11-12 Dear friends, I urge you, as aliens and strangers in the world, to abstain from sinful desires, which war against your soul. 12 Live such good lives among the pagans that, though they accuse you of doing wrong, they may see your good deeds and glorify God on the day he visits us.

(NIV) 1 Peter 4:1-5 Therefore, since Christ suffered in his body, arm yourselves also with the same attitude, because he who has suffered in his body is done with sin. 2 As a result, he does not live the rest of his earthly life for evil human desires, but rather for the will of God. 3 For you have spent enough time in the past doing what pagans choose to do- living in debauchery, lust,

drunkenness, orgies, carousing and detestable idolatry. 4 They think it strange that you do not plunge with them into the same flood of dissipation, and they heap abuse on you. 5 But they will have to give account to him who is ready to judge the living and the dead.

(NIV) Romans 12:1-2 Therefore, I urge you, brothers, in view of God's mercy, to offer your bodies as living sacrifices, holy and pleasing to God- this is your spiritual act of worship. 2 Do not conform any longer to the pattern of this world, but be transformed by the renewing of your mind. Then you will be able to test and approve what God's will is- his good, pleasing and perfect will.

These verses tell us that we must avoid sin in our fleshly bodies, and keep ourselves holy. This is our spiritual service of worship; to avoid sin and renew our minds, and follow God's will.

The next verse re-enforces the idea that we must lead a holy life.

(NIV) 2 Corin. 7:1 Since we have these promises, dear friends, let us purify ourselves from everything that contaminates body and spirit, perfecting holiness out of reverence for God.

Is there an easier way to avoid sinning? Yes, by following God.

(NIV) Galatians 5:16 So I say, live by the Spirit, and you will not gratify the desires of the sinful nature.

(NIV) Ephesians 4:22-24 You were taught, with regard to your former way of life, to put off your old self, which is being corrupted by its deceitful desires; 23 to be made new in the attitude of your minds; 24 and to put on the new self, created to be like God in true righteousness and holiness.

(NIV) Colossians 3:1-10 Since, then, you have been raised with Christ, set your hearts on things above, where Christ is seated at the right hand of God. 2 Set your minds on things above, not on earthly things. 3 For you died, and your life is now hidden with Christ in God. 4 When Christ, who is your life appears, then you will also appear with him in glory. 5 Put to death, therefore, whatever belongs to your earthly nature: sexual immorality, impurity, lust, evil desires and greed, which is idolatry. 6 Because of these, the wrath of God is coming. 7 You used to walk in these

ways, in the life you once lived. 8 But now you must rid yourselves of all such things as these: anger, rage, malice, slander, and filthy language from your lips. 9 Do not lie to each other, since you have taken off your old self with its practices 10 and have put on the new self, which is being renewed in knowledge in the image of its Creator.

These last few verses are very powerful. They say that once you become a Christian, you must avoid sin, and focus on God. God is working in us each and everyday to perfect us. He helps us to avoid sin. We only need to follow Him and trust in His ways.

(NIV) Proverbs 2:6-11 For the Lord gives wisdom, and from his mouth come knowledge and understanding. 7 He holds victory in store for the upright, he is a shield to those whose walk is blameless, 8 for he guards the course of the just and protects the way of his faithful ones. 9 Then you will understand what is right and just and fair-every good path. 10 For wisdom will enter your heart, and knowledge will be pleasant to your soul. 11 Discretion will protect you, and understanding will guard you.

Once we chose to become Christians and gave our lives to Jesus we decided to give up our old sinful natures by renewing our minds and spirits by following God's ways, and trying to live by the example that our Lord and Savior Jesus Christ set for us throughout his lifetime. He died so that we might have the opportunity to follow Him. In return it is our duty to live out the rest of our lives avoiding sin.

References

Discipline

The narrow path of the Lord leads to Heaven. There will be no more pain, tears, death, or suffering there. To get there we must walk the straight and narrow path of the Lord, which will require discipline while we are on the earth. Both self-discipline and the discipline of the Lord will be involved. Before we get into the discipline of the Lord we will first examine how we are to raise and discipline our own children.

> **(KJV) Deuteronomy 6:6-7 And these words, which I command thee this day, shall be in thine heart: 7 And thou shalt teach them diligently unto thy children, and shalt talk of them when thou sittest in thine house, and when thou walkest by the way, and when thou liest down, and when thou risest up.**

We are to instruct our children to observe the commandments of God.

> **(KJV) Colossians 3:20-21 Children, obey your parents in all things: for this is well pleasing unto the Lord. 21 Fathers, Ephesians 6:4 And, ye fathers, provoke not your children to wrath: but bring them up in the nurture and admonition of the Lord. provoke not your children to anger, lest they be discouraged.**

Children are to obey their parents in all things, and parents are to be careful not to discourage their children. We are to nurture and discipline our children, and raise them up to be in subjection to the Lord. Provoking your children to anger or wraith does not mean that you are not to discipline them. A child might be provoked to anger or become discouraged if they witness their parents being hypocrites; if see them coming home drunk every night, or gambling away all of their family's money.

Parents are to set an example for their children to follow. If they are doing this and raising their children in a loving home then their children will not be provoked to wraith, and will learn from the discipline. As you read this study look at yourself in the place of both the parent and as the child. You may have your own children who are to obey you in all things, but you are also a child of God and must obey Him in all things.

> **(KJV) Proverbs 22:15 Foolishness is bound in the heart of a child; but the rod of correction shall drive it far from him**

Children need to be disciplined. They are not yet wise enough to understand the decisions they make, and are prone to make bad choices. When they do make bad decisions it is their parent's duty to correct them so that they do not continue to make the same mistakes in the future.

(KJV) Proverbs 29:15 The rod and reproof give wisdom: but a child left to himself bringeth his mother to shame.

(KJV) Proverbs 29:17 Correct thy son, and he shall give thee rest; yea, he shall give delight unto thy soul.

If we leave our children to their own devices they will bring us shame, but if we correct them they will be a delight to our souls. When you place yourself in the above verses as God's child you can see that if God allowed us to wander too far off the straight and narrow path then it would be hard to find our way back, but if He corrects us right away and we return to a life of obedience to the Lord, His heart would rejoice.

(KJV) Proverbs 13:24 He that spareth his rod hateth his son: but he that loveth him chasteneth him betimes.

If you do not discipline your children then you are doing them a grave injustice equivalent to hating them. If you truly love your children you would correct them when you need to in order to provide them every opportunity in life.

(KJV) Proverbs 19:18 Chasten thy son while there is hope, and let not thy soul spare for his crying.

You are to discipline your children while there is still hope. Don't let them get so set in their ways that there is no coming back. You need to be strong and remember that it is for their good that you discipline them. No body wants to hurt the ones they love, but you must discipline them for their own good. As Proverbs 13:24 states if you don't discipline them then you are doing them an injustice equal to hating them.

(KJV) Proverbs 23:13-14 Withhold not correction from the child: for if thou beatest him with the rod, he shall not die. 14 Thou shalt beat him with the rod, and shalt deliver his soul from hell.

Your children will not die from being disciplined, and through your correction you can save your children from hell. The Lord disciplines us in the same way. The above example refers to spanking your child, but the idea is that of discipline. Whether it is through grounding your child or having them take a time out, disciplining your child now will save them from worse things to come in the future. God does not spank us to discipline us, but the discipline He gives us sometimes stings or affects us on an emotional level. Discipline may seem painful at the time but it is for our on edification, and is intended to straighten us up and have us return to the straight and narrow path of the Lord; as opposed to the broad path that leads to hell.

(KJV) Proverbs 22:6 Train up a child in the way he should go: and when he is old, he will not depart from it.

(KJV) 1 Timothy 5:8 But if any provide not for his own, and specially for those of his own house, he hath denied the faith, and is worse than an infidel.

As Christians we are to train our children and provide for them. This is our duty as parents. If we fulfill our responsibilities our children will follow our instructions when they are older, and we can save their souls from hell.

All of the above verses apply to us as parents, and as children of God. Now we will look at verses that relate specifically to the discipline of the Lord.

(KJV) Deuteronomy 8:5-6 Thou shalt also consider in thine heart, that, as a man chasteneth his son, so the LORD thy God chasteneth thee. 6 Therefore thou shalt keep the commandments of the LORD thy God, to walk in his ways, and to fear him.

(KJV) Job 5:17 Behold, happy is the man whom God correcteth: therefore despise not thou the chastening of the Almighty:

The above verses state that in the same way that a man corrects his son, God corrects us. We are to keep the commandments of the Lord. The discipline of the Lord is done in our best interest, and if we learn from it we will find happiness.

(KJV) Proverbs 3:11-13 My son, despise not the chastening of the LORD; neither be weary of his correction: **12** For whom the LORD loveth he correcteth; even as a father the son in whom he delighteth. **13** Happy is the man that findeth wisdom, and the man that getteth understanding.

Do not be dismayed by the correction of the Lord. It is done out of love for us, and will bring us wisdom, understanding, and happiness.

(KJV) Hebrews 12:5-7 And ye have forgotten the exhortation which speaketh unto you as unto children, My son, despise not thou the chastening of the Lord, nor faint when thou art rebuked of him: **6** For whom the Lord loveth he chasteneth, and scourgeth every son whom he receiveth. **7** If ye endure chastening, God dealeth with you as with sons; for what son is he whom the father chasteneth not? **8** But if ye be without chastisement, whereof all are partakers, then are ye bastards, and not sons.

Being disciplined by the Lord is proof that He has accepted you as His son. If you did not receive discipline from the Lord then you are not considered one of His sons.

(KJV) Hebrews 12:9-11 Furthermore we have had fathers of our flesh which corrected us, and we gave them reverence: shall we not much rather be in subjection unto the Father of spirits, and live? **10** For they verily for a few days chastened us after their own pleasure; but he for our profit, that we might be partakers of his holiness. **11** Now no chastening for the present seemeth to be joyous, but grievous: nevertheless afterward it yieldeth the peaceable fruit of righteousness unto them which are exercised thereby.

(KJV) 1 Corinthians 11:32 But when we are judged, we are chastened of the Lord, that we should not be condemned with the world.

(KJV) Relevelations 3:19-21 As many as I love, I rebuke and chasten: be zealous therefore, and repent. **20** Behold, I stand at the door, and knock: if any man hear my voice, and open the door, I will come in to him, and will sup with him, and he with me. **21** To him that overcometh will I grant to sit with me in my throne, even as I also overcame,

The discipline of the Lord is for our own good. We may go through hard times, face difficult challenges, and they may seem grievous at the time, but they are proof that we are accepted by God; it will bring us happiness on the earth, and will allow us to be partakers of His holy kingdom to come.

(KJV) Romans 12:1-2 I beseech you therefore, brethren, by the mercies of God, that ye present your bodies a living sacrifice, holy, acceptable unto God, which is your reasonable service. 2 And be not conformed to this world: but be ye transformed by the renewing of your mind, that ye may prove what is that good, and acceptable, and perfect, will of God.

Now that you have begun your Christian walk you must present your body as a living sacrifice, and live according to the will of God. You are to overcome the world and follow Christ.

(KJV) Matthew 16:24 Then said Jesus unto his disciples, If any man will come after me, let him deny himself, and take up his cross, and follow me.

(KJV) John 10:27-28 My sheep hear my voice, and I know them, and they follow me: 28 And I give unto them eternal life; and they shall never perish, neither shall any man pluck them out of my hand.

(KJV) John 12:26 If any man serve me, let him follow me; and where I am, there shall also my servant be: if any man serve me, him will my Father honour.

The instructions we are given are to follow Christ, and live a life after His teachings according to the scriptures. During our journey we will have to overcome temptations, have our faith tried, and will be disciplined by the Lord. The discipline of the Lord may seem difficult at the time, but God will not allow us to endure more than we can handle and will always provide us with a way out.

(KJV) 1 Corinthians 10:13 There hath no temptation taken you but such as is common to man: but God is faithful, who will not suffer you to be tempted above that ye are able; but will with the temptation also make a way to escape,

(KJV) James 1:2-4 My brethren, count it all joy when ye fall into divers temptations; 3 Knowing this, that the trying of your faith worketh patience. 4 But let patience have her perfect work, that ye may be perfect and entire, wanting nothing.

(KJV) 1 Peter 1:6-7 Wherein ye greatly rejoice, though now for a season, if need be, ye are in heaviness through manifold temptations: 7 That the trial of your faith, being much more precious than of gold that perisheth, though it be tried with fire, might be found unto praise and honour and glory at the appearing of Jesus Christ:

We are instructed to overcome temptations with patience so that we may be made perfect, wanting nothing, and we will receive honor and glory at the second coming of Christ.

(KJV) 1 Peter 4:12-14 Beloved, think it not strange concerning the fiery trial which is to try you, as though some strange thing happened unto you: 13 But rejoice, inasmuch as ye are partakers of Christ's sufferings; that, when his glory shall be revealed, ye may be glad also with exceeding joy. 14 If ye be reproached for the name of Christ, happy are ye; for the spirit of glory and of God resteth upon you: on their part he is evil spoken of, but on your part he is glorified.

When we suffer trials and temptations on this earth we are sharing in the sufferings of Christ. If we suffer because of our faith we should rejoice because it is proof that the spirit of God rests upon us.

(KJV) Philippians 4:13 I can do all things through Christ which strengtheneth me.

Christ will provide you with the strength to endure and trials or disciplines that you might face.

2 Peter 1:4-8 Whereby are given unto us exceeding great and precious promises: that by these ye might be partakers of the divine nature, having escaped the corruption that is in the world through lust. 5 And beside this, giving all diligence, add to your faith virtue; and to virtue knowledge; 6 And to knowledge temperance; and to temperance patience; and to patience

godliness; 7 And to godliness brotherly kindness; and to brotherly kindness charity. 8 For if these things be in you, and abound, they make you that ye shall neither be barren nor unfruitful in the knowledge of our Lord Jesus Christ.

As we walk the narrow path of the Lord we are to seek to add virtue, knowledge, self-control, endurance, righteousness, kindness, and charity to our personal characteristics.

(KJV) Daniel 10:12 Then said he unto me, Fear not, Daniel: for from the first day that thou didst set thine heart to understand, and to chasten thyself before thy God, thy words were heard, and I am come for thy words.

The very moment you set out to understand and discipline yourself before God, He will be there to support you. You will not have to walk the straight and narrow path alone. God will be there to support you, to strengthen you, and to correct you when you start to stray from the path. Accept His discipline with joy, knowing that it is for your own good, and that He will not give you more than you can handle.

(KJV) John 6:37 All that the Father giveth me shall come to me; and him that cometh to me I will in no wise cast out.

(KJV) John 6:44 No man can come to me, except the Father which hath sent me draw him: and I will raise him up at the last day.

(KJV) Romans 8:28 And we know that all things work together for good to them that love God, to them who are the called according to his purpose.

If you are seeking God it is because God has chosen you. If you follow Him He will not cast you out, and will accept you into Heaven. All things will work together for the good of those that love God.

(KJV) Matthew 11:28-30 Come unto me, all ye that labour and are heavy laden, and I will give you rest. 29 Take my yoke upon you, and learn of me; for I am meek and lowly in heart: and ye shall find rest unto your souls. 30 For my yoke is easy, and my burden is light.

(KJV) Matthew 6:33 But seek ye first the kingdom of God, and his righteousness; and all these things shall be added unto you.

(KJV) Philippians 4:5 In nothing be anxious; but in everything by prayer and supplication with thanksgiving let your requests be made known unto God.

Go to Christ with your troubles, and He will give you rest. Follow Christ, obey the commandments of God, and learn from them. Seek the kingdom of God first and all of your physical needs on earth will also be provided for.

(KJV) Colossians 2:6 As ye have therefore received Christ Jesus the Lord, so walk ye in him:

(KJV) 2 John 1:6 And this is love, that we walk after his commandments. This is the commandment, That, as ye have heard from the beginning, ye should walk in it.

(KJV) 2 Thessalonians 3:3 But the Lord is faithful, who shall stablish you, and keep you from evil.

God will be with us during our Christian walks, but we will still be disciplined and have trials. No one is perfect. It is a hard path for anyone to walk, but the Lord is faithful and will be with us on our journey. To help you understand further the discipline of the Lord we will examine the lives of Abraham, and Peter.

(KJV) Romans 4:3 For what saith the scripture? Abraham believed God, and it was counted unto him for righteousness.

(KJV) Galatians 3:6-9 Even as Abraham believed God, and it was accounted to him for righteousness. 7 Know ye therefore that they which are of faith, the same are the children of Abraham. 8 And the scripture, foreseeing that God would justify the heathen through faith, preached before the gospel unto Abraham, saying, In thee shall all nations be blessed. 9 So then they which be of faith are blessed with faithful Abraham.

Abraham is remembered because of his faith, and considered righteous because he believed God. Let's examine Abraham's faith more closely, and look at the trials that he went through.

(KJV) Genesis 12:1-5 Now the LORD had said unto Abram, Get thee out of thy country, and from thy kindred, and from thy father's house, unto a land that I will show thee: 2 And I will make of thee a great nation, and I will bless thee, and make thy name great; and thou shalt be a blessing: 3 And I will bless them that bless thee, and curse him that curseth thee: and in thee shall all families of the earth be blessed. 4 So Abram departed, as the LORD had spoken unto him; and Lot went with him: and Abram was seventy and five years old when he departed out of Haran. 5 And Abram took Sarai his wife, and Lot his brother's son, and all their substance that they had gathered, and the souls that they had gotten in Haran; and they went forth to go into the land of Canaan; and into the land of Canaan they came.

Abram (later renamed Abraham) was called by God, and he obeyed. He was promised that he would be made into a great nation, that he would be blessed, and that God would curse those who curse him. Abraham brought his wife Sarai and his nephew Lot with him, as well as his servants and possessions. Abraham had faith in God and went where God told him to go. Now we will look at Abraham's first trial.

(KJV) Genesis 12:10-13 And there was a famine in the land: and Abram went down into Egypt to sojourn there; for the famine was grievous in the land. 11 And it came to pass, when he was come near to enter into Egypt, that he said unto Sarai his wife, Behold now, I know that thou art a fair woman to look upon: 12 Therefore it shall come to pass, when the Egyptians shall see thee, that they shall say, This is his wife: and they will kill me, but they will save thee alive. 13 Say, I pray thee, thou art my sister: that it may be well with me for thy sake; and my soul shall live because of thee.

A famine hit and Abraham had to move to Egypt to survive. God promised to make Abraham into a great nation, but he would be disciplined and face some trials before that happened. His first trial was the need to travel to Egypt due to a famine that came across the land. Before he got to Egypt Abraham convinces his wife to lie for him, and claim to be his sister so that the Egyptians would not kill him to take Sarai from him.

(KJV) Genesis 12:14-16 And it came to pass, that, when Abram was come into Egypt, the Egyptians beheld the woman that she was very fair. 15 The princes also of Pharaoh saw her, and

commended her before Pharaoh: and the woman was taken into Pharaoh's house. 16 And he entreated Abram well for her sake: and he had sheep, and oxen, and he asses, and menservants, and maidservants, and she asses, and camels.

When they made it to Egypt it happened just as Abraham had predicted. Pharaoh wanted Sarai, and because he believed that she was unwed he bought her from Abraham. This was the first test that Abraham faced after God called him, and Abraham failed. God promised to make Abraham a great nation. God would not be able to make Abraham into a great nation if Abraham were dead. Abraham believed God and left his country, but at the first trying of his faith, out of fear he sold his wife to Pharaoh. God remained faithful in His promise.

(KJV) Genesis 12:17-20 And the LORD plagued Pharaoh and his house with great plagues because of Sarai Abram's wife. 18 And Pharaoh called Abram, and said, What is this that thou hast done unto me? why didst thou not tell me that she was thy wife? 19 Why saidst thou, She is my sister? so I might have taken her to me to wife: now therefore behold thy wife, take her, and go thy way. 20 And Pharaoh commanded his men concerning him: and they sent him away, and his wife, and all that he had.

God was faithful in His promise to Abraham, and cursed those who would have cursed Abraham. God plagued Pharaoh with great plagues and Pharaoh returned Sarai to Abraham. Everything works to the glory of God. Through Abraham's weakness God was able to display His faithfulness. How could a God of justice allow someone to lie and profit from it? God used this opportunity to prove that He will make good on His promises. He blessed Abraham and cursed those that were against him. As far as this event not being fair to Pharaoh that depends on how you look at it. Losing a few servants and some animals does not seem to compare to the justice Pharaoh should have received for routinely murdering travelers, and taking their wives as his own.

(KJV) Genesis 15:4-6 And, behold, the word of the LORD came unto him, saying, This shall not be thine heir; but he that shall come forth out of thine own bowels shall be thine heir. 5 And he brought him forth abroad, and said, Look now toward heaven, and tell the stars, if thou be able to number them: and he said unto him, So shall thy seed be. 6 And he believed in the LORD; and he counted it to him for righteousness.

God appeared to Abraham again and this time promised him that his offspring shall be as innumerable as the stars. Abraham believed God and it was credited to him as righteousness.

(KJV) Genesis 16:1-3 Now Sarai Abram's wife bare him no children: and she had an handmaid, an Egyptian, whose name was Hagar. 2 And Sarai said unto Abram, Behold now, the LORD hath restrained me from bearing: I pray thee, go in unto my maid; it may be that I may obtain children by her. And Abram hearkened to the voice of Sarai. 3 And Sarai Abram's wife took Hagar her maid the Egyptian, after Abram had dwelt ten years in the land of Canaan, and gave her to her husband Abram to be his wife.

(KJV) Genesis 16:11-12 And the angel of the LORD said unto her, Behold, thou art with child, and shalt bear a son, and shalt call his name Ishmael; because the LORD hath heard thy affliction. 12 And he will be a wild man; his hand will be against every man, and every man's hand against him; and he shall dwell in the presence of all his brethren.

(KJV) Genesis 16:15 And Hagar bare Abram a son: and Abram called his son's name, which Hagar bare, Ishmael.

Abraham had a promise from God that his offspring would be as innumerable as the stars, but they became impatient waiting for God to fulfill His promise, and Abraham had a child with Sarai's servant girl. Many Arabs claim Ishmael as their forefather to this day. They believe that Ishmael was the firstborn and therefore the true heir of Abraham. Isaac is Abraham's son through Sarah (Sarai) and is the forefather of Israel. Isaac is considered as Abraham's true heir because he is the one that was promised by God, and since Ishmael was the son of a servant he is considered illegitimate and not entitled to the rights of the firstborn son.

In Genesis 16:12 the angel of the Lord said that Ishmael's hand would be against everyone and everyone's hand will be against him. The Arabs and Jews have been fighting this war for thousands of years. This on going war is the direct result of Abraham's sin. When Abraham lied about Sarai being his wife and sold her to Pharaoh he received Hagar as a servant for the price of his wife. It is likely that this is when Abraham and Sarah acquired Hagar as their servant because Hagar was an Egyptian, and this was Abraham's first trip to Egypt. Before that time they lived in Ur of the

Chaldeens, and Haran in the land of Canaan. If Abraham had not lied about Sarai being his sister, Hagar would not have been Sarai's maid, and the years of conflict and bloodshed that exist between the descendents of the two brothers would have never come to pass.

The impatience of Abraham in waiting for God to fulfill His promise is the second time that Abraham's faith failed. It is a combination of Abraham selling his wife to Pharaoh, and him impregnating his wife's servant girl that resulted in a feud between the Muslims and the Jews that is still going on to this day (Galatians 4:29).

> **(KJV) Genesis 17:1-5 And when Abram was ninety years old and nine, the LORD appeared to Abram, and said unto him, I am the Almighty God; walk before me, and be thou perfect. 2 And I will make my covenant between me and thee, and will multiply thee exceedingly. 3 And Abram fell on his face: and God talked with him, saying, 4 As for me, behold, my covenant is with thee, and thou shalt be a father of many nations. 5 Neither shall thy name any more be called Abram, but thy name shall be Abraham; for a father of many nations have I made thee.**

> **(KJV) Genesis 17:15-16 And God said unto Abraham, As for Sarai thy wife, thou shalt not call her name Sarai, but Sarah shall her name be. 16 And I will bless her, and give thee a son also of her: yea, I will bless her, and she shall be a mother of nations; kings of people shall be of her.**

> **(KJV) Genesis 17:19 And God said, Sarah thy wife shall bear thee a son indeed; and thou shalt call his name Isaac: and I will establish my covenant with him for an everlasting covenant, and with his seed after him. 20 And as for Ishmael, I have heard thee: Behold, I have blessed him, and will make him fruitful, and will multiply him exceedingly; twelve princes shall he beget, and I will make him a great nation. 21 But my covenant will I establish with Isaac, which Sarah shall bear unto thee at this set time in the next year.**

God appeared to Abraham again, and clarified His promise to Abraham even further. God changed Abram's name to Abraham, and Sarai's name to Sarah. God tells Abraham that Sarah will be the mother of nations, and will give birth to Isaac. Isaac is the son that God will establish His covenant with, and He will give the Promised Land to the descendants Isaac.

Ishmael will be blessed also and he will become a great nation, but of Ishmael's line there would be princes, and from Isaac's line there would be kings (including Jesus). Because Abraham became impatient with God's last promise God was much more clear with this one. Abraham will have a son named Isaac, Sarah will be his mother, and it will take place within the time frame of one year.

> **(KJV) Genesis 20:1-7 And Abraham journeyed from thence toward the south country, and dwelled between Kadesh and Shur, and sojourned in Gerar. 2 And Abraham said of Sarah his wife, She is my sister: and Abimelech king of Gerar sent, and took Sarah. 3 But God came to Abimelech in a dream by night, and said to him, Behold, thou art but a dead man, for the woman which thou hast taken; for she is a man's wife. 4 But Abimelech had not come near her: and he said, Lord, wilt thou slay also a righteous nation? 5 Said he not unto me, She is my sister? and she, even she herself said, He is my brother: in the integrity of my heart and innocency of my hands have I done this. 6 And God said unto him in a dream, Yea, I know that thou didst this in the integrity of thy heart; for I also withheld thee from sinning against me: therefore suffered I thee not to touch her. 7 Now therefore restore the man his wife; for he is a prophet, and he shall pray for thee, and thou shalt live: and if thou restore her not, know thou that thou shalt surely die, thou, and all that are thine.**

God actually spoke to Abraham and promised him that Sarah would have Abraham's child within the next year, and for a second time Abraham lied and said that Sarah was his sister and gave her over to another man. God was faithful and protected Abraham again, and withheld King Abimelech from defiling Sarah. God dealt fairly with King Abimelech and basically told him what was going on and to let Sarah return to her husband. King Abimelech did as God instructed him.

> **(KJV) Genesis 21:2 For Sarah conceived, and bare Abraham a son in his old age, at the set time of which God had spoken to him.**

God fulfilled His promise and Sarah gave birth to Abraham's son Isaac at the set time that God promised.

(KJV) Genesis 22:1-2 And it came to pass after these things, that God did tempt Abraham, and said unto him, Abraham: and he said, Behold, here I am. 2 And he said, Take now thy son, thine only son Isaac, whom thou lovest, and get thee into the land of Moriah; and offer him there for a burnt offering upon one of the mountains which I will tell thee of.

(KJV) Genesis 22:9-12 And they came to the place which God had told him of; and Abraham built an altar there, and laid the wood in order, and bound Isaac his son, and laid him on the altar upon the wood. 10 And Abraham stretched forth his hand, and took the knife to slay his son 11 And the angel of the LORD called unto him out of heaven, and said, Abraham, Abraham: and he said, Here am I. 12 And he said, Lay not thine hand upon the lad, neither do thou any thing unto him: for now I know that thou fearest God, seeing thou hast not withheld thy son, thine only son from me.

The Bible doesn't say why God tempted Abraham with the sacrifice of his son Isaac, but it can be surmised that it was to test Abraham's faith since Abraham allowed his wife to be taken into a King's harem for a second time. Abraham had the promise of God that he would live to have a child with Sarah, yet Abraham still feared man over God. God gave Abraham another chance to prove his faith, and this time Abraham passed.

Events like these are what can be expected in your Christian walk. You will be tested and sometimes will fail. You will have to deal with the results of your sin, but God will give you other opportunities to make amends. I am not saying that there are an infinite number of second chances, but that if you slip, you can get back up.

(KJV) Matthew 24:43-44 But know this, that if the goodman of the house had known in what watch the thief would come, he would have watched, and would not have suffered his house to be broken up. 44 Therefore be ye also ready: for in such an hour as ye think not the Son of man cometh.

As a Christian you are always called to be ready to meet your maker. Along your path you may stumble, but you need to get right back on the path and be prepared for the coming of the Lord. Now we will examine some areas of the life of the apostle Peter.

(KJV) Matthew 16:16-18 And Simon Peter answered and said, Thou art the Christ, the Son of the living God. 17 And Jesus answered and said unto him, Blessed art thou, Simon Barjona: for flesh and blood hath not revealed it unto thee, but my Father which is in heaven. 18 And I say also unto thee, That thou art Peter, and upon this rock I will build my church; and the gates of hell shall not prevail against it.

Peter is credited as being the first one to make the good confession, the confession that Jesus Christ is the Son of God. It is a confession of faith, and it is through this confession that John the Baptist stated that God could raise up descendants of Abraham out of stones (Matthew 3:9). Abraham is considered righteous because of his faith, and the good confession is a way of demonstrating our faith in Jesus Christ.

(KJV) Matthew 10:32 Whosoever therefore shall confess me before men, him will I confess also before my Father which is in heaven.

Jesus states in Matthew 16:18 that it is upon this rock that he will build His church, and Jesus gave Simon the name Peter at this time. The word Peter actually means rock. The Catholic Church interprets Matthew 16:18 to mean that Peter would be the one to establish the church, and considers the Catholic Church to be the one true church because Peter is said to have baptized and establish the first Pope of the Catholic Church.

(KJV) Matthew 26:33-35 Peter answered and said unto him, Though all men shall be offended because of thee, yet will I never be offended. 34 Jesus said unto him, Verily I say unto thee, That this night, before the cock crow, thou shalt deny me thrice. 35 Peter said unto him, Though I should die with thee, yet will I not deny thee. Likewise also said all the disciples.

Peter told Christ that he would die before he would deny Him, and Jesus predicted that Peter would deny him three times that night, before the cock crowed. After this Jesus was taken prisoner and would later be crucified. Peter stayed behind, but followed those that took Jesus.

(KJV) Matthew 26:69 Now Peter sat without in the palace: and a damsel came unto him, saying, Thou also wast with Jesus of Galilee. 70 But he denied before them all, saying, I know not what thou sayest. 71 And when he was gone out into the porch,

another maid saw him, and said unto them that were there, This fellow was also with Jesus of Nazareth. 72 And again he denied with an oath, I do not know the man. 73 And after a while came unto him they that stood by, and said to Peter, Surely thou also art one of them; for thy speech bewrayeth thee. 74 Then began he to curse and to swear, saying, I know not the man. And immediately the cock crew. 75 And Peter remembered the word of Jesus, which said unto him, Before the cock crow, thou shalt deny me thrice. And he went out, and wept bitterly.

(KJV) Luke 22:61-62 And the Lord turned, and looked upon Peter. And Peter remembered the word of the Lord, how he had said unto him, Before the cock crow, thou shalt deny me thrice. 62 And Peter went out, and wept bitterly.

Just as Jesus predicted Peter denied Him three times before the cock crowed. The very man that was the first person to make the good confession was also the first person to deny Christ. Peter stated earlier that he would die before doing so, but when the pressure was on he failed. There is no doubt that Peter loved Jesus, and he immediately went out and wept bitterly and repented. Peter walked with the Son of God for the past three years; he had witnessed Jesus raise people from the dead (John 11:44), and had even walked on water with Jesus (Matthew 14:28). There is no doubt that Peter knew Jesus was the Son of God, but Peter failed in this situation and denied Him three times.

After Jesus' resurrection He visited the disciples again and gave Peter a chance to redeem himself.

John 21:15-17 So when they had dined, Jesus saith to Simon Peter, Simon, son of Jonas, lovest thou me more than these? He saith unto him, Yea, Lord; thou knowest that I love thee. He saith unto him, Feed my lambs. 16 He saith to him again the second time, Simon, son of Jonas, lovest thou me? He saith unto him, Yea, Lord; thou knowest that I love thee. He saith unto him, Feed my sheep. 17 He saith unto him the third time, Simon, son of Jonas, lovest thou me? Peter was grieved because he said unto him the third time, Lovest thou me? And he said unto him, Lord, thou knowest all things; thou knowest that I love thee. Jesus saith unto him, Feed my sheep.

Jesus came to Peter and gave Peter three chances to proclaim his love for Him. This was to make up for the three times that Peter denied

Christ. Jesus knew that Peter loved him, and He knew that Peter repented for his mistake; so Jesus gave Peter the opportunity to get back on the right path, but there are always consequences when we fall away.

> **(KJV) John 21:18-19 Verily, verily, I say unto thee, When thou wast young, thou girdedst thyself, and walkedst whither thou wouldest: but when thou shalt be old, thou shalt stretch forth thy hands, and another shall gird thee, and carry thee whither thou wouldest not. 19 This spake he, signifying by what death he should glorify God. And when he had spoken this, he saith unto him, Follow me.**

Peter would be given another chance to fulfill the things that he spoke. He did as Christ commanded and followed Christ. Peter traveled around preaching the Gospel and eventually would be taken prisoner and executed for it. This time Peter was faithful to his word, he confessed Christ before men, and gave his life before he would deny Him.

During our Christian walk we will face trials and temptations in the same way that Abraham and Peter did. We will suffer, be disciplined, and endure rough times and hardships. Not every trial will have to do with overcoming sin, but may be normal trials involved in everyday life. The trials could be trouble at work, at home, or in your spiritual life. We must put our faith in God and patiently endure them, knowing that God only disciplines those He loves, and is only doing it for our own edification. God will be there with us, He will give us the strength to overcome the trial, He will not ask of us more than we can endure, and He will always give us a means of escape.

These trials and testings that you will endure during your Christian walk are the very reason for your existence. They are the very meaning of life. Think of your life as a big test to see whether you deserve to go to Heaven or to Hell. This is an open book test, because all of the answers to it are contained in the Bible, which you can reference anytime that you please. Your task is to pass the test by purifying your soul, and improving the areas of your life where you are lacking. You are to follow Christ and live your life in accordance with the scriptures.

Some people wonder how a loving God could sentence people to hell for making a few mistakes. The answer is He doesn't. Everyday that a person is alive they are either being tested, or given the opportunity to prepare for the day that they will be tested. You do not go to hell for getting one answer wrong on a test. The test is over your entire lifetime, and if you fail the test for eighty or ninety years (when you are even given the answers to the test) it should be of no great surprise that you would go to hell.

Today is the day to prepare your soul to meet your maker. Now is your chance to prove yourself. Your Christian walk will require patience and endurance, but it will be worth it in the long run. God actually spoke to Abraham. Peter lived with Christ for three years, but you have something they didn't. You have the word of God written down in the Bible outlining how you are to live and what you are supposed to do.

(KJV) James 1:12 Blessed is the man that endureth temptation: for when he is tried, he shall receive the crown of life, which the Lord hath promised to them that love him.

Before we conclude this study we will look at one more example of the discipline of the Lord, and a trial that someone successfully passed. We will look at the encounter between David and Goliath. Goliath was the champion of the Philistines, and was an enormous man that the armies of Israel were afraid to face. Goliath stood in defiance to the armies of the Lord (1 Samuel 17:10) profaning the name of God.

(KJV) 1 Samuel 17:32-37 And David said to Saul, Let no man's heart fail because of him; thy servant will go and fight with this Philistine. 33 And Saul said to David, Thou art not able to go against this Philistine to fight with him: for thou art but a youth, and he a man of war from his youth. 34 And David said unto Saul, Thy servant kept his father's sheep, and there came a lion, and a bear, and took a lamb out of the flock: 35 And I went out after him, and smote him, and delivered it out of his mouth: and when he arose against me, I caught him by his beard, and smote him, and slew him. 36 Thy servant slew both the lion and the bear: and this uncircumcised Philistine shall be as one of them, seeing he hath defied the armies of the living God. 37 David said moreover, The LORD that delivered me out of the paw of the lion, and out of the paw of the bear, he will deliver me out of the hand of this Philistine. And Saul said unto David, Go, and the LORD be with thee.

David went to King Saul and said that he would defend God, and represent his nation against Goliath. Saul told David that he was not capable of fighting with Goliath because Goliath was a man of war, and David was just a boy. David had faith in God and told Saul how in the past he had killed both a lion and a bear. David's argument convinced Saul, and Saul allowed David to represent the entire army of Israel (Besides, no one else was volunteering).

> **(KJV) 1 Samuel 17:42-50 And when the Philistine looked about, and saw David, he disdained him: for he was but a youth, and ruddy, and of a fair countenance. 43 And the Philistine said unto David, Am I a dog, that thou comest to me with staves? And the Philistine cursed David by his gods. 44 And the Philistine said to David, Come to me, and I will give thy flesh unto the fowls of the air, and to the beasts of the field. 45 Then said David to the Philistine, Thou comest to me with a sword, and with a spear, and with a shield: but I come to thee in the name of the LORD of hosts, the God of the armies of Israel, whom thou hast defied. 46 This day will the LORD deliver thee into mine hand; and I will smite thee, and take thine head from thee; and I will give the carcases of the host of the Philistines this day unto the fowls of the air, and to the wild beasts of the earth; that all the earth may know that there is a God in Israel. 47 And all this assembly shall know that the LORD saveth not with sword and spear: for the battle is the Lord's, and he will give you into our hands. 48 And it came to pass, when the Philistine arose, and came and drew nigh to meet David, that David hasted, and ran toward the army to meet the Philistine. 49 And David put his hand in his bag, and took thence a stone, and slang it, and smote the Philistine in his forehead, that the stone sunk into his forehead; and he fell upon his face to the earth. 50 So David prevailed over the Philistine with a sling and with a stone, and smote the Philistine, and slew him; but there was no sword in the hand of David. 51 Therefore David ran, and stood upon the Philistine, and took his sword, and drew it out of the sheath thereof, and slew him, and cut off his head therewith. And when the Philistines saw their champion was dead, they fled.**

David had faith in the Lord and bravely walked into the middle of the two armies to face a veteran warrior much bigger than himself. David slew Goliath with one stone, and since a boy was able to destroy the strongest and greatest warrior the Philistines had the rest of the Philistines ran for their lives.

David found the courage to face Goliath through faith in God, but the Lord had prepared David for this day. God disciplined David earlier in his life by having him successfully face a lion and a bear. God built David up.

David learned from the discipline of the Lord, and was prepared on the day God called him to meet Goliath. This is why David was considered a man after God's own heart (1 Samuel 13:14).

We need to be patient during our trials, have faith, and trust in God.

References

Scripture taken from the KING JAMES VERSION OF THE BIBLE, (KJV) Public Domain 1611

Dressing Up For Church

I had questions about what to wear to church; should I dress up in my finest clothes? If I dress up for church am I dressing up for God's benefit or the other members of the church? If I don't dress up and it causes the other churchgoers to look down on me, am I being a stumbling block and causing them to sin? If I do dress up, do I make others who can't afford to dress up a stumbling block by condoning wearing your nicest clothes to church?

Is it not my heart that goes to church and not my wardrobe? Doesn't Christ live in me 24 hours a day, and if I should dress up for church to be in God's presence then shouldn't I always be dressed up, because isn't God with me always? If the reason I dress up when I go to church is because the church is the house of God, isn't the body the temple of the Lord that is always with me, and if so should I always be dressed up, or should I go to church in my everyday clothes?

These are the questions that were going through my mind. I went to the Bible to find the answers.

(NASB) James 2:2-4 For if a man comes into your assembly with a gold ring and dressed in fine clothes, and there also comes in a poor man in dirty clothes, 3 and you pay special attention to the one who is wearing fine clothes, and say,"You sit here in a good place," and say to the poor man,"You stand over there, or sit down by my foot stool," 4 have you not made distinctions among yourselves, and become judges with evil motives?

By reading James 2:2-4 you see that you should not judge people by their appearances, but treat everyone equally. Now comes another question, if when people judge you by what you are wearing makes them sin; should you dress in a manner that you think they won't judge you to prevent them from sinning, or should you not dress up for them and rebuke them if they judge you to prevent them from sinning in the future? It is possible that people might judge you regardless of what you wear.

(NASB) 1Tim 2:9 Likewise, I want women to adorn themselves with proper clothing, modestly and discreetly, not with braided hair and gold or pearls or costly garments,

(NASB) 1 Peter 3:3-4 Your adornment must not be merely external braiding the hair, and wearing gold jewelry, or putting on dresses; 4 but let it be the hidden person of the heart, with the

imperishable quality of a gentle and quiet spirit, which is precious in the sight of God.

(NASB) 1Peter 5:5 You younger men, likewise, be subject to your elders: and all of you, clothe yourselves with humility toward one another, for GOD IS OPPOSED TO THE PROUD, BUT GIVES GRACE TO THE HUMBLE.

1 Peter 3:3-4 says that God doesn't care about your outward appearance, but it's what is in your heart that counts. 1 Peter 5:5 says to be humble. Dressing up in your finest clothes is more prideful than humble.

(NASB) Jonah 3:5 Then the people of Nineveh believed in God; and they called a fast and put on sackcloth from the greatest to the least of them.

(NASB) Jeremiah 6:26 O daughter of my people, put on sackcloth and roll in ashes; Mourn as for an only son, A lamentation most bitter. For suddenly the destroyer Will come upon us.

(NASB) Daniel 9:3 So I gave my attention to the Lord God to seek Him by prayer and supplications, with fasting, sackcloth and ashes.

(NASB) Luke 10:13 Woe to you , Chorazin! Woe to you, Bethsaida! For if the miracles had been performed in Tyre and Sidon which occurred in you, they would have repented long ago, sitting in sackcloth and ashes.

The previous verses describe how people in the past dressed to please the Lord. They dressed in sackcloth to humble themselves before the Lord. Sackcloth is dark goat hair used in making sacks, and worn in times of mourning.

The following Bible verses have to do with those who dress up to impress other people.

(NASB) Mark 12:38 In His teaching He was saying:"Beware of the scribes who like to walk around in long robes, and like respectful greetings in the market places,

(NASB) Matt 23:5 But they do all their deeds to be noticed by men; for they broaden their phylacteries and lengthen the tassels of their garments.

The following verses state not to worry about what you wear; because all that is important is you seek the Kingdom of God. Follow God with your hearts, and not with the garments you put on your body.

(NASB) Matt 6:25-32 For this reason I say to you,do not be worried about your life, as to what you will eat or what you will drink; nor for your body, as to what you will put on. Is not life more than food, and the body more than clothing.28 And why are you worried about clothing? Observe how the lilies of the field grow; they do not toil nor do they spin, 29 yet I say to you that not even Solomon in all his glory clothed himself like one of these. 30 "But if God so clothes the grass of the field , which is alive today and tomorrow thrown into the furnace, will He not much more clothe you? You of little faith! 31 "Do not worry then, saying,"What will we eat? or"What will we drink?"or "What will we wear for clothing?" 32 "For the Gentiles eagerly seek all these things; for your heavenly Father knows that you need all these things.33 "But seek first His kingdom and His righteousness, and all these things will be added to you.

(NASB) Joel 2:12-13 "Yet even now," declares the LORD,"Return to Me with all your heart, And with fasting , weeping and mourning;13 And rend your heart and not your garments."

(NASB) 2 Corinth 5:12 We are not again commending ourselves to you but are giving you an occasion to be proud of us, so that you will have an answer for those who take pride in appearance and not in heart.

The next few verses remind us that we are in Christ always. 2 Corinth. 10:7 reminds us to look inwardly and not outwardly. Just as one person in a church is in Christ so are we all. We should not judge other members of Christ's body by only looking at them outwardly.

(NASB) 2 Corinth. 10:7 You are looking at things as they are outwardly. If anyone is confident in himself that he is Christ's, let him consider this again within himself, that just as he is Christ's, so also are we

(NASB) 1Corinth 6: 19 Or do you not know that your body is a temple of the Holy Spirit who is in you, whom you have from God, and that you are not your own?

(NASB) 1 Corinth 6:15 Do you not know that your bodies are members of Christ? Shall I then take away the members of Christ and make them members of a prostitute? May it never be!

We as members of Christ's body are always in His presence, and there is no time that we are instructed to dress differently than any other time. God wants us to worship Him with our hearts and motives, not with the clothing we put on. This opinion is based on the scriptures we have just read in the Bible. I am not saying that you shouldn't dress up. You can dress however you like. I don't think how you dress matters, but if you decide to dress up for church, you should examine your motives, and not judge others by their appearances. God is the only judge. It is not our place to judge anybody; especially on merely his or her outward appearance.

(NASB) Matt 11:6 " And blessed is he who does not take offense at Me"

References

Work Behavior

This Bible Study has to do with Work. The Bible is very specific about how a Christian is to behave at work, and the necessity for a Christian to support himself. There are many people that feel they are too good to work certain jobs, or earn minimum wage. In this Bible study we will find out why Christians must work, how they are to behave at work, and who they are really working for. We will begin with, why Christians need to work.

(KJV) Ge 3:17-19 And unto Adam he said, Because thou hast hearkened unto the voice of thy wife, and hast eaten of the tree, of which I commanded thee, saying, Thou shalt not eat of it: cursed is the ground for thy sake; in sorrow shalt thou eat of it all the days of thy life; 18 Thorns also and thistles shall it bring forth to thee; and thou shalt eat the herb of the field; 19 In the sweat of thy face shalt thou eat bread, till thou return unto the ground; for out of it wast thou taken: for dust thou art, and unto dust shalt thou return.

Because of Adam's original sin man has been forced to work to provide for the basic needs we need in order to stay alive. It is our pennants for tasting the fruit of the Tree of Knowledge of Good and Evil. Not much has changed since the time of the original sin. We may not have to grow our own food, but we still must work to pay for our food and the houses we live in; in order to maintain a healthy life. Genesis 3:19 not only tells us that we will need to work in order to provide for ourselves until we die, but it also tells us how we are supposed to work. We are to work by the sweat of our faces, meaning we are to work hard. The Bible is very specific in regards to how hard a Christian is expected to work, behave at work, and why they should work in this way.

(KJV) Eph 6:5-7 Servants, be obedient to them that are your masters according to the flesh, with fear and trembling, in singleness of your heart, as unto Christ;:6 Not with eyeservice, as menpleasers; but as the servants of Christ, doing the will of God from the heart; 7 With good will doing service, as to the Lord, and not to men:

(KJV) Tit 2:9-10 Exhort servants to be obedient unto their own masters, and to please them well in all things; not answering again; 10 Not purloining, but shewing all good fidelity; that they may adorn the doctrine of God our Saviour in all things.

The above verses tell Christians how they are to behave at work. Christians need to be outstanding employees, and not talk back to their bosses. They need to do a good job, be a trusted employee, be obedient, not be eye pleasers (meaning only working hard when the boss is watching), and have good will doing service. Be happy and pleasant at work, not pouting or complaining. The above verses tell us that when we are working, we are working for the Lord. We are to perform for our earthly bosses in the same manner that we would if we were working for God.

God is our real boss; by being outstanding employees we bring praise to God. As Christians we represent God, and are to work wholeheartedly so that we make the Christian faith look good and bring glory to God. If you are a Christian and are lazy, rude, not taking your job seriously, and are a bad employee, the others at work will judge you and you would give Christians a bad name.

(KJV) 1Pe 2:15 For so is the will of God, that with well doing ye may put to silence the ignorance of foolish men:

(KJV) 1Pe 2:18-20 Servants, be subject to your masters with all fear; not only to the good and gentle, but also to the froward. 19 For this is thankworthy, if a man for conscience toward God endure grief, suffering wrongfully. 20 For what glory is it, if, when ye be buffeted for your faults, ye shall take it patiently? but if, when ye do well, and suffer for it, ye take it patiently, this is acceptable with God.

(KJV) Col 3:22-24 Servants, obey in all things your masters according to the flesh; not with eyeservice, as menpleasers; but in singleness of heart, fearing God: 23 And whatsoever ye do, do it heartily, as to the Lord, and not unto men; 24 Knowing that of the Lord ye shall receive the reward of the inheritance: for ye serve the Lord Christ.

(KJV) He 6:10 For God is not unrighteous to forget your work and labour of love, which ye have shewed toward his name, in that ye have ministered to the saints, and do minister

Work is a way for you to serve God. By having a job you have the opportunity to represent God to others. At work you represent the entire Christian faith, and 1 Peter 2:15 states that it is God's will that by proving yourself through hard work you prevent others from putting down the faith. 1 Peter 2:18 goes on to say that you need to be the best employee that you can be regardless of if your boss is nice. If you have a mean boss and you still work whole-heartedly it is acceptable and thankworthy to God. You need to remember God is the one that is really your boss, and He is the one that you are working for. If your earthly boss is mean, and you still give one hundred percent everyday the mean boss will have nothing bad to say about you. Work hard for your earthly bosses even if they are mean. God will reward you for your work. God will not forget your work, and He can reward you in many aspects of your life.

(KJV) 1Pe 2:12 Having your conversation honest among the Gentiles: that, whereas they speak against you as evildoers, they may by your good works, which they shall behold, glorify God in the day of visitation.

(KJV) Phi 2:14-15 Do all things without murmurings and disputings: 15 That ye may be blameless and harmless, the sons of God, without rebuke, in the midst of a crooked and perverse nation, among whom ye shine as lights in the world;

(KJV) Tit 2:7-8 In all things shewing thyself a pattern of good works: in doctrine shewing uncorruptness, gravity, sincerity, 8 Sound speech, that cannot be condemned; that he that is of the contrary part may be ashamed, having no evil thing to say of you.

(KJV) 1Th 2:9-10 For ye remember, brethren, our labour and travail: for labouring night and day, because we would not be chargeable unto any of you, we preached unto you the gospel of God. 10 Ye are witnesses, and God also, how holily and justly and unblameably we behaved ourselves among you that believe:

The above verses reinforce the need to work hard and to be a good example at everything you do. You are to be honest, trusted, and be an example, so that others cannot find anything to complain about you. These attitudes are to be applied in your entire life not just at work. 1TH 2:9 is a demonstration of the qualities a Christian should possess. Paul did not freeload off of the people that he was preaching to. He earned his own keep, and conducted himself unblameably among the people around him.

He did this as an example for them to follow. If Paul would have preached to the people, but also freeloaded, ate all their food, and demonstrated bad behavior in their presence, no one that he preached to would have taken him seriously. They would have resented him, ignored what he said, and probably would never invite him back or trust what he said again. By Paul earning his own keep, and behaving well while among the people he proved himself to be a stand up guy, and the people were willing to listen to him. First he proved himself, and then the people were willing to listen to him. He earned their respect first.

(KJV) Col 4:1 Masters, give unto your servants that which is just and equal; knowing that ye also have a Master in heaven.

The above verse has to do with how you need to behave when you are the boss. You are to be fair and just. If you are the one in charge you need to remember that you still have a boss in heaven that you will have to give an account of your actions to.

(KJV) Ga 6:2 Bear ye one another's burdens, and so fulfil the law of Christ. 3 For if a man think himself to be something, when he is nothing, he deceiveth himself. 4 But let every man prove his own work, and then shall he have rejoicing in himself alone, and not in another. 5 For every man shall bear his own burden.

Gal 6:3 is directed towards the people that put themselves above others. There are many people that believe they are too good to do some jobs. They think that if they can't instantly be the CEO of a company then why should they work at all. Many people think they are above cleaning toilets, moping floors, or even earning minimum wage. There are people that refuse to get a job that they feel is beneath them. Of course they are wrong. It doesn't matter what job you do. You always have the same boss (God).

If you think that you are too good to work a certain job, then you are deceiving yourself. As Christians we are supposed to be humble. If you are not humble perhaps being the CEO of a company is not a good job for you to have. As Christians we are on this planet to serve God, and learn the lessons given to us in the Bible. We are expected to work and bear our own burdens. It doesn't matter what job we have all that matters is the amount of effort we put into our jobs, and how we behave.

If you work hard in the fast food industry you can have self-respect in the job that you do. It doesn't matter if the job is considered a high status job by the media and mundane world; all that matters is how hard you work at your job. If you are the President of a company or work manual labor God is still your boss, and how good you are doing spiritually is based on if God finds the work you do acceptable. Not if the World does.

The above verses tell us to help each other out. Don't get a big ego and place yourself above others. We are all equal servants of God. We need to look out for each other, and each of us must bear our own burden. Gal 6:4

tells us that after we prove ourselves then we will have self-respect. It is better to earn self-respect by proving yourself through your work, than to think you're something that you are not.

(KJV) Ec 3:13 And also that every man should eat and drink, and enjoy the good of all his labour, it is the gift of God.

The above verse tells us to enjoy our job and the fruits of our labor. What you earn is yours. Enjoy it. Enjoy the house that you live in and the life that you live. They are a gift from God. Working is not a mere punishment that we must endure because Adam ate the forbidden fruit. There are many wonderful benefits from working. Work gives us the opportunity to serve God, and also gives us the means to enjoy our lives and have self-respect.

God is a rewarder of those that diligently seek Him. If you put God first everything else will be added unto you. Work hard at everything you do, and enjoy the life that God has given you.

(KJV) Ec 10:18 By much slothfulness the building decayeth; and through idleness of the hands the house droppeth through

The above verse tells us not to be lazy. If you are lazy your life will fall apart. I included this verse to point out that it is necessary to work. There are many verses in the Bible like the above verse, but I feel it is redundant to include them in this Bible study.

The Bible tells us exactly how hard we are to work, and how we are to behave while at work. It is obvious that work is necessary, and that we must bear our own burdens. I included the above verse merely to point out that being lazy will have an adverse affect on your life. If you do not work or are a lazy employee, then you are not fulfilling the requirements of work listed in the Bible.

So far in this Bible study we have been examining the responsibilities of men at work, and women that choose to work. Women were not instructed to work due to eating the forbidden fruit. The punishment given to women for tasting the fruit is pain in childbirth. However, if a woman chooses to work, she is subject to all of the same requirements for Christians at work listed in the Bible verses covered so far. Now we will look at the responsibilities given to women in the Bible.

(KJV) Tit 2:4-5 That they may teach the young women to be sober, to love their husbands, to love their children, 5 To be

discreet, chaste, keepers at home, good, obedient to their own husbands, that the word of God be not blasphemed.

(KJV) Tit 2:7-8 In all things shewing thyself a pattern of good works: in doctrine shewing uncorruptness, gravity, sincerity,:8 Sound speech, that cannot be condemned; that he that is of the contrary part may be ashamed, having no evil thing to say of you.

As you can see from the above verses women have the same requirements as men, but there duties have to do with working in the home. They are to offer love and support to their families, and teach and raise their children well. By being a good homemaker women are given the opportunity to serve God. They are to live a good life, and be examples to others. Women are responsible for displaying proper behavior so that they do not make the faith look bad, or give anyone reason to speak badly of them.

Proverbs Chapter 31 is an example of what women are to strive for. She should be loyal and trustworthy. She is responsible for ensuring that her family is clothed, and for providing food for her house (cooking it and/or earning it). She should be generous and willing to work until her tasks are complete. She can work from home (or a job) to help support her family. She should give good advice, and display kindness. She is to take care of her household, and not be lazy. She shall earn the respect of her family and others.

You must first earn others respect before they will be willing to accept your advice. Proverbs 31:30 has to do with vanity, it states that obedience to the Lord is the real virtue not your appearance or the services you can provide. Proverbs 31:31 states that women are entitled to the fruits of their labor. A homemaker should enjoy the fruits of her labor as much as the husband that earns the money. She should be shown respect by her family, and enjoy her life. It is a gift from God.

(KJV) Ec 3:13 And also that every man should eat and drink, and enjoy the good of all his labour, it is the gift of God.

References

Scripture taken from the KING JAMES VERSION OF THE BIBLE, (KJV) Public Domain 1611

Listening, Anger, and Speech

The scriptures I am going to be discussing are from the book of James. We will be discussing James 1:19-21 taken from The New American Standard Version of the Bible. These verses are very important not only do they give you guidelines on how to control your emotions, but also how to achieve or not achieve the Righteousness of God. This message is very important because as it is stated in James 1:21, it is able to save your soul.

(NASB) James 1:19-21 This you know, my beloved brethren. But everyone must be quick to hear, slow to speak and slow to anger; 20 for the anger of man does not achieve the righteousness of God. 21 Therefore, putting aside all filthiness and all that remains of wickedness, in humility receive the word implanted, which is able to save your souls.

You must listen to God's word, don't speak rashly, and you must learn to control your emotions. If you give into anger and hatred, you are not following God's word, or the example that God has set for us. If you don't control your emotions and your deeds you are not on the path of righteousness. James 1:21 goes on to tell us how to achieve the righteousness of God; by removing all sin, anger, and all things unclean from our lives that may lead us to sin. In humility we are to receive God's word implanted, which if followed will save our souls.

To further study these verses I have broken them down into three different subjects; Anger, Speech, and Hearing and Following God's will.

Anger

James 1:19 says to be slow to anger. This not only tells us to control our emotions, but also to follow God's example.

(NASB) Psalm 145:8-9 The Lord is gracious and merciful; slow to anger and great in loving kindness. 9 The Lord is good to all; and his mercies are over all his works.

(NASB) Ephesian 4:30-32 Do not grieve the Holy Spirit of God, by whom you were sealed for the day of redemption. 31 Let all bitterness and wrath and anger and clamor and slander be put away from you, along with all malice. 32 Be kind to one another, tenderhearted, forgiving each other, just as God in Christ also has forgiven you.

(NASB) Nehemiah 9:17 They refused to listen, and did not remember Your wondrous deeds which you had performed among them; So they became stubborn and appointed a leader to return to their slavery in Egypt. But You are a god of forgiveness, gracious, and compassionate, Slow to anger and abounding in loving kindness; And You did not forsake them.

I have selected the following verses to demonstrate **WHY** you should be slow to anger.

(NASB) Proverbs 14:17 A quick tempered man acts foolishly, and a man of evil devices is hated

When you are quick to anger you act foolishly. You cause others to hate you. By causing someone to hate you are cause them to sin and stumble. Matthew 18:7 warns us not to be a stumbling block to others.

(NASB) Matthew 18:7 Woe to the world because of it's stumbling blocks! For it is inevitable that stumbling blocks come; but woe to that man through whom the stumbling block comes!

(NASB) Psalm 37:8-9 Cease from anger and forsake wrath; Do not fret; it leads only to evildoing. 9 For evildoers will be cut off, but those who wait for the Lord, they will inherit the land.

The following verses are examples of how to overcome anger.

(NASB) Hosea 14:4 I will heal their apostasy, I will love them freely, For my anger has turned away from them.

(NASB) Romans 12:21 Do not be overcome by evil, but overcome evil with good.

(NASB) Proverbs 19:11 A man's discretion makes him slow to anger, And it is his glory to overlook a transgression.

(NASB) James 4:7 Submit therefore to God. Resist the Devil and he will flee from you.

What this is saying is to overcome anger and evil with love, goodness, forgiveness, and to trust and be obedient to God.

Speech

Now we study a few verses on **WHY** you should be slow to speak, and what can come from speaking in haste.

(NASB) Proverbs 15:1-2 A gentle answer turns away wrath, But a harsh word stirs up anger. 2 The tongue of the wise makes knowledge acceptable, But the mouth of fools spouts folly.

(NASB) James 1:26 If anyone thinks himself to be religious, and yet does not bridle his tongue but deceives his own heart, this man's religion is worthless.

(NASB) Matthew 5:22 But I say to you that everyone who is angry with his brother shall be guilty before the court; and whoever says to his brother, "You good-for-nothing" shall be guilty before the supreme court; and whoever says,"You fool" shall be guilty enough to go into the fiery hell.

What you say can either turn away wrath, or cause anger. If you do not watch what you say, and you speak from your emotions and not God's truth your religion is worthless. If you don't control your anger, but instead speak from it, you are guilty before the Supreme Court, which I interpret as God, and it is enough of an offence that it merits being thrown into Hell fire.

Hearing/Following God's Will

The next subject we will cover is Hearing, or listening to God's word, and following it with obedience.

(NASB) Acts 3:22-23 Moses said, "The Lord God will raise up for you a Prophet like me from your own brethren; To him you shall give heed to everything he says to you.23 And it will be that every soul that does not heed that prophet shall be utterly destroyed from among the people.

(NASB) John 6:53 So Jesus said to them, Truly, Truly, I say to you, unless you eat the flesh of the Son of Man and drink his blood, you have no life in yourselves.

In the first set of verses Moses predicts the coming of Jesus, and states that if you don't listen to him you will be utterly destroyed. In the second verse Jesus says that without Him you have no life.

(NASB) John 5:25 Truly, Truly, I say to you, an hour is coming and now is, when the dead will hear the voice of the Son of God, and those who hear will live.

In John 5:25 those how hear Jesus will have life. The dead in this verse refers to those in John 6:53 who aren't in Jesus.

(NASB) James 1:22 But prove yourselves doers of the word, and not merely hearers who delude themselves.

This verse (James 1:22) demonstrates that the true hearers of the word do what it says. Those who delude themselves in this verse might be compared to those Jesus speaks of in Matthew 7:22-23.

(NASB) Matthew 7:22-24 Many will say to me on that day Lord, Lord, did we not prophecy in your name, and in your name perform many miracles? 23 And then I will declare to them, I never knew you; Depart from me you who practice lawlessness. 24 Therefore everyone who hears these words of mine and acts on them , may be compared to a wiseman who built his house on the rock

(NASB) James 1:25 But one who looks intently at the perfect law, the law of liberty, and abides by it, not having become a forgetful hearer but an effectual doer, this man will be blessed in what he does

(NASB) Luke 11:28 But he said," On the contrary, blessed are those who hear the word of God and observe it.

(NASB) Matthew 13:9 He who has ears, let him hear

The followers of Jesus are the ones who hear His words and observe His commands.

(NASB) Matthew 13:16 But blessed are your eyes, because they see, and your ears because they hear

(NASB) John 10:3-4 To him the doorkeeper opens, and the sheep hear his voice and he calls his sheep by name and leads them out. 4 When he puts forth all his own, he goes ahead of them, and the sheep follow him because they know his voice

John 10:3-4 states that it is the Christian who hears Jesus' voice, and follows Him. Jesus goes ahead of them to death and is crucified, but the Christians of modern times still are able to follow Him because they know His voice. The word in the Bible.

(NASB) John 10:15-16 Even as the Father knows Me and I know the Father; and I lay down my life for the sheep. 16 I have other sheep , which are not of this fold; I must bring them also, and they will hear My Voice; and they will become one flock with one shepherd.

In John 10:15-16 Jesus dies for our sins (all those who hear him). The other sheep He will also bring refers to all nations; Jews and Gentiles will all be one flock with one shepherd, our Lord Jesus Christ.

(NASB) John 10:27 My sheep hear my voice, and I know them, and they know me, And I give eternal life to them, and they will never perish; and no one will snatch them out of my hand

It is clear that the Hearers (Christians) are the ones who listen to God's word, and do what it says. James 1:19 says you should be quick to follow God.

James 1:21 says, *"in humility receive the word implanted, which is able to save your souls."* The word "humility" in this passage is referring to meekness like that of a child. Forsaking all your pride, all of your preconceived ideas, your thoughts that you know what is right, forsake all those ideas and start over, fresh, and except the word of God as the only truth and abide in it. Receive the kingdom of God like a child. A child trusts its Father and obeys His commands.

(NASB) Mark 10:15 "Truly I say to you, whoever does not receive the kingdom of God like a child will not inter it at all."

References

Confessing Christ

One day while I was at work, I overheard a conversation that four co-workers were having. One of the employees had just mentioned that he had come to work directly after leaving church. The other employees immediately began to mock him saying, "You go to church?" I began listening to their conversation more closely, because I had recently become a Christian myself. The other three co-workers began to make fun of the employee who had come to work from church. As they continued mocking him, I felt very conflicted as to what I should do. Should I ignore what was going on so the conversation will not be dragged on, or should I confess my faith in God and support my fellow Christian?

I didn't speak up, and the employee who said that he went to church gave into the other employee's ridicule. He eventually said that he doesn't believe in God and only goes to church because his parents make him. Once I got home from work I felt like I had failed my fellow man by not supporting him, and made him feel alone to the extent that he denied his faith. As the week progressed, the employee that once said that he went to church began coming to work and blaspheming God the entire time he was at work in an effort to gain the respect of the other employees. I was very upset with myself and began to ask myself questions about what I should have done. When is the right time to make the good confession and express your religious beliefs?

I justified my actions to myself by scriptures that say things like, "Don't cast your pearls before swine", but I kept coming back to verses thirty-two and thirty-three in the book of Matthew chapter ten. In Matthew 10:32-33 Jesus says, "Whosoever therefore confesses me before men, him will I confess also before my Father which is in heaven. But whosoever shall deny me before men, him will I also deny before my Father which is in heaven." To some people the above mentioned event may seem like a trivial thing that happened one day at work, but to others it is the moment of truth, a decision that makes the difference between heaven and hell.

Since then I have done a great deal of soul searching as to what I should have done. I came to the conclusion that it is up to every individual to stand up for their own beliefs, because "everyone will be judged according to their own deeds" (Rev.20: 12). In the book of 1Peter chapter 3:15, we are told to always be ready to give an answer to others regarding our faith; regardless of others being there that will support our statement. It is easy to make the good confession at church or in front of other believers who share the same beliefs as you. The true test is to confess your faith in front of unbelievers. We need to follow Jesus' example, who made the good confession even in front of Pontius Pilate (1 Tim.6:13). Jesus was mocked, beaten, and still made the good confession in front of Pontius Pilate, who was the one that ordered Jesus' crucifixion.

Standing up for our beliefs in front of people who might make fun of us isn't that big of a deal. As it says in Hebrews 12:4, *"we have not yet resisted to the point of shedding blood."* The next time that I am in a similar situation, I think that I will speak up and confess my faith, not because I feel that it is my duty, but to help prevent a fellow Christian from making a decision that they will regret later (Matthew 25:45). We are to be there for others in need, but at the same time the choice to confirm or deny Christ is the responsibility of each individual.

Soldier

Can a Christian be a soldier? Is it wrong to be in the Military? Some Christians feel that it is sinful to serve in a profession that may require you to kill. To find out if it is okay for a Christian to serve in such a profession we must examine the scriptures.

> **(KJV) Ro 13:1-5 Let every soul be subject unto the higher powers. For there is no power but of God: the powers that be are ordained of God. 2 Whosoever therefore resisteth the power, resisteth the ordinance of God: and they that resist shall receive to themselves damnation. 3 For rulers are not a terror to good works, but to the evil. Wilt thou then not be afraid of the power? do that which is good, and thou shalt have praise of the same: 4 For he is the minister of God to thee for good. But if thou do that which is evil, be afraid; for he beareth not the sword in vain: for he is the minister of God, a revenger to execute wrath upon him that doeth evil. 5 Wherefore ye must needs be subject, not only for wrath, but also for conscience sake.**

> **(KJV) 1Pe 2:13-14 Submit yourselves to every ordinance of man for the Lord's sake: whether it be to the king, as supreme;:14 Or unto governors, as unto them that are sent by him for the punishment of evildoers, and for the praise of them that do well.**

The above scriptures tell us that we are to obey the rulers that are on earth. The scriptures tell us that all governments are instituted by God. If we are law-abiding citizens then we have no reason to fear the government. The governments were set up by God to prevent evil. To do this governments need people to aid in keeping the peace. These people are soldiers and policemen. As we read in Romans 13:4 and 1 Peter 2:14 these soldiers are instituted by God, and may be required to kill in order to keep the peace and stop evil.

A big concern of some Christians is if by killing you are breaking one of the Ten Commandments, which says, *"Thou shalt not murder."* Some translations of the Bible use the word, "Kill" in place of the word, "Murder", and this leads to confusion. Common sense tells us that if the word, "Kill" was used then the commandment would be impossible to keep. In the Old Testament the tribes of Israel were often ordered by God to kill.

In the New Testament Peter had a vision in which he saw several animals lowered on a blanket from heaven and God told him to kill and eat.

People must kill simply to eat. In the Bible God often tells us to obey all of His commandments. God does not contradict Himself. He wouldn't tell us not to do something, and then turn around and tell us to do the thing that he told us not to do. If for some reason you think that if you kill animals that you are not really killing, I suggest that you read the Bible study on animals also found in this book. If the word, "murder" is used in the commandment it makes perfect sense.

(KJV) 1John 3:15 Whosoever hateth his brother is a murderer: and ye know that no murderer hath eternal life abiding in him.

To murder is to kill somebody for evil reasons. Not because of food, not to protect yourself, but for reasons like to rob the person or because you hate the person or some other evil motive. Before we examine the need for soldiers, and what the job entails we will first look at whether or not it is possible for a Christian to be a soldier.

(KJV) Lu 3:14 And the soldiers likewise demanded of him, saying, And what shall we do? And he said unto them, Do violence to no man, neither accuse any falsely; and be content with your wages.

Reading the above scripture you notice that when John the Baptist was asked by the soldiers what they could do he told them to be just in their job, and dealings with people. If it was wrong to be a soldier, John the Baptist could have easily said to them, "*stop being soldiers.*"

(KJV) Lu 7:6-9 Then Jesus went with them. And when he was now not far from the house, the centurion sent friends to him, saying unto him, Lord, trouble not thyself: for I am not worthy that thou shouldest enter under my roof: 7 Wherefore neither thought I myself worthy to come unto thee: but say in a word, and my servant shall be healed. 8 For I also am a man set under authority, having under me soldiers, and I say unto one, Go, and he goeth; and to another, Come, and he cometh; and to my servant, Do this, and he doeth it. 9 When Jesus heard these things, he marvelled at him, and turned him about, and said unto the people that followed him, I say unto you, I have not found so great of faith, no, not in Israel.

In the above verses Jesus does not rebuke the soldier for being a soldier, but instead pointed out how great of faith the man had. As you can see you can be a soldier, and be a follower of Christ.

(KJV) Mt 26:53 Thinkest thou that I cannot now pray to my Father, and he shall presently give me more than twelve legions of angels?

(KJV) Rev 9:15-16 And the four angels were loosed, which were prepared for an hour, and a day, and a month, and a year, for to slay the third part of men. 16 And the number of the army of the horsemen were two hundred thousand thousand: and I heard the number of them.

The above verses let us know that there are even soldiers and armies in Heaven. On this planet there are evil people, and it is the policeman or soldier's job to protect people from evil.

(KJV) Acts 23:10 And when there arose a great dissension, the chief captain, fearing lest Paul should have been pulled in pieces of them, commanded the soldiers to go down, and to take him by force from among them, and to bring him into the castle.

(KJV) Acts 23:23-24 And he called unto him two centurions, saying, Make ready two hundred soldiers to go to Caesarea, and horsemen threescore and ten, and spearmen two hundred, at the third hour of the night; 24 And provide them beasts, that they may set Paul on, and bring him safe unto Felix the governor.

In the above verses we read how the soldiers protected Paul from those who wanted to kill him. Soldiers are protectors and are used to keep the peace and establish law and order.

(KJV) Rom 12:18 If it be possible, as much as lieth in you, live peaceably with all men.

(KJV) Ec 3:8 A time to love, and a time to hate; a time of war, and a time of peace.

The above verses tell us that we are to do our best to live at peace as much as it is in our power. They also tell us that there are times of war that we cannot avoid. This is when soldiers are necessary.

Now we will look at what the job of a soldier entails.

(KJV) Mt 26:52 Then said Jesus unto him, Put up again thy sword into his place: for all they that take the sword shall perish with the sword.

The above scripture has a lot to do with soldiers. If you decide go draw your weapon and go into battle there is a very good chance that you may be killed. If you are a soldier or a policeman you are a fool if you don't recognize that your job is dangerous. To be a soldier you must be willing to risk death to protect others. You must put the safety of others before yourself.

(KJV) 1 John 3:16 Hereby perceive we the love of God, because he laid down his life for us: and we ought to lay down our lives for the brethren.

The above scripture tells us that we should take on the same attitude of Christ, and be willing to die to save others. Soldiers have to put this teaching into practice, and be willing to give their lives for their brethren, families, country, and countrymen. If you begin to think to yourself, *"who would die for this Country (for whatever your reason)"*, remember that Christ died for us when we were all sinners. So if you think that you shouldn't die to protect a country or a people remember that Christ gave his life for people that didn't deserve it. He died that we might have the chance to straighten out our lives and correct the things that are wrong.

The following verses are from the book of Judges; I feel that by reading these verses you would understand not only the need for soldiers, but also see the sacrifices that they are willing to make in a effort to keep justice in the world. This is a tale about a traveler and his fiancé.

(KJV) Jud 19:22 Now as they were making their hearts merry, behold, the men of the city, certain sons of Belial, beset the house round about, and beat at the door, and spake to the master of the house, the old man, saying, Bring forth the man that came into thine house, that we may know him.

By know him, they mean rape him.

(KJV) Jud 19:23-24 And the man, the master of the house, went out unto them, and said unto them, Nay, my brethren, nay, I pray you, do not so wickedly; seeing that this man is come into mine house, do not this folly. 24 Behold, here is my daughter a maiden, and his concubine; them I will bring out now, and humble ye them, and do with them what seemeth good unto you: but unto this man do not so vile a thing.

The owner of the house pleaded that they leave his guest alone; just as Lot did in Sodom & Gomorrah (even willing to sacrifice his own daughter).

(KJV) Jud 19:25-28 But the men would not hearken to him: so the man took his concubine, and brought her forth unto them; and they knew her, and abused her all the night until the morning: and when the day began to spring, they let her go. 26 Then came the woman in the dawning of the day, and fell down at the door of the man's house where her lord was, till it was light. 27 And her lord rose up in the morning, and opened the doors of the house, and went out to go his way: and, behold, the woman his concubine was fallen down at the door of the house, and her hands were upon the threshold. 28 And he said unto her, Up, and let us be going. But none answered. Then the man took her up upon an ass, and the man rose up, and gat him unto his place.

The evil men took the travelers fiancé, and gang raped her and abused her all night long until she died from her injuries. We don't know exactly what horrors they put her through, but it was so much that she died from the abuse.

(KJV) Jud 19:29-30 And when he was come into his house, he took a knife, and laid hold on his concubine, and divided her, together with her bones, into twelve pieces, and sent her into all the coasts of Israel. 30 And it was so, that all that saw it said, There was no such deed done nor seen from the day that the children of Israel came up out of the land of Egypt unto this day: consider of it, take advice, and speak your minds.

The traveler sent pieces of his fiancés body all over the country trying to get justice for her death.

(KJV) Jud 20:3-8 (Now the children of Benjamin heard that the children of Israel were gone up to Mizpeh.) Then said the children of Israel, Tell us, how was this wickedness? 4 And the Levite, the husband of the woman that was slain, answered and said, I came into Gibeah that belongeth to Benjamin, I and my concubine, to lodge. 5 And the men of Gibeah rose against me, and beset the house round about upon me by night, and thought to have slain me: and my concubine have they forced, that she is dead. 6 And I took my concubine, and cut her in pieces, and sent her throughout all the country of the inheritance of Israel: for they have committed lewdness and folly in Israel. 7 Behold, ye are all children of Israel; give here your advice and counsel. 8 And all the people arose as one man, saying, We will not any of us go to his tent, neither will we any of us turn into his house.

Israel formed an army to bring the evil men to justice.

(KJV) Jud 20:12-14 And the tribes of Israel sent men through all the tribe of Benjamin, saying, What wickedness is this that is done among you? 13 Now therefore deliver us the men, the children of Belial, which are in Gibeah, that we may put them to death, and put away evil from Israel. But the children of Benjamin would not hearken to the voice of their brethren the children of Israel: 14 But the children of Benjamin gathered themselves together out of the cities unto Gibeah, to go out to battle against the children of Israel.

The men of Benjamin decided not to hand over the evil men to be punished for their crimes, but decided to form an army and fight to defend the evil men.

(KJV) Jud 20:20-25 And the men of Israel went out to battle against Benjamin; and the men of Israel put themselves in array to fight against them at Gibeah.:21 And the children of Benjamin came forth out of Gibeah, and destroyed down to the ground of the Israelites that day twenty and two thousand men. 22 And the people the men of Israel encouraged themselves, and set their battle again in array in the place where they put themselves in array the first day. 24 And the children of Israel came near against the children of Benjamin the second day. 25 And Benjamin went forth against them out of Gibeah the second day, and destroyed down to the ground of the children of Israel again eighteen thousand men; all these drew the sword.

As you can see Israel is losing the war. Although they are fighting to prevent evil they are still losing thousands of men to bring a few criminals to justice. In Judges 20:25 it states that the men who died are men who drew the sword.

(KJV) Jud 20:34-35 And there came against Gibeah ten thousand chosen men out of all Israel, and the battle was sore: but they knew not that evil was near them. 35 And the Lord smote Benjamin before Israel: and the children of Israel destroyed of the Benjamites that day twenty and five thousand and an hundred men: all these drew the sword.

(KJV) Jud 20:44-48 And there fell of Benjamin eighteen thousand men; all these were men of valour. 45 And they turned and fled toward the wilderness unto the rock of Rimmon: and

they gleaned of them in the highways five thousand men; and pursued hard after them unto Gidom, and slew two thousand men of them. 46 So that all which fell that day of Benjamin were twenty and five thousand men that drew the sword; all these were men of valour. 47 But six hundred men turned and fled to the wilderness unto the rock Rimmon, and abode in the rock Rimmon four months. 48 And the men of Israel turned again upon the children of Benjamin, and smote them with the edge of the sword, as well the men of every city, as the beast, and all that came to hand: also they set on fire all the cities that they came to.**

In the end Israel won the war, but you can see that thousands of men died trying to bring a few evil men to justice. I don't know why the tribe of Benjamin didn't hand over the criminals, perhaps in their minds they were doing what they felt was right. As you can see many soldiers were willing to die to stop the spread of evil, and get justice for the poor woman who suffered such a horrible death by those evil men. It seems like the war was a waste of thousands of good men's lives, but it wasn't.

Justice needs to be established on the earth. If evil was to spread and people were allowed to do any evil thing that they wanted to do to any body that they wanted to do evil to then this world would be a horrible place. Every society must be careful not to let evil get out of control. In order to do this, governments need people who are willing to risk their own lives to make the world a safer place to live in for others. Preventing evil and crime is everyone's job. Do your part; if you see a crime take place do not look the other way. If nothing else call the police.

Are there bad soldiers and bad cops? Yes! Like any group of people or any profession some people are evil.

(KJV) Mr 15:16-20 And the soldiers led him away into the hall, called Praetorium; and they call together the whole band. 17 And they clothed him with purple, and platted a crown of thorns, and put it bout his head, 18 And began to salute him, Hail, King of the Jews! 19 And they smote him on the head with a reed, and did spit upon him, and bowing their knees worshipped him. 20 And when they had mocked him, they took off the purple from him, and put his own clothes on him, and led him out to crucify him.

The soldiers in the above scriptures are obviously bad. They abused their power and acted evilly.

(KJV) Ro 14:2-4 For one believeth that he may eat all things: another, who is weak, eateth herbs.:3 Let not him that eateth despise him that eateth not; and let not him which eateth not judge him that eateth: for God hath received him. 4 Who art thou that judgest another man's servant? to his own master he standeth or falleth. Yea, he shall be holden up: for God is able to make him stand.

(KJV) Ro 14:22-23 Hast thou faith? have it to thyself before God. Happy is he that condemneth not himself in that thing which he alloweth. 23 And he that doubteth is damned if he eat, because he eateth not of faith: for whatsoever is not of faith is sin.

The above scripture has to do with motives and choices. If you think that something is bad and you still do it, then that is wrong of you. If you don't do something that doesn't mean that it is bad for others to do. I included the above scriptures to let you know that in the end it is up to you. If you feel that it is wrong to be a soldier don't be one. Just understand that soldiers and policemen are necessary to keep the world a somewhat safe place to live in. Remember the world needs soldiers and police regardless of their beliefs. Personally I'd rather have Christians be the soldiers, because as you know there are good guys and bad guys in every profession, I would rather have the good guys be the ones in charge of my protection.

(KJV) 2Ti 2:3-5 Thou therefore endure hardness, as a good soldier of Jesus Christ. 4 No man that warreth entangleth himself with the affairs of this life; that he may please him who hath chosen him to be a soldier. 5 And if a man also strive for masteries, yet is he not crowned, except he strive lawfully.

(KJV) Lu 22:36 Then said he unto them, But now, he that hath a purse, let him take it, and likewise his scrip: and he that hath no sword, let him sell his garment, and buy one.

(KJV) Ps 144:1 Blessed be the Lord my strength, which teacheth my hands to war, and my fingers to fight:

References

Scripture taken from the KING JAMES VERSION OF THE BIBLE, (KJV) Public Domain 1611

Magnum Opus

There are many things you can do in your leisure time, but the very best thing to do in your leisure time, is to work. I'm not talking about the nine to five work that you do to make a living, but Magnum Opus, or the great work. In the past alchemists tried making gold. Spiritual alchemy is the process of turning your soul into gold metaphorically speaking. In short, instead of working on paying your bills and putting bread on the table, you should spend all of the time you can working on the perfection of your soul, by doing the will of your Father, the Creator of all things visible and invisible.

The Bible says in 2 Timothy 2:15, "Be diligent to present yourself approved to God as a workman who does not need to be ashamed, accurately handling the word of truth." This tells me, that we must strive to do our very best and live a life pleasing to God. How do you do this? By studying the Bible so that you can accurately handle the word of truth. How can you do God's will if you don't know what he wants from you? Many times in the Bible Jesus tells us exactly how, by following Him. Jesus is the Light of the world; He came to the world in human form and lived a sinless life as an example to us all. He says to follow Him, but we can't do that unless we take the time to familiarize ourselves with His word. If you take the time to familiarize yourself with His word, you will know how to act in accordance to God's will, regardless of the situation, whether at work or at home.

Colossians 3:16 says to let the word of Christ richly dwell within you. Colossians 3:17 says," Whatever you do in word or in deed, do all in the name of the Lord Jesus, giving thanks through Him to God the Father." These two verses tell us that we need to know what we are supposed to do, so that we will be prepared to do what is right, under any given circumstance. For example, Colossians 3:22-23 tells us how we are supposed to act at work. It says, "*22 Slaves, in all things obey those who are your masters on earth, not with external service, as those who merely please men, but with sincerity of heart, fearing the Lord. 23 Whatever you do, do your work heartily, as for the Lord rather than for men.*" The Bible is full of examples of how to live every aspect of our lives in a manner pleasing to God, if we only take the time to read it. Of course there is never enough time to read and understand everything in the Bible. The Bible is a big book, and no matter how many times you read it you always learn something new.

Do not deceive yourself; thinking that just reading through the Bible one time is enough. Learning and understanding is an on going process. You can't be shown how to swim at an early age, and expect to win an Olympic swimming competition years later. You must be diligent in your training, work hard, and do your best to win such a competition. How much more important is the preservation of your soul, than a swimming contest. Yet people will spend their entire lives trying to get ahead in this world, seeking their own glory and selfish pride, and pay little attention to their spiritual progress. They are too busy to worry about their souls.

In the book of Matthew, Jesus speaks a parable about a king that gave a wedding feast. This parable is about the return of Jesus. It has to do with people who are invited to come to Him, but they are too wrapped up in their own lives, to have time for Him. In this parable, the king sends out his servants to call all who have been invited to his feast to join him, but this is what happened, "*Matthew 22:5 But they paid no attention and went there way, one to his own farm, another to his business.*" These people are like us all; following our vain pursuits in this world, and that is something we all go through in this life. However, we need to find a middle ground. In our lives we need to work, and earn a living by the sweat of our faces, because of Adam and the original sin (Genesis 3:18-19), but at the same time we must incorporate Christ in every aspect of our lives; never forgetting that it is because of God that we have a life in the first place.

The Ten Commandments (Exodus 20:3-17) tell us how to live a righteous life; by not lying, stealing, murdering, and coveting what our neighbor has, but the first commandment is that you shall not have any other gods before God. If you remember this, then you can apply it to your life. Who is your God? Is it money? Is it power? Are you seeking your own glory, or are you putting God first in your life? Most of the commandments can be looked at as a moral system that helps us exist among other humans, but the first commandment of loving God above everything else forces us to look at our lives on a broader scale. Not abstaining from stealing so that we don't get put in jail, but following God's commandments, seeking to please Him. Exodus 20:5 basically says that those who don't obey His commandments will face the anger of God, but Exodus 20:6 says that God will show loving kindness to all those who keep His commandments.

In this world there is always something we can spend our time doing instead of studying God's word. We get wrapped up in school, work, hobbies, video games, and if nothing else watching television. The world is full of distractions, and after a hard day's work we might not feel like studying. We need to find time! Is watching television more important than learning what God wants you to do?

In Mark 12:6 a scribe asked Jesus, what the most important commandment was. His answer was this, Mark 12:30 "*AND YOU SHALL*

LOVE THE LORD YOUR GOD WITH ALL YOU HEART, AND WITH ALL YOUR SOUL, AND WITH ALL YOUR MIND, AND WITH ALL YOUR STRENGTH." This is the most important commandment that you are to follow. You must put God first in your life, loving Him with all your heart, meaning you should desire to do God's will. Loving Him with all your mind, meaning to keep your thoughts on Him focusing on Him all day long. This will help you to act in accordance with His will in any situation you find yourself in. A very important part of this commandment that we should focus on when we feel too tired, or too busy to study God's word is the end of this commandment. To love Him with all your strength; this is very important.

You need to find the strength to study the plan of your salvation. Strength is very important in your journey through life. You need to have the strength not to succumb to peer-pressure, that might cause you to sin. You need the strength to fight off your thoughts of lust and greed, and the strength to do what is right. It takes strength to stand up for your beliefs, to confess your love for God in a room full of non-believers. Jesus says, in Mark 8:38 that whoever is ashamed to confess Him in front of men, He will also be ashamed to confess him in front of God. Where do we get this strength? Psalm 28:7, Philippians 4:13, and 1 Peter 4:11 says that God will supply us with the strength. The strength that we are to demonstrate does not require much effort on our parts, because God will give us the strength.

If you look at the history of Christianity you will see that lots of people had the strength to stand up against incredible odds; even dying for their beliefs. Jesus himself had the strength to die on the cross, and the strength to forgive those who crucified Him (Luke 23:34). In light of the strength that Jesus demonstrated by dying on the cross for us, how can we in good conscience, say to ourselves that we can't find the time or the strength to study the Bible, which is only in our best interest anyways?

We must determine who we serve in this life. Is it our ambition for the things in this world, or God and our eternal salvation? We need to learn to exist in the world, but not be apart of this world. 1 John 2:15 says, "*Do not love the world or the things in the world. If anyone loves the world, the love of the Father is not in him.*" 1 John 2:17 says, "*The world is passing away, and also its lust; but the one who does the will of God lives forever.*" You can see that although presently we must live in this world, we must focus on the big picture. No matter what you achieve in this world when the world ends, all you have achieved will be gone. (Matthew 6:19-20)

When the world ends the only thing that you will have left is your relationship with God, and where you will spend eternity. 1 John 2:17 says that those who do God's will will live forever. The only way to know what

God's will is, is to study your Bible. Don't be confused thinking that only the people who follow Christ will live forever; everyone will exist for eternity. It's just that only the followers of Christ will exist in a state that would be considered living. Matthew 25:46 says, *"These will go away into eternal punishment, but the righteous into eternal life."* Revelation 21:7-8 says," *He who overcomes will inherit these things, and I will be his God and he will be My son. 8 But for the cowardly and unbelieving and abominable and murderers and immoral persons and sorcerers and idolaters and all liars, their part will be in the lake that burns with fire and brimstone, which is the second death."* You know by the last few verses (Matthew 25:46 & Revelation 21:8) that everyone will live forever. It's just that some will live forever in paradise, and some will live forever in eternal punishment and torment.

When you die, or the world ends, everything you have acquired in this life will not amount to anything. The only thing that is important is how you have lived. Revelation 20:12 says that everyone will be judged by their deeds; weather they spend eternity in bliss, or eternal torment. The choice is yours, and the time is now, for you to decide your eternity. No one knows when the world will end, (Matthew 24:36) so you need to be prepared for it always. What would you do if the world ended right now? Where would you spend eternity? Are you confident that you have put God first in your life, and that you are living in accordance with His will? If not I urge you to read your Bible, find out what God's will is and live by it (James 1:22-25).

Certainly it would be better to spend your time seeking God and eternal life, than the material goods this world has to offer. Use your time wisely, go to work, and to school, but you must also find time to learn how to live forever. It all comes down to putting God first; of course, you still must work and earn a living it's just a question of your priorities. Matthew 6:31-33 tells you, that if you seek God first He will give you all of the material things you need to survive.

(KJV) Matthew 6:31-33 Do not worry then, saying,' What will we eat?' or What will we drink?' or 'What will we wear for clothing?" 32 For the Gentiles eagerly seek all these things; for your heavenly Father knows that you need all these things. 33 But seek first His kingdom and His righteousness, and all these things will be added to you."

References

Scripture taken from the KING JAMES VERSION OF THE BIBLE, (KJV) Public Domain 1611

Meditation

(KJV) Psalm 63:6 When I remember thee upon my bed, and meditate on thee in the night watches

Psalm 119:97 O how love I thy law! it is my meditation all the day.

In the Bible meditations are used as a means of renewing your mind. Most of the time when the word meditation is used in the Bible, it is used in the context of pondering, contemplating, or reflecting on scripture in an effort to overcome sin and abide by God's commandments. There are many different Greek and Hebrew words for meditation in the Bible. Some have been translated as; musing, revolving in the mind, murmur, ponder, pray, sing, or study. Different versions of the Bible translate the words differently. For example, one version might say a person went off to pray, another version might say they went off to ponder, and another might say that the person went off to meditate. In this study we will only be dealing with the pondering aspect of meditation in an effort to grow.

(KJV) Jas 1:19-21 Wherefore, my beloved brethren, let every man be swift to hear, slow to speak, slow to wrath: 20 For the wrath of man worketh not the righteousness of God. 21 Wherefore lay apart all filthiness and superfluity of naughtiness, and receive with meekness the engrafted word, which is able to save your souls.

What these verses are about is learning to control your emotions, and actually changing your behavioral patterns by receiving the word ENGRAFTED. These verses were taken from the King James Version of the Bible, in the American Standard Version the word engrafted is substituted with IMPLANTED, and in the Latin Vulgate Version the word that is used means planted. This idea of planting words in your mind seems very familiar to me. When I worked as a hypnotherapist, I planted suggestions in people's sub-conscious minds all of the time in an effort to help them change their old negative behavioral patterns into newer more positive ones. There are also other Bible verses that refer to changing your way of thinking. Let's look at some of them.

(KJV) Eph 4:23 And be renewed in the spirit of your mind;

(KJV) Ro 12:2 And be not conformed to this world: but be ye transformed by the renewing of your mind, that ye may prove what is that good, and acceptable, and perfect, will of God.

The previous verses state that you change by renewing your minds; this is similar to the following verses.

(KJV) 1Ti 4:15 Meditate upon these things; give thyself wholly to them; that thy profiting may appear to all.

(KJV) Phi 4:8 Finally, brethren, whatsoever things are true, whatsoever things are honest, whatsoever things are just, whatsoever things are pure, whatsoever things are lovely, whatsoever things are of good report; if there be any virtue, and if there be any praise, think on these things.

(KJV) Ps 119:11 Thy word have I hid in mine heart, that I might not sin against thee.

(KJV) Ps 119:59 I thought on my ways, and turned my feet unto thy testimonies.

(KJV) Ps 119:15 I will meditate in thy precepts, and have respect unto thy ways.

The first two verses above have to do with meditating on positive things for your own benefit; the second two verses have to do with meditating on the Bible so that you will not sin against God. The following verses have to do with meditating on God's word in the Bible to overcome your emotions in times of crisis (when a lot of people might be plotting vengeance or their defense). These verses are a good example of overcoming your emotions and instead benefiting by gaining wisdom.

(KJV) Ps 119:23 Princes also did sit and speak against me: but thy servant did meditate in thy statutes

(KJV) Ps 119:78 Let the proud be ashamed; for they dealt perversely with me without a cause: but I will meditate in thy precepts.

(KJV) Ps 119:98-99 Thou through thy commandments hast made me wiser than mine enemies: for they are ever with me. 99 I have more understanding than all my teachers: for thy testimonies are my meditation.

(KJV) Ps 143:5 I remember the days of old; I meditate on all thy works; I muse on the work of thy hands.

(KJV) Ps 49:3 My mouth shall speak of wisdom; and the meditation of my heart shall be of understanding.

(KJV) Ps 77:12 I will meditate also of all thy work, and talk of thy doings.

The following verses reinforce all of the previous verses in stating that you should meditate on God's word in the Bible for your own good, and to enable you to avoid sin and make your way prosperous.

(KJV) Jos 1:8 This book of the law shall not depart out of thy mouth; but thou shalt meditate therein day and night, that thou mayest observe to do according to all that is written therein: for then thou shalt make thy way prosperous, and then thou shalt have good success.

(KJV) Ps 1:2 But his delight is in the law of the Lord; and in his law doth he meditate day and night.

Basically the Bible says that meditating on God's word is a good way to change your thinking patterns for your own benefit. As a hypnotherapist I've seen how meditating and putting yourself into a trance state makes it very easy to change your thought patterns so that you are able to think and act the way you want to. The Bible also refers to trance states, for example Adam fell into a deep sleep before God removed his rib and created Eve.

The following are two verses in which God induced a trance. Trances induced by God are different than a trance state that you put yourself into. I'm not saying that you can't receive a vision from God by a self-induced trance, but simply mean that just because you put yourself into a trance that doesn't mean that you will. The trances that God induces in people are induced for His specific purpose. Although by putting yourself into a trance you probably won't receive a vision from God, you still will receive great benefits from putting yourself into a trance. For example, it will make it much easier for you to change your thinking patterns, and as you know from the above verses that you can gain wisdom and help in times of crisis.

(KJV) Jos 1:8 This book of the law shall not depart out of thy mouth; but thou shalt meditate therein day and night, that thou mayest observe to do according to all that is written therein: for then thou shalt make thy way prosperous, and then thou shalt have good success.

(KJV) Ps 1:2 But his delight is in the law of the Lord; and in his law doth he meditate day and night.

The following verses are taken from the Apocrypha

(KJV) Sir 14:20 Blessed is the man that doth meditate good things in wisdom, and that reasoneth of holy things by his understanding

(KJV) Sir 39:1 But he that giveth his mind to the law of the most High, and is occupied in the meditation thereof, will seek out the wisdom of all the ancient, and be occupied in prophecies.

(KJV) Sir 6:37 Let thy mind be upon the ordinances of the Lord and meditate continually in his commandments: he shall establish thine heart, and give thee wisdom at thine owns desire.

Before I go into how to meditate on scripture, I will first help you to find and connect verses in order to understand what they mean. Take the following verses for example.

(KJV) Mt 22:10-14 So those servants went out into the highways, and gathered together all as many as they found, both bad and good: and the wedding was furnished with guests. 11 And when the king came in to see the guests, he saw there a man which had not on a wedding garment: 12 And he saith unto him, Friend, how camest thou in hither not having a wedding garment? And he was speechless. 13 Then said the king to the servants, Bind him hand and foot, and take him away, and cast him into outer darkness; there shall be weeping and gnashing of teeth. 14 For many are called, but few are chosen.

The first time you read this parable it seems very confusing. If the King invited all these people to the wedding feast, why did he throw out one of the guest that he invited? The answer is in the following set of verses.

(KJV) Rev 19:7-8 Let us be glad and rejoice, and give honour to him: for the marriage of the Lamb is come, and his wife hath made herself ready. 8 And to her was granted that she should be arrayed in fine linen, clean and white: for the fine linen is the righteousness of saints.

By comparing these two sets of verses we are able to understand the original parable. The wedding feast represents Jesus' return to earth. The people invited to the feast represent the people of earth having their opportunity to enter heaven. The guest was thrown out of the feast and into outer darkness (outer darkness represents getting thrown into hell) because he did not have on the appropriate apparel on. We know from reading Rev. 19:8 that the correct apparel represents the righteous acts of the saints. So now we know that the guest was not thrown into hell because of the way he was dressed, but because of the deeds he did in his life. This makes the Mt 22:14 make sense.

As you can see by the above example, linking verses together will greatly benefit you in understanding any verse you are researching. An easy way to link verses together is to use a concordance. A concordance is a book that lists every word in the Bible, and tells you every single verse in the Bible that the word is included in. For example, if you wanted to do a Bible study on fish, you can look up the word fish in a concordance, and you will know every verse in the Bible that contains the word fish. This helps you find several other related Bible verses to what you are studying, and also gives you a better understanding of how that word is used in the Bible.

At one time I attended a church that had very strong ideas about how to take communion. Their main argument was that communion must be taken out of only one cup. This is because at the Lord's Supper the Bible says that Jesus took THE CUP, so this church believed that other churches that use plural cups are taking communion wrong. For me to make my own decision as to which churches were right, I used a concordance and read every verse in the Bible that had the word cup in it. What I found is that in the Bible the word cup is only used two times in which it is referring to an actual drinking vessel.

Every other time the word CUP is used in the Bible it is used metaphorically to represent a person's destiny. Example, *"you must drink the cup of God's wrath"* or, *"Shall I not drink the cup my father has prepared for me."* In the Bible the word cup meant much more than just a drinking vessel and I came to the conclusion that communion was more than just drinking grape juice on Sunday, but was more like declaring that you take responsibility for your destiny, and reflecting on how to serve God better.

I decided that it was not necessary for everyone in church to drink out of the same cup because the communion is not with the other church members, but is a communion between you and God on a higher spiritual level than everybody just drinking grape juice together.

You can also use a Topical Bible, which lists Bible verses by their subject, but I recommend using a concordance. It seems more effective, and allows you to research every verse with the same words in them where as in Topical Bibles it is up to the author to decide what verses they feel are relative to the subject.

By doing a Bible study with a concordance to understand what one particular verse means you will probably read several Bible verses. You can then meditate on the verse you did the Bible study on or any other verse you found interesting while doing your research. As you know from reading the above Bible verses having to do with meditation, you understand that to meditate on the verses means to contemplate or ponder them. Just by pondering the verses that you have read you will benefit from studying them. The Bible contains pretty deep stuff so you will likely already be in a state of focused concentration just by trying to figure out what the verses mean. Once you understand what the verses mean you can meditate on them even further to help you to IMPLANT OR ENGRAFT the information into your mind.

To meditate on the verse even further simply relax, close your eyes and think to yourself how these verses apply to your life. Are you wearing the wrong wedding clothes? What must you do to change this? In Proverbs there is a verse that says, *"wine is a mocker and strong drink is a brawler"* (Proverbs 20:1). You can apply this verse to your life by thinking about how people loose control when they drink; some people are easily angered when they are drunk and get into fistfights. Some people seem to become meaner when they drink and insult people, or spread nasty rumors about other people that they wouldn't spread if they were sober. Meditate on whatever verse you are interested in, ponder how it applies to your life, and see what you can learn from it.

After you have pondered the verse for a while you can visualize yourself in a situation where that verse would apply. For example, if the verse you are meditating on says, *"cease from anger and forsake wrath, fret not it leads only to evil doing"* you can visualize yourself in a situation where you would normally get angry, but instead visualize yourself overcoming your emotions and realizing that getting angry and loosing control won't help the situation, but probably would only make it worse. By doing this you are giving your mind a blue print to work with so that if a similar situation arises you will be able to stay in control. As a hypnotherapist I can reassure you that you do not need to be in a deep trance for you to change your thoughts and behavioral patterns to the thoughts and ideas that you want to live by. By simply using the pondering and visualization skills listed above you will find that your Christian meditations have a profound and beneficial effect on your life, your dealings with other people, and most importantly your relationship with God.

(KJV) Ps 19:14 Let the words of my mouth, and the meditation of my heart, be acceptable in thy sight, O Lord, my strength, and my redeemer.

References

Scripture taken from the KING JAMES VERSION OF THE BIBLE, (KJV) Public Domain 1611

Do Animals Have A Soul?

Do animals have a soul? Will there be animals in Heaven? A lot of people say no. I decided to do this Bible study to correct the misconception that many Christians share with unbelievers. I have met several people who not only believe that animals don't have a soul and won't go to Heaven, but also believe that animals don't think or have emotions. These people think that it is fine to leave their pets out in the rain with no food, and that although pets are fun to have around sometimes, they don't experience any of the things that humans do. There are also people who believe that hunting is a sport, and that it is okay to murder animals for *fun* (not for food). The believe animals are not human and therefore can't feel the things that we feel, like; fear of getting hunted, the pain of getting shot etc.. Guinea Pigs are animals that Scientists have no remorse about torturing, and conducting experiments on. People raise cows in stalls that they don't even have enough room to turn around in. The cows are raised in these stalls until they are large enough to be killed and have their flesh sold for profit.

People who have views like the above mentioned, believe these things simply because animals don't communicate with humans the way that humans communicate with each other. For some reason they think that because animals don't speak the same language as humans that they can't think. This is not a new way of thinking. Africans were enslaved by the Americans at one time, and were also treated as less than human. Just because they spoke a different language than the slave owners of the time and looked different, slave owners believed that their slaves weren't as intelligent and treated them as those they were inhuman; having no qualms about treating them in any inhumane condition. In the past nations had no qualms about going to war with other nations and murdering thousands of people; believing that it is okay because the enemy is so culturally different that they seemed like another species. Making it okay to do any evil desire you want to them. Hitler tortured and murdered millions of Jews in W.W.II he viewed Jews as inferior. In America women barely started receiving equal rights with men in the last century.

Another Christian once told me that I was, "*Stupid*" and that, "*as much as she would like to believe that animals had a soul, they are only beast of instinct and cannot think.*"

I don't understand how people could be so blind, especially if they have a pet. If they can look into another human's eyes and tell that they have a soul, why can't they do the same thing with animals? I have had several animals, and they do THINK. They have emotions; they can get angry, be happy, playful, protective, sad, stressed out, compassionate, and all of the other emotions that HUMANS have. If you watch them interact with other animals you can witness that sometimes they are friends, sometimes they irritate each other, and sometimes they fight and need to make up with each other. Sometimes one of the animals is even too prideful to make up with the other animal for a while, just like humans. It doesn't take a rocket scientist to see that animals THINK.

They not only think, but also are able to communicate with us. If they did not have the capability to think and reason how is it that they are able to respond to our vocal commands, SIT for example? Animals are able to understand our words (sit, come, stay, etc..) we are the ones with the communication problem. You are able to communicate with animals if you try; they know if you are mad at them, if you want to play with them, and if you are sad or hurt they will show you compassion and try to comfort you. You need to remember that if you are going to communicate with an animal then you must at least be as smart as the animal you are trying to communicate with.

If you were to meet a deaf human would you think that just because the deaf person doesn't seem to understand your words that they must be to stupid to communicate with you? Would you consider them merely a beast of instinct? Another obvious example that animals think is the fact that they are able to move around. If they were just these things that could move around without thinking they would walk around bumping into everything. But the fact is that animals do think enough to know where they are going, and they have an idea of why they are going there, (to hunt, to join their family, to play, to get something, etc..).

Some animals travel in packs, and act as a team when they hunt. If they were only beasts of instinct they wouldn't commune with each other. Wouldn't they just try to eat each other instead of hunting together, and maybe going home hunger? As humans we are also creatures of instinct, seeking the basic necessities of life, the same ones the animals seek. The difference is only that we choose to live in houses and destroy God's creation. Animals hunt and eat other animals for food, but so do we. The difference is only that animals don't kill for money, and don't raise humans in little boxes from the time the human is born until they are big enough to eat or have their flesh sold for profit like humans do.

The above information is self-evident that animals think, have emotions, feelings, and souls. The above information I wrote to explain it to you using common sense alone. You should be able to see these things for yourself by merely observing an animal's behavior. Now if you want further proof we will look to the Bible for the answers.

In this study I cross reference the Latin Vulgate and the King James Version of the Bible to help you better understand what the Bible says about animals. I chose the Latin Vulgate because it was translated directly out of Hebrew in the Old Testament, and Greek in the New Testament. It was also written in 300 A.D. in one of the languages that were spoken in Christ's lifetime. Unlike Greek and Hebrew, the Latin language is still spoken today having only minimal changes over the years.

The first verses I would like to examine are the ones that prove that animals have a Soul.

(KJV) Ge 2:7 And the Lord God formed man of the dust of the ground, and breathed into his nostrils the breath of life; and man became a """"living soul"""".

(Latin Vulgate) Ge 2:7 formavit igitur Dominus Deus hominem de limo terrae et inspiravit in faciem eius spiraculum vitae et factus est homo in """"animam viventem""""

Notice the words that I put quotations around. They are the words that mean "Living Soul". Notice that the word used for soul is animam a conjugation of the word "anima" meaning soul. You might recognize the other word "viventem" meaning *living*, from sayings like, "Viva Las Vegas" meaning long live Las Vegas. The above verses describe how God created Adam. Now lets look at how God created animals.

(KJV) Ge 2:19 And out of the ground the Lord God formed every beast of the field, and every fowl of the air; and brought them unto Adam to see what he would call them: and whatsoever Adam called every """"living creature"""", that was the name thereof.

(Latin Vulgate) Ge 2:19 formatis igitur Dominus Deus de humo cunctis animantibus terrae et universis volatilibus caeli adduxit ea ad Adam ut videret quid vocaret ea omne enim quod vocavit Adam """"animae viventis"""" ipsum est nomen eius

As you can see by reading the above verses God created animals the same way that He created man; out of the ground He formed them, and animals also became a """"Living SOUL"""". Why did the KJV translate the same word anima differently in Gen 2:19 and Gen. 2:7, well I don't know why. Why would the KJV translate the word for SOUL as CREATURE in Gen 2:19? In Latin there is another word that means creature, which we will look at later. The Latin word for creature is, "creatura".

When I first became a Christian the evangelist I was meeting with used the two above verses to tell me that man became a living soul, and animals became a living creature. He used these verses to prove to me that animals are less than we are; they don't have a soul and won't go to heaven. As you can see by studying the above verses before they were translated into English that he was wrong. The above verses state that animals were created out of the dust of the ground, and became a SOUL just like Adam did. The only difference is that God breathed into Adams nostrils, but I think the fact that animals breath air like we do that God might have also given them the *breath of life.* In the following verses when God flooded the earth, many different animals are described and said to have possessed the *Breath of Life* in their *Nostrils.*

> **(KJV) Ge 7:21-22 And all flesh died that moved upon the earth, both of fowl, and of cattle, and of beast, and of every creeping thing that creepeth upon the earth, and every man: 22 All in whose nostrils was the breath of life, of all that was in the dry land, died.**

The Latin word "Anima" means soul, I've included the following set of verses for you to see for yourself.

> **(KJV) De 10:12 And now, Israel, what doth the Lord thy God require of thee, but to fear the Lord thy God, to walk in all his ways, and to love him, and to serve the Lord thy God with all thy heart and with all thy """"soul""""**

> **(Latin Vulgate) De 10:12 et nunc Israhel quid Dominus Deus tuus petit a te nisi ut timeas Dominum Deum tuum et ambules in viis eius et diligas eum ac servias Domino Deo tuo in toto corde tuo et in tota """"anima"""""" tua**

As you can see the word Anima means soul. In Gen.2:19 they used the word anima conjugated to the word, """"Animae"""" to mean soul. To allow you to be sure that elsewhere in the Bible that conjugation of anima means soul and not animal or creature I've included the following verses.

> **(KJV) Acts 2:41 Then they that gladly received his word were baptized: and the same day there were added unto them about three thousand """"souls"""".**

(Latin Vulgate) Acts 2:41 qui ergo receperunt sermonem eius baptizati sunt et adpositae sunt in illa die """"animae"""" circiter tria milia

As you can see the word animae means soul, otherwise Acts 2:41 would say that on that day three thousand animals were added to them.

I believe that God created the Garden of Eden as perfection, and God created animals in the Garden of Eden. There are similarities to the Garden of Eden and Heaven. Both have a river flowing through them, and both have the Tree of Life in them. Now that you understand that animals have souls, we will now look at what evidence the Bible gives us about animals being in Heaven.

(KJV) Rev 19:17 And I saw an angel standing in the sun; and he cried with a loud voice, saying to all the fowls that fly in the midst of heaven, Come and gather yourselves together unto the supper of the great God; 18 That ye may eat the flesh of kings, and the flesh of captains, and the flesh of mighty men, and the flesh of horses, and of them that sit on them, and the flesh of all men, both free and bond, both small and great.

In the above verses, you can see that the fowls of the air will still exist after the Apocalypse. If they didn't they wouldn't be able to eat the flesh of those who die in the battle.

(KJV) Rev 19:11 And I saw heaven opened, and behold a white horse; and he that sat upon him was called Faithful and True, and in righteousness he doth judge and make war.

(KJV) Rev 19:14 And the armies which were in heaven followed him upon white horses, clothed in fine linen, white and clean.

The above verses state that heaven will open and Jesus will ride out of Heaven on a horse. Many of the verses in Revelations are metaphoric, and I will include how animals are used in the Bible metaphorically in this study as well, but I do not see any reason not to take the above verses literally. After all Jesus did ride into Jerusalem on a literal cult, and not a symbolic one. If so, the above verses refer to horses being in Heaven.

(KJV) Lu 12:4-7 And I say unto you my friends, Be not afraid of them that kill the body, and after that have no more that they can do.5 But I will forewarn you whom ye shall fear: Fear him, which after he hath killed hath power to cast into hell; yea, I say

unto you, Fear him. 6 Are not five sparrows sold for two farthings, and not one of them is forgotten before God? 7 But even the very hairs of your head are all numbered. Fear not therefore: ye are of more value than many sparrows.

The above verses teach us that God loves us, and that we should not fear anybody but Him. To make this point clear Jesus points out that we are worth more than many sparrows. I didn't include these verses to reinforce the idea that we are better than animals, (in this study we will look at verses that say that we are to rule over animals and have domination over them), but to remind you that even though we are more important than animals God still hasn't FORGOTTEN them. If God hasn't forgotten the sparrows why would you think that they wouldn't be in Heaven?

(KJV) Rev 5:13 And every creature which is in heaven, and on the earth, and under the earth, and such as are in the sea, and all that are in them, heard I saying, Blessing, and honour, and glory, and power, be unto him that sitteth upon the throne, and unto the Lamb for ever and ever.

The above verse states that all the creatures in heaven and on earth and in the sea shall say blessings and praises to the Lord. Indicating that fish and all the creatures in the sea, and on earth, and the ones IN HEAVEN, will praise Him. In Heaven could mean that there are animals in heaven, or it could be referring to angels, which are also creatures. I mentioned earlier that I would also go over the uses of the Latin word """"creatura"""" to help you get a better understanding of whom it applies to. The word """"Creatura"""" means, created thing or creation. Lets now look at some Bible verses that use that word to help us to understand what the creatures in the above verse is referring to.

(KJV) Rev 8:9 And the third part of the """"creatures"""" which were in the sea, and had life, died; and the third part of the ships were destroyed.

(Latin Vulgate) Rev 8:9 et mortua est tertia pars """""creatura""""" quae habent animas et tertia pars navium interiit

As you can see the Latin word for creature is referring to creatures in the sea like fish and whales etc... The word creatura doesn't only include animals but all of creation. In the following verses you will see that the word creature is used to describe all of creation including humans.

(KJV) 1Ti 4:4 For every creature of God is good, and nothing to be refused, if it be received with thanksgiving:

(KJV) 2Co 5:17 Therefore if any man be in Christ, he is a new creature: old things are passed away; behold, all things are become new.

(KJV) Col 1:15 Who is the image of the invisible God, the firstborn of every creature:

(KJV) Ga 6:15 For in Christ Jesus neither circumcision availeth any thing, nor uncircumcision, but a new creature.

(KJV) Mr 16:15 And he said unto them, Go ye into all the world, and preach the gospel to every creature.

So Rev 5:13 refers to there being more of God's creations in heavens than just humans. Now that you can see how much is included in the word creature you might want to re-examine your thoughts about the meaning of the verse Mark 16:15 were as Christians we are instructed to preach the gospel to all of creation. Creation here doesn't mean all over the earth, because in the same verse we are to go all over the world to preach to the creation.

Jesus could have easily said to all of mankind (which the Latin word HOMO meaning humans would have been used), but he didn't. He used the word creature. I don't know what our duty is regarding that verse; are we supposed to preach to animals, trees, fish, and every other aspect of creation? I don't know, but I think it is something that we should contemplate. Jesus said this after He had risen from the dead so it should be something that we should take seriously.

To help us understand why God would want animals in heaven, I have decided to include some verses that have to do with how God cares about animals.

(KJV) Ge 6:18-21 But with thee will I establish my covenant; and thou shalt come into the ark, thou, and thy sons, and thy wife, and thy sons' wives with thee. 19 And of every living thing of all flesh, two of every sort shalt thou bring into the ark, to keep them alive with thee; they shall be male and female. 20 Of fowls after their kind, and of cattle after their kind, of every creeping thing of the earth after his kind, two of every sort shall come unto thee, to keep them alive. 21 And take thou unto thee of all

food that is eaten, and thou shalt gather it to thee; and it shall be for food for thee, and for them.

(KJV) Ge 7:2-3 Of every clean beast thou shalt take to thee by sevens, the male and his female: and of beasts that are not clean by two, the male and his female. 3 Of fowls also of the air by sevens, the male and the female; to keep seed alive upon the face of all the earth.

In the above verses God cared enough about the animals to make sure that they survived the flood. He says that He did this to keep their seed alive on the earth. God didn't tell Noah to bring the animals in the Ark so that they could be eaten, in Gen.6: 21 God instructs Noah to bring food for himself and for the animals. God didn't create animals for food. Before the fall of man neither animals nor man ate animals for food. We didn't start eating animals until after sin entered the world. The animals in the Garden of Eden were created as companions to man before God created woman.

(KJV) De 22:6 If a bird's nest chance to be before thee in the way in any tree, or on the ground, whether they be young ones, or eggs, and the dam sitting upon the young, or upon the eggs, thou shalt not take the dam with the young:

(KJV) De 23:18 Thou shalt not bring the hire of a whore, or the price of a dog, into the house of the Lord thy God for any vow: for even both these are abomination unto the Lord thy God.

In the above verses God says not to take the mother bird along with her eggs. In Deut. 23:18 God says not to bring money that was made by being a whore, or selling a dog, into His house. He says that this would be an abomination. Both acts involve selling a life for the money to give to God, and He says that it is wrong to do this. This is a good example of God caring for dogs as much as He cares about not wanting humans to sin. It would be like robbing someone, or selling your children, and donating the money to the church. That is not an acceptable fellowship offering.

(KJV) Ex 22:19 Whosoever lieth with a beast shall surely be put to death.

The above verse is self-evident

(KJV) Nu 22:23-34 And the ass saw the angel of the Lord standing in the way, and his sword drawn in his hand: and the ass turned aside out of the way, and went into the field: and

Balaam smote the ass, to turn her into the way. 24 But the angel of the Lord stood in a path of the vineyards, a wall being on this side, and a wall on that side. 25 And when the ass saw the angel of the Lord, she thrust herself unto the wall, and crushed Balaam's foot against the wall: and he smote her again. 26 And the angel of the Lord went further, and stood in a narrow place, where was no way to turn either to the right hand or to the left. 27 And when the ass saw the angel of the Lord, she fell down under Balaam: and Balaam's anger was kindled, and he smote the ass with a staff. 28 And the Lord opened the mouth of the ass, and she said unto Balaam, What have I done unto thee, that thou hast smitten me these three times? 29 And Balaam said unto the ass, Because thou hast mocked me: I would there were a sword in mine hand, for now would I kill thee. 30 And the ass said unto Balaam, Am not I thine ass, upon which thou hast ridden ever since I was thine unto this day? was I ever wont to do so unto thee? And he said, Nay. 31 Then the Lord opened the eyes of Balaam, and he saw the angel of the Lord standing in the way, and his sword drawn in his hand: and he bowed down his head, and fell flat on his face.32 And the angel of the Lord said unto him, Wherefore hast thou smitten thine ass these three times? behold, I went out to withstand thee, because thy way is perverse before me: 33 And the ass saw me, and turned from me these three times: unless she had turned from me, surely now also I had slain thee, and saved her alive. 34 And Balaam said unto the angel of the Lord, I have sinned; for I knew not that thou stoodest in the way against me: now therefore, if it displease thee, I will get me back again.

The above verse shows God's mercy toward animals. The ass was being beaten wrongfully, so God allowed the ass to be able to speak with a human's voice. The angel also rebuked Balaam; told him that the ass saved his life, and that if the ass didn't turn away then the angel would have killed Balaam and let his animal live. These are very good verses that prove that God doesn't like to see animals mistreated. What these verses also prove is that animals can think. If the ass was unable to think how could it have made the decision to turn away from the angel's sword? Not only did the ass think and make its own decision, but it also had compassion and feelings for Balaam, or else she wouldn't have made the decision to protect Balaam from the angel to the point that she put her own life at risk of Balaam killing her. The following verse also shows that animals can have feelings for humans and show compassion.

(KJV) Lu 16:21 And desiring to be fed with the crumbs which fell from the rich man's table: moreover the dogs came and licked his sores.

The above verse shows us that sometimes animals can be more humane than humans.

(KJV) Mt 10:16 Behold, I send you forth as sheep in the midst of wolves: be ye therefore wise as serpents, and harmless as doves.

The above verse uses animals in metaphoric terms, but even so it still proves that animals can think and act. You couldn't use animals metaphorically if they didn't have certain characteristics. If snakes weren't cunning and doves weren't gentle, you couldn't make up metaphors based on their personality traits.

(KJV) Is 56:10 His watchmen are blind: they are all ignorant, they are all dumb dogs, they cannot bark; sleeping, lying down, loving to slumber.

(KJV) 2Pe 2:12-16 But these, as natural brute beasts, made to be taken and destroyed, speak evil of the things that they understand not; and shall utterly perish in their own corruption; 13 And shall receive the reward of unrighteousness, as they that count it pleasure to riot in the day time. Spots they are and blemishes, sporting themselves with their own deceivings while they feast with you; 14 Having eyes full of adultery, and that cannot cease from sin; beguiling unstable souls: an heart they have exercised with covetous practices; cursed children: 15 Which have forsaken the right way, and are gone astray, following the way of Balaam the son of Bosor, who loved the wages of unrighteousness; 16 But was rebuked for his iniquity: the dumb ass speaking with man's voice forbad the madness of the prophet.

The above verses are also metaphoric uses of animals. In this verse the people are compared to dumb dogs. In this verse the dogs are not dumb because dogs are stupid, but because they can't bark. So the metaphor is meaning something along the lines that people can act dumber than animals. In the Peter verses above, man is metaphorically compared to brute beasts, the *Brute* isn't used because animals are brutes, but is used because of all of the sin of man. In the verse Peter 2: 16 when Balaam's ass is called dumb, I it is done in a sarcastic way. Balaam was considered a wise man and was even able to talk to God. Balaam was hired to put a curse on the children of Israel, but in all of Balaam's wisdom he couldn't see the truth as well as his ass (donkey), which was considered far dumber than he.

> **(KJV) Rev 5:5-9 And one of the elders saith unto me, Weep not: behold, the Lion of the tribe of Juda, the Root of David, hath prevailed to open the book, and to loose the seven seals thereof. 6 And I beheld, and, lo, in the midst of the throne and of the four beasts, and in the midst of the elders, stood a Lamb as it had been slain, having seven horns and seven eyes, which are the seven Spirits of God sent forth into all the earth. 7 And he came and took the book out of the right hand of him that sat upon the throne. 8 And when he had taken the book, the four beasts and four and twenty elders fell down before the Lamb, having every one of them harps, and golden vials full of odours, which are the prayers of saints. 9 And they sung a new song, saying, Thou art worthy to take the book, and to open the seals thereof: for thou wast slain, and hast redeemed us to God by thy blood out of every kindred, and tongue, and people, and nation;**

The above verses are more metaphoric uses of animals.

Now I would like to talk about another pretty common reason Christians have given me as to why animals aren't important, and won't go to heaven. Their reason is that man was created in the image of God. Because of this reason I've even heard some Christians claim that we as humans are in God's bloodline, and are His actual children just like Christ. They are wrong. We are adopted children of God, and saved by His grace. Being made in the image of God is different than being God's true child. Jesus is God's ONLY begotten son. We are adopted children. I could make an image of myself out of clay, but that doesn't make it in my bloodline. You can look at yourself in a mirror and you will be able to see your image, but your image is not actually in the same bloodline as you. In the following verses we will examine how God formed man and animal.

> **(KJV) 1Co 15:38-40 But God giveth it a body as it hath pleased him, and to every seed his own body. 39 All flesh is not the same flesh: but there is one kind of flesh of men, another flesh of beasts, another of fishes, and another of birds. 40 There are also celestial bodies, and bodies terrestrial: but the glory of the celestial is one, and the glory of the terrestrial is another.**

The above verses simply tell us that God made every creature different; the way He saw fit to.

Ge 1:26-27 And God said, Let us make man in our image, after our likeness: and let them have dominion over the fish of the sea, and over the fowl of the air, and over the cattle, and over all the earth, and over every creeping thing that creepeth upon the earth. 27 So God created man in his own image, in the image of God created he him; male and female created he them.

Above is the account of God forming man in His image. He also gave us dominion over all the animals. Yes, we are higher in status than animals and worth more than many sparrows, but just because we have dominion over them that doesn't mean that they cannot think or that they aren't important to God. The people I mentioned earlier who place so much value on form should pay close attention to the following verses.

(KJV) Jo 1:32 And John bare record, saying, I saw the Spirit descending from heaven like a dove, and it abode upon him.

(KJV) Lu 3:22 And the Holy Ghost descended in a bodily shape like a dove upon him, and a voice came from heaven, which said, Thou art my beloved Son; in thee I am well pleased.

(KJV) Mr 1:10 And straightway coming up out of the water, he saw the heavens opened, and the Spirit like a dove descending upon him:

The above verses state that the Holy Spirit descended in BODILY FORM (not metaphoric) as a dove. That does not mean that the Holy Spirit is in the line of birds. So maybe the package isn't as important as what is inside. This is another verse that also says that an animal came out of heaven like the earlier verse where Jesus rides out of heaven on a horse. Now lets look at how God created animals.

(KJV) Ge 1:21 And God created great whales, and every living creature that moveth, which the waters brought forth abundantly, after their kind, and every winged fowl after his kind: and God saw that it was good. 22 And God blessed them, saying, Be fruitful, and multiply, and fill the waters in the seas, and let fowl multiply in the earth.

In the above verses, you can see that God created these creatures AFTER their kind. The same way that God created man after His image, He created animals after THEIR kind. This might be referring to preexistent animals living with God that have earthly animals created after their images, and if so it is a great example of animals being in heaven.

Now I would like to address something a little off the subject, but it is still God's instructions to us for dealing with lost animals.

(KJV) De 22:1-2 Thou shalt not see thy brother's ox or his sheep go astray, and hide thyself from them: thou shalt in any case bring them again unto thy brother. 2 And if thy brother be not nigh unto thee, or if thou know him not, then thou shalt bring it unto thine own house, and it shall be with thee until thy brother seek after it, and thou shalt restore it to him again.

The above verses tell you what you are to do if you find a lost animal (dogs more likely in cities). You are to return it to its owner. If you don't know who the owner is then you are to bring the animal home with you and take care of it until you are able to return it to its owner. Read the newspaper to see if there are any lost animal flyers, and look around your neighborhood for lost animal signs hanging up. If you have no luck hang up signs yourself saying that you found an animal. If you don't find the owner, take care of the animal yourself if you are able to, or look for a home for it with someone you know. If all else fails you can take the animal to an animal shelter and they will care for it and give it a few more weeks to find a home. Remember that animals have FEELINGS; it is probably terrified to be away from home, and scared of the danger on the streets. It is not safe for a small child to live on the streets, so it's not okay to let a frightened animal be forced to live in them either. Remember that Jesus said what you have done for the least of these you have done for me. Don't be like the sinners who tell Jesus, *"when did we see you thirsty"*, if you see an abandoned animal on the street starving, thirsty, and petrified with fear. Help the animal, take it into your home, and take care of it until its owner comes.

I hope that this Bible study has helped you to realize that animals have souls and feelings just like you do, and are not to be mistreated. You don't have to agree with all of my interpretations of the above scriptures, but if you just use common sense you will be able to see that animals think, have souls, and emotions just by watching them. Take care of your pets. I believe that God gave us animals so that we may better understand our relationship with Him.

Sometimes our pets cause us to get angry at them, sometimes our pets fight with each other and we feel sad wishing that they could just get along, and sometimes our pets show us incredible amounts of love; thanking us for the food and love that we give them. Our relationship to our pets is a good metaphor to help us understand our relationship with God, because although sometimes our pets are disobedient to us, we still forgive them. We might stay mad at them longer if they don't seem to be sorry for what they did. But we forgive our pets, because THEY KNOW NOT WHAT THEY DO (in the same way as humans regarding their sins).

We can learn a lot from our pets just like Balaam could have learned some things from his donkey; if we would only pay attention to our pets and not have our vanity so threatened that they might also have a soul and be loved by God. Remember it was man's sin that destroyed the world, not animals. Don't mistreat animals; love them as God loves you. Don't be so full of vanity that you believe that humans are the only emotional, thinking, and feeling creatures on the planet.

(KJV) Ec 1:2 Vanity of vanities, saith the Preacher, vanity of vanities; all is vanity.

I have heard many Christians state that Jesus died for our sins only, and since the Bible doesn't spell out a path of salvation for animals they don't think animals could be saved?

The answer is to this question is that Animals did not eat from the tree of Knowledge of Good and Evil. Man is the one that is responsible for the bringing sin into the world. Jesus is the second Adam, which removed the curse from us. Since animals did not eat from the same tree as Adam, why do you think that animal need to be forgiven for Adam eating from it? Animals are in the state they are in because of man. Jesus removed the curse of original sin; animals were apart of that curse as well as the earth. There is no reason to believe that animals needed forgiveness in the first place, and if you come to the conclusion that they do then Jesus would have removed their curse/sin along with the curse of original sin. Through one man's disobedience sin entered the world, and through one man's faith sin was overcome. If you still feel that animals need their own path to salvation then share the Gospel with them. We are after all told to preach the Gospel to every creature (Mark 16:15).

References

Scripture taken from the KING JAMES VERSION OF THE BIBLE, (KJV) Public Domain 1611

Scripture taken from the LATIN VULGATE VERSION OF THE BIBLE, Public Domain

Magick and Divination

Before we begin this Bible study on magick I would like to tell you something about myself. Before I became a Christian for many years I studied all sorts of different philosophies seeking understanding of the universe. I did do a great deal of research into the occult, and I studied several different aspects of magick. I never dealt with demons or angels or sacrificed anything to anybody, but I did study magick to some degree.

I mainly am writing this Bible study for magicians. To let them know what the Bible says about magick, and what the Bible considers to be wrong with it. Magick is a very touchy subject because everybody has their own opinion as to what exactly magick is. Some people believe magick is a satanic practice, but magick is not based on Satan. Mostly it is based on a distorted view of God. For example in conjuring (not every magician is a conjurer) a magician summons forth spirits to communicate with. The magician does this by commanding the spirit to manifest trapped inside a magick circle or triangle so that the magician can't be harmed.

Conjurers believe that there is a hierarchy among spirits, and that the lower spirits respond by commanding them in the name of the higher spirits. Therefore the conjurer commands the spirit to manifest in the name of God or Jesus, because they are the highest in the hierarchy. The belief in controlling lower spirits by commanding them in the name of higher spirits is reflected in the Bible (Matthew 12:24). The Pharisees accuse Jesus of casting out devils in the name of Beelzebub (their prince). Jesus corrects them by stating that the devils were cast out in the name of God (Matthew 12:28).

The following verses are an example of what happened when some exorcists in the Bible tried commanding demons in the name of Jesus.

(KJV) Acts 19:13-16 Then certain of the vagabond Jews, exorcists, took upon them to call over them which had evil spirits the name of the LORD Jesus, saying, We adjure you by Jesus whom Paul preacheth. 14 there were seven sons of one Sceva, a Jew, and chief of the priests, which did so. 15 And the evil spirit answered and said, Jesus I know, and Paul I know; but who are ye? 16 And the man in whom the evil spirit was leaped on them, and overcame them, and prevailed against them, so that they fled out of that house naked and wounded.

Jesus and His disciples were able to drive out demons in Jesus' name, but not everybody who tries commanding spirits in Jesus' name is able to do so. Some modern magicians claim that the above exorcists failed because they didn't first evoke Jesus (as is done in ceremonial magick). It is more likely that Jesus' disciples were able to cast out demons because they were Christians, and Christ already lived in their hearts. There is no need to evoke Him if He dwells within you. So it is possible for Christians to cast out demons if they had need to (Luke 9:49-50), but in the Bible we are not instructed to seek out demons to cast out. In the Bible a girl that was a fortuneteller, and was also possessed by a demon, was following Paul around. He waited days before he decided to cast it out, and he only did so then because he became annoyed.

> **(KJV) Acts 16:16-18 And it came to pass, as we went to prayer, a certain damsel possessed with a spirit of divination met us, which brought her masters much gain by soothsaying: 17 The same followed Paul and us, and cried, saying, These men are the servants of the most high God, which shew unto us the way of salvation. 18 And this did she many days. But Paul, being grieved, turned and said to the spirit, I command thee in the name of Jesus Christ to come out of her. And he came out the same hour.**

The following verses show you that there is nothing to be gained by conjuring spirits, and that God is the one you should consult.

> **(KJV) Isaiah 8:19 And when they shall say unto you, Seek unto them that have familiar spirits, and unto wizards that peep, and that mutter: should not a people seek unto their God? for the living to the dead?**

The above verse points out that it does you no good to consult the dead on behalf of the living. Why consult anybody other than God? Would you really want to take the advice of a demon anyways? The next verse is from the book of Daniel. Daniel was appointed chief of all the magicians, astrologers, and soothsayers. Daniel did not practice any magical arts. He only consulted God for the answers to His problems, and He was considered wiser than all the magicians in the land.

> **(KJV) Daniel 1:20 And in all matters of wisdom and understanding, that the king enquired of them, he found them ten times better than all the magicians and astrologers that were in all his realm.**

The following verses contain further warnings not to consult mediums and spiritualists. In doing so you will turn the Lord against you, He will prove them to be wrong, you will be rejected from God's people, and He will show the nations your disgrace.

(KJV) Lev 19:31 Regard not them that have familiar spirits, neither seek after wizards, to be defiled by them: I am the LORD your God.

(KJV) Lev 20:6 And the soul that turneth after such as have familiar spirits, and after wizards, to go a whoring after them, I will even set my face against that soul, and will cut him off from among his people.

(KJV) Nahum 3:4-5 Because of the multitude of the whoredoms of the wellfavoured harlot, the mistress of witchcrafts, that selleth nations through her whoredoms, and families through her witchcrafts. 5 Behold, I am against thee, saith the LORD of hosts; and I will discover thy skirts upon thy face, and I will shew the nations thy nakedness, and the kingdoms thy shame.

(KJV) 2 Chron 33:6 And he caused his children to pass through the fire in the valley of the son of Hinnom: also he observed times, and used enchantments, and used witchcraft, and dealt with a familiar spirit, and with wizards: he wrought much evil in the sight of the LORD, to provoke him to anger.

(NIV) Hosea 4:12 They consult a wooden idol and are answered by a stick of wood. A spirit of prostitution leads them astray; they are unfaithful to their God.

(KJV) Deut 18:10-14 There shall not be found among you any one that maketh his son or his daughter to pass through the fire, or that useth divination, or an observer of times, or an enchanter, or a witch. 11 Or a charmer, or a consulter with familiar spirits, or a wizard, or a necromancer. 12 For all that do these things are an abomination unto the LORD: and because of these abominations the LORD thy God doth drive them out from before thee. 13 Thou shalt be perfect with the LORD thy God. 14 For these nations, which thou shalt possess, hearkened unto observers of times, and unto diviners: but as for thee, the LORD thy God hath not suffered thee so to do.

As you can see by the above verses all magical practices are detestable to God. You need to put God first in your life. If you have a problem look to God for the answers. If you need help, call on God, and He will provide for your needs. My life is thousands of times better now that I seek God's aid instead of practicing magick. I still get into situations where practicing magick could be used, but now all I do is pray and God provides me with what I need far better than any magical effect possibly could. If you trust in God you will have no need to ever practice magick. Magick cannot compare to the power of God, as you will see in the following verses.

> **(KJV) Exod 7:11-12 Then Pharaoh also called the wise men and the sorcerers: now the magicians of Egypt, they also did in like manner with their enchantments. 12 For they cast down every man his rod, and they became serpents: but Aaron's rod swallowed up their rods.**

> **(KJV) Exod 8:18-19 And the magicians did so with their enchantments to bring forth lice, but they could not: so there were lice upon man, and upon beast. 19 Then the magicians said unto Pharaoh, This is the finger of God: and Pharaoh's heart was hardened, and he hearkened not unto them; as the LORD had said.**

In the above verses the magicians of Egypt tried to compete with God, but they could not. *Is magick real*? The Bible portrays magick as being real. The magicians of Egypt were able to turn their staffs into snakes, but God is much more powerful, and that is why Aaron's staff swallowed the magician's staves up. Several people in the Bible did things that might be considered magick. The above verses are an example of Aaron changing His staff into a snake just as the magicians did, but Aaron's technique is considered a miracle and the magician's considered witchcraft.

Many churches today still practice the laying on of hands. The Old Testament prophets received insight by using the Urim and Thummim, and the Bible is full of miracles. The disciples cast lots to determine who would replace Judas as one of the twelve, and Daniel was a dream interpreter. So how do you know which magick is okay and which magick is not okay? The answer to this question is also the answer to what is wrong with magick.

The magick that the prophets and the disciples performed were done to bring glory to God. The magick that magicians perform is done to bring glory to themselves. Christians no longer perform miracles because there is no longer a need for them. In the early church, miracles were performed to help people to believe, but now that the world has so many believers in it Christians no longer need to go to such extremes to convert people to Christianity. The Bible says that if you have faith you can move a mountain, but why would you need that power? How would moving a mountain glorify

God? By moving a mountain, only the person that did so would get the glory, and it would be like showing off.

Magick is vanity. If you are a magician examine your motives; what were the reasons that you chose to study magick in the first place? If you are seeking power, look to God, He is the highest power there is. The problem I had that caused me to take so long to become a Christian was also vanity; vanity in knowledge (wanting to know what others didn't). Vanity is everywhere, and that is why there are so many other religious books and religious practices. Books like the Book of Mormon, the Koran, the Lost Books of the Bible, the 6th & 7th Books of Moses, and The lesser keys of King Solomon. People are full of vanity and want to believe that they know more than the other religions do.

The above books are a good example of this. The members of these religions or sects want to believe that they know more about God or are closer to Him than the other religions that worship the same God. The above-mentioned books are only the extra books written about God. There are also hundreds of magick books on the shelves of bookstores full of little tidbits of information that make the reader feel like they have a deeper understanding of the universe than everybody else. The Bible says, "*Vanity vanity all is vanity*", and this is true. It is basic human nature to want to feel smarter or have more knowledge than other people do. At Churches I've witnessed Christians arguing over scripture in an effort to exalt themselves, and feel that they have a better understanding of the Bible than the other Christians do. Debates like this also happen between denominations.

I've even seen elders engage in these arguments over how to interpret scripture. The reason there are so many different denominations of Christians is because everyone wants to feel that their denomination is the right one. Magick is just another way to exalt yourself. The true power is with God. The following verse is an example of what people who practiced magick did when they figured out that God is the number one power.

(KJV) Acts 19:19 Many of them also which used curious arts brought their books together, and burned them before all men: and they counted the price of them, and found it fifty thousand pieces of silver.

The following set of verses are about Simon the magician

(KJV) Acts 8:9-24 But there was a certain man, called Simon, which beforetime in the same city used sorcery, and bewitched the people of Samaria, giving out that himself was some great

one: 10 To whom they all gave heed, from the least to the greatest, saying, This man is the great power of God. 11 And to him they had regard, because that of long time he had bewitched them with sorceries. 12 But when they believed Philip preaching the things concerning the kingdom of God, and the name of Jesus Christ, they were baptized, both men and women. 13 Then Simon himself believed also: and when he was baptized, he continued with Philip, and wondered, beholding the miracles and signs which were done. 14 Now when the apostles which were at Jerusalem heard that Samaria had received the word of God, they sent unto them Peter and John: 15 Who, when they were come down, prayed for them, that they might receive the Holy Ghost: 16 (For as yet he was fallen upon none of them: only they were baptized in the name of the Lord Jesus.) 17 Then laid they their hands on them, and they received the Holy Ghost. 18 And when Simon saw that through laying on of the apostles' hands the Holy Ghost was given, he offered them money, 19 Saying, Give me also this power, that on whomsoever I lay hands, he may receive the Holy Ghost. 20 But Peter said unto him, Thy money perish with thee, because thou hast thought that the gift of God may be purchased with money. 21 Thou hast neither part nor lot in this matter: for thy heart is not right in the sight of God. 22 Repent therefore of this thy wickedness, and pray God, if perhaps the thought of thine heart may be forgiven thee. 23 For I perceive that thou art in the gall of bitterness, and in the bond of iniquity. 24 Then answered Simon, and said, Pray ye to the LORD for me, that none of these things which ye have spoken come upon me.

In the above verses Simon, who is said to have been a great magician, realized that the power of God was far greater than any magick he could do. He followed the disciples, and was constantly amazed. Simon's problem was also with vanity. He wanted to pay money so that he can have the same power as the Apostles. Vanity and pride are emotions that are hard to over come. This is why the Bible speaks so much about being humble.

Before I became a Christian I had the same opinion that a lot of non-Christians share. I saw the hypocrisy of many people that claimed to be Christians (people who claim to be Christians, but were really sinners, and hypocrites). To me magick seemed like the answer. I thought that Christians were hypocrites, and that magicians had a closer relationship to God; understanding His secrets that the hypocritical Christian did not understand. I believed that as a magician I would be a servant of God, but with a higher status than the people who merely called themselves Christians.

I read shelves full of books on magick, and thought that I had tons of knowledge and understanding. I was wrong. I was full of vanity. I wasted my time reading all sorts of books that contained nothing but nonsense. The Bible says that man's wisdom is foolishness to God, and I had spent many years studying and memorizing that foolishness.

Once I finally began reading the Bible I understood the mysteries that I thought I was finding in the books written by men. Remember the above verse that said, "*Why consult the dead on behalf of the living*", well that applies here also; why consult the philosophies of men to understand the mysteries of God? Why not read the book that God had inspired? Finally, after several years I figured that out, and began reading the Bible.

One of the first things that I learned was that those hypocritical Christians who I so much didn't want to have anything to do with; weren't Christians at all. This was an enlightening realization for me. For many years I judged Christians as hypocrites, because of what I saw people who *claimed* to be Christians do. I was wrong. The Bible tells us exactly how to be a Christian, and if you do not meet the Biblical standards then you are not a Christian; no matter how much you claim to be.

The Bible speaks a great deal about hypocrites, and also about being humble. Now I joyfully call myself a Christian, and if I witness hypocrites I will rebuke them with kindness. Now that I understand that being a magician is detestable to God, I no longer practice magick. If you are a Christian you don't need to practice magick, because God takes care of all your needs. As a Christian all you need to do is try to live a righteous life, avoid sinning, and God will take care of the rest. If you practice magick I ask you to examine yourself; does your magical practices glorify God, or your own vanity? Don't answer yet; take some time to think about it.

Now we will examine divination. In the Old Testament the Urim and Thummim were used to gain information and guidance from God. Joseph Smith also claims to have translated the Book of Mormon with these stones. How was it okay to gain information by these stones, but wrong for the pagans to use divination? What is the difference? One difference is that only Priests used the Urim and Thummim, and all credit and glory was given to God. The pagans were consulting other gods and doing it for their own vanity and profit.

Another thing that is important to remember is that once Jesus came, He became mediator between God and man. We no longer need to practice divination to gain information from God, because now all that we have to do is pray and God will provide us the answer. We live in a time where we have easy access to the Bible. We are able to read the Bible to get answers from God so we don't need to use tarot cards or dowsing rods in order to get this information.

Now we have the Holy Spirit to guide us. The time when God communicated to us through divination is over. In my opinion even when the 11 disciples cast lots to replace Judas with Mathias was wrong of them. I think that the fact that Mathias is never again mentioned in the Bible is because He was not supposed to be the replacement. Paul is the replacement for Judas, and Paul was selected by God when God chose to select a replacement.

Divination is wrong because it demands an answer from God right then. Who are we to demand anything from God? How can we say to God, "*I am going to cast a lot and you must give me the answer now*"? Divination is vanity because it makes the diviner believe that they have a power to see the future that no one else possesses. They also become stumbling blocks to others. They lead people astray by having the people turn to them instead of to God. They cause others to play the harlot to God, and they place themselves into God's shoes. Nobody should be vain enough to believe that they could fill God's shoes.

If you are a diviner, astrologer, conjurer, magician, medium, or dowser remember that YOU are causing people to commit adultery to God, and He will hold you accountable for it. Sometimes divination can be quite impressive, it can even be somewhat accurate, but if you've ever practiced it you would know that a great deal of the time it is wrong. Psychic advice isn't even one hundred percent accurate; yet they lead people away from God, and have them seek answers from them (for profit in most cases). If you are performing magick it must be for the glory of God, and not your own. The same thing applies to all Christians. If your church practices faith healing, is it done for the glory of God, or for the glory of your church or its members?

If you are a Christian don't be quick at judging other people's practices before you examine your own, or those of your church. A lot of magick practices are related to the scriptures. Occultists are not Satanists, as most Christians believe. Occultists are simply people who study obscure subjects trying to gain knowledge outside of the mainstream. In doing so they are probably being led astray, because man's wisdom is foolishness to God. These people do not need people accusing them of being something they are not. They need guidance from Christians to be led back onto the right path, and not brainless accusations.

Many of the books on the Occult found in Christian bookstores are poorly written, and they really frustrate me. These books are written by Christians, who for the most part are sincerely trying to help out their brethren, but most of the time they don't have any facts, are completely wrong, and make Christians look like hypocrites or fools. *How can someone that is supposed to possess the truth write books that are full of lies, falsehood, and ignorance?*

The books I am talking about are books written to protect Christians from getting mixed up with cults and/or the occult (which they say means Satanism). Most of the books I've read written in this manner I have found to be grossly inaccurate, and completely useless for what it is designed to do. For example, I learned that a *serpent* gave Joseph Smith the Book of Mormon. You can probably imagine how foolish I looked when Mormons knocked on my door and I told them that.

They looked at me like I was the biggest idiot on the planet. Making a false statement immediately discredits a person, and then others become reluctant to take the person's advice. Another example is in regards to *Hypnotism*. Every Christian book I've read so far has said that Hypnotism is either from the devil, or is an occult practice. I happen to have gone to school for hypnotism while working on my degree in Psychology. I understand all of the principles of hypnotic suggestion, and can assure you that it has nothing to do with the devil or the occult. I have also investigated the occult, and occultist and magicians do not use hypnotism (it would take away from their vanity).

Doctors and the scientific community used hypnotism for one hundred years before Hollywood started making movies that portrayed it in a bad light. If hypnotism is from the devil and that is why Christians tell you to be scared of it, WHY if these people are such good Christians are they watching devil movies in the first place? These books I've been discussing fail to achieve their purpose. If your children met someone from one of the cults in these books the cult would have no trouble convincing the child that their parents are wrong, and that they (the cult) have the true answers.

If their parents had the truth in them they should easily know that the angel Moroni gave Joseph Smith the book of Mormon, and not a snake. If their parents are wrong about such a simple thing how can they be trusted to know the truth about important things? I'm not saying that Christians should not warn their kids about the danger of false teachings; I'm just saying that you should understand a *basic overview of a subject* (especially if you are going to write a book on it) before you make ignorant statements. You don't want make Christians look like imbeciles and hypocrites. The following verses are about not being misled by dream interpreters, false prophets, and miracles.

> **(KJV) Deut 13:1-4 If there arise among you a prophet, or a dreamer of dreams, and giveth thee a sign or a wonder, 2 And the sign or the wonder come to pass, whereof he spake unto thee, saying, Let us go after other gods, which thou hast not known, and let us serve them; 3 Thou shalt not hearken unto the words of that prophet, or that dreamer of dreams: for the LORD your God proveth you, to know whether ye love the LORD your God with all your heart and with all your soul. 4 Ye shall walk after the LORD your God, and fear him, and keep his commandments, and obey his voice, and ye shall serve him, and cleave unto him.**

The above verses tell us that even if someone's divination turns out to be true, not to be lead astray. Always trust in God first, and never play the harlot. Interpreting dreams is another matter requiring discernment as to whether it is from God or from Magick. Jacobs's son Joseph interpreted dreams, and so did Daniel. Peter had a vision that did away with circumcision. My advice is to realize that there are many different types of dreams. Not all dreams and visions are signs from God, and you had better be sure before you claim one to be.

A trance that you put yourself into by meditating is different than a trance induced by God. You might interpret your dreams to find out your sub-conscious ramblings, but that is different than God giving you a dream of prophecy. I have never had a dream or trance induced by God so I'm not sure what the difference would be, but I'm sure that God would make it clear to you if it was from Him. I'd say that you should be sure before you claim that you received a message from God.

The dream interpreters in the Bible had their dreams in times of great need. God may answer your questions in your dreams, but that doesn't mean that you are to spread it around like you are God's spokesperson on earth. In the book of Revelations John is carried off in the spirit; there is a big difference between God carrying you off in the spirit, and self-willed astral projection (out of body experiences).

I hope that I have helped you to understand what the Bible says is wrong with magick. If you are someone who currently practices magick, I ask you to contemplate what I wrote every deeply. If you have been practicing magick for a long time these things might be hard to accept at first, but it is the TRUTH. You have probably wasted many years studying what I am now telling you is worthless. You probably have your own ideas and philosophies that make perfect sense to you, and they have likely become apart of your belief system.

I have been there. It was very hard for me to accept the truth. I spent so much time, money, energy, and effort to learn a forbidden practice that I now consider foolishness. I assure you that if you trust in God, and study the Bible, magick will seem useless and unnecessary to you. You will come to know what you may now consider wisdom as foolishness.

I searched the scriptures for a long time trying to find a verse that says that magick is okay, but it isn't anywhere to be found. If you are not ready to give up magick, search the scriptures anyways to learn about God. You may find that the God of the scriptures is different than the idea that you currently hold about who God is. If you practice magick you are probably full of vanity, which the Bible can help you with. If you consider yourself to be a very spiritual person, then you would really enjoy reading the Bible anyways. If you are a seeker of wisdom I assure you that you will find plenty of wisdom in the Bible. Whatever the case, please read the Bible and decide for yourself if your practices are right or wrong. Meet with someone from a church, and learn more about Christianity before you decide that you have all of the answers. Once you gain true wisdom the false wisdom of man will be useless to you.

If you are a Christian I hope I have provided you with information about magick, and given you something to think about. I hope this Bible study will cause you to examine your practices, and the practices of your church. Maybe you won't accuse someone falsely of being a Satanist, but will realize that a lot of people are just lost. They think that they are serving God, but they are confused. You should show compassion to them, and help them get on the correct path of following Christ.

Know what you are talking about before you make false statements that might lead others to think that the truth is not in you. If you don't know something ask the person to explain it to you first, and then you can use scripture to show them the error of their ways. Just don't show them the error of something you think they are doing when they're not doing it. All that does is make the person think it is a waste of time talking to you, and they won't listen to your advice. It would be like if someone told you that they had a flat tire on their car, and you tell them that it is because they shouldn't have been flying a sub-marine in the first place. If you rebuke someone with such an inaccurate statement, do you think they will allow you to teach them about God?

The following verses tell us what God has in store for magicians and astrologers. As Paul stated in Acts 18:6 after he had preached the gospel, *"Your blood be on your own heads! I am clear of my responsibility."* I have shared with you the scriptures that have to do with magick. Now it is up to you to accept them or reject them.

(KJV) Rev 21:8 But the fearful, and unbelieving, and the abominable, and murderers, and whoremongers, and sorcerers, and idolaters, and all liars, shall have their part in the lake which burneth with fire and brimstone: which is the second death.

(KJV) Isaiah 47:10-14 For thou hast trusted in thy wickedness: thou hast said, None seeth me. Thy wisdom and thy knowledge, it hath perverted thee; and thou hast said in thine heart, I am, and none else beside me. 11 Therefore shall evil come upon thee; thou shalt not know from whence it riseth: and mischief shall fall upon thee; thou shalt not be able to put it off: and desolation shall come upon thee suddenly, which thou shalt not know. 12 Stand now with thine enchantments, and with the multitude of thy sorceries, wherein thou hast laboured from thy youth; if so be thou shalt be able to profit, if so be thou mayest prevail. 13 Thou art wearied in the multitude of thy counsels. Let now the astrologers, the stargazers, the monthly prognosticators, stand up, and save thee from these things that shall come upon thee. 14 Behold, they shall be as stubble; the fire shall burn them; they shall not deliver themselves from the power of the flame: there shall not be a coal to warm at, nor fire to sit before it.

References

Scripture taken from the KING JAMES VERSION OF THE BIBLE, (KJV) Public Domain 1611

The Trinity

In this Bible study we will be discussing the Trinity. Is there One God that exists in three persons, three Gods that are co-equal in one Godhead, or is there One God (the father) who has a son (Jesus), which has been given authority by His father, and the Holy Spirit which is sent by God at the request of Jesus to do the will of the Father?

The Holy Trinity has been taught as a matter of fact for centuries, and is accepted by the majority of Protestant/Catholic churches, yet the scriptural basis for such a belief is highly debatable. Most of the scriptures used to support the Trinity are found in the King James Version of the Bible, and do not exist in most other Bibles either before or after the King James Version. The writers of the King James Version of the Bible took the liberty to include beliefs found in hymns and sermons of the earlier church into the Bible; believing that if something were taught by some of the early churches then that is justification to include those beliefs in the Bible. This led to the inclusion of doctrines regardless of if the beliefs were actually recorded as scripture throughout the years.

The King James Version was translated out of the **Textus Receptus** a Greek Manuscript that was written only a few years prior to the King James Version. This approach (finding early Christian hymns or sermons to support a belief as legitimate) doesn't take into account the Arian Controversy in which the Christian churches of the time were divided over the belief in the Trinity. The result of the Arian Controversy was the construction of the Nicene Creed, which was a man-made document designed to summarize the belief system of a certain sect of Christianity. Creeds such as the Nicene Creed could be looked at as the introduction to man's doctrines and church dogma into Christianity. They can be looked at to represent the beginning of denominationalism.

The Nicene Creed laid the foundation for other non-scriptural introductions that worked their way into the Christian belief system not through the scriptures, but through man-made creeds. The Holy Spirit was not considered as God even at Nicene. The Holy Spirit and Mary as the Mother of God, Queen of Heaven were added in other Creeds shortly there after. Our modern translations of the Bible are tainted by these man-made doctrines. Even people that claim to practice Sola Scriptura (Scripture only) read the scriptures with the traditional interpretations taught in the Creeds of 300-400 A.D.

For example "Word" in John 1:1 is capitalized in most modern translations of the Bible leading the reader to believe that the WORD is referring to a person (Jesus as a pre-existent deity), as opposed to the PLAN, LOGIC, or FOREORDINATION of God. The early English Bibles such as the Geneva and Tyndale Bibles translate John 1:1 with "word" in lowercase letters and from then on use the word IT instead of HIM (as the KJV does). The capitalized letter and the use of the word HIM instead of IT greatly changes the meaning of John's statement.

Using "word" in the lowercase sense John 1:1 would more closely be translated to mean, "*In the beginning God had a Plan, God has always had a plan, the Plan was God's, everything takes place according to God, and apart from God's plan nothing has taken place that has taken place*". It is the difference from Predestination which is clearly taught in the Bible and Pre-existence, which is inferred into the Bible only when looking at the Bible with theology tainted by the early Creeds. The above paraphrase is a different interpretation than most people are taught in the modern day churches, but it conforms to the scripture much better than the translations tainted by the Nicene Creed.

The debate over the existence of the Trinity has been taking place ever since the third century A.D. This Bible study is not meant to tell you which way to believe, but is presented in order for the reader to benefit from the research that I have completed in my own search for the truth. Do not take something on faith that is not in the Bible, just because someone in a church says they believe it. Research it and decide for yourself.

I first began my search for the truth by speaking to a Baptist minister who had the KJV (King James Version) only philosophy. I have been trying to understand the KJV only philosophy, and the concept of the Trinity. One of the main arguments used by KJV believers is that the KJV was needed to make the Bible available to the English-speaking people. They have a theory that the Catholic Church prevented English-speaking people from reading the Bible in order to control them. The problem with this idea is that there already were English Bibles available at the time the KJV was written.

The idea is that the Catholic Church was keeping the Bible from the people to control them, but the Catholic Church released an English Bible before the KJV came out. The Douay-Rheims Bible published in 1582. The pastor I was meeting with let me borrow a book called "*Way of Life Encyclopedia of the Bible and Christianity*" it has a large history of the KJV. It is where I obtained much of my information, which I later verified on the

Internet. In this book the author states that 4/5 to 9/10 of the KJV was taken directly from the William Tyndale Translation.

I am not sure how much I trust the Tyndale translation as he is said to have added his own tracts and distributed them with his Bibles printed inside with the text. All of the Bibles written at the time of the reformation I find suspect. Yes, they may have been men devoted to God willing to stand up against the church, but at the same time they were men who may have been arrogant and seeking to establish their names in history (for writing the first English Bible etc..) Several of the Reformers wrote their own Bibles and started their own denominations in their own names (not the actions of someone solely devoted to God). So I am not impressed that 90% of the KJV is taken straight out of the Tyndale Bible.

In this same book it states that the KJV has a superior translation of the Old Testament taken out of Ben Chayyim's translation of 1525 (Daniel Bomberg addition or the Second Great Rabbinic Bible) and not the false translation by Ben Asher. I found this information disturbing as well. I have been told that the KJV was good because it used the original manuscripts, but I am now finding that 90% of it was taken from the Tyndale Bible of 1530 and the Old Testament translation was from 1525. These ancient manuscripts that were used to write the KJV Bible only existed for 80 years before being used to create the KJV. From what I have read the *Textus Receptus* (the other source of Greek text used in the KJV) was also created in this same time period.

The pastor I have been meeting with claims that the Latin Vulgate is corrupt, but at least it has been in existence since somewhere between 150-350 A.D. From my research the Vulgate was even used to create the KJV. David Otis Fuller author of "*Which Bible*" stated that one of the reasons for his faith in the *Textus Receptus* is that it conferred diligently with the Latin Vulgate. Tyndale being a former priest probably used it in his translations as well.

Another question I have is in regards to the Apocrypha. If the KJV was the true and perfectly preserved word of God (as many claim) then why did it originally include the Apocrypha in it, and then later take it out? The Apocrypha was included in the Septuagint, which was the Bible that was used by Christ and the Apostles. The Apostles warn us so much to beware of false doctrines that it would seem that if there was several false books included in the Bible that they would mention it.

I have read everything I can in support of the Trinity and it just doesn't make sense to me. Why would God say to Himself, "*this is my beloved son in whom I am well pleased?*" Why would He say that to Himself? Why would Jesus say that He came to do the will of His Father, if he is talking about Himself and doing His own will? I don't understand this concept. To me it seems like a man-made philosophy for Polytheist to attempt to claim to be Monotheistic.

I try to take the Bible at its word and don't find it prudent to trust other people just because they say something is true. I read in the Bible that God is the Father who sent His son to die for the sins of the world. After Jesus prayed to His father, He ascended into Heaven and all authority in Heaven and on Earth was given to Him. He now sits besides His father (at His right hand). The belief in the Trinity as I understand it asks us to believe that none of the above is true, but that God pretended and role-played different characters because our human minds were too weak to understand the concept that He was really all three persons of a Trinity.

When speaking with people that have been enculturated into this belief, once they become stumped and unable to explain their own philosophy they tell me, "*Some things you need to take on faith*", which is faulty logic because the Bible warns us not to be led astray by the false doctrines of man. The Bible also states not to trust someone that comes to us with a different Gospel. We are to have blind faith in things that are not found in scripture. Another huge problem I have with the Trinity is that I cannot find anything in the Bible that leads me to believe that the Holy Spirit is God. I do not deny the work of the Holy Spirit, but I do not see that the Holy Spirit is presented as a coequal with God and Jesus. The Bible states that Jesus was given authority by His father, but the only arguments that I have seen to support the Holy Spirit as equal is that he shares some traits with God or Jesus.

Another interesting fact that I discovered recently is that the culture of people that lived in Rome prior to the Roman Catholic Church were Trinitarians and believed in three gods. It is easy to see how this philosophy could have crept into the Catholic Church over the years in the same way the worship of the Virgin Mary Mother of God concept crept into the church to replace the pagan worship of the goddess Diana. The more research I do the more confused I become, and the less trust I have in the sources I read.

(KJV) 1 John 5:7 For there are three that bear record in heaven, the Father, the Word, and the Holy Ghost: and these three are one.

The above scripture comes from the KJV of the Bible. The KJV is one of the only versions of the Bible that contains this verse. This is one of the main verses used to support the Trinity, but most scholars including Trinitarians admit that this verse is spurious.

I believe that the truth can be found in the Bible if you study it, and look hard enough for it. Seek and you will find is promised in the word of God (Matt. 7:8). The problem with the Trinity is that I have read the proof verses everyone uses to prove the Trinity and it just doesn't make sense to me. I trust that the Holy Spirit dwells within me and guides me into all understanding, and I am not being called to believe in the Trinity.

My first question is **WHY** if the Trinity were true is it not taught **CLEARLY** in the New Testament? Why if there is only one God that exists in three separate but coequal parts didn't any of the authors of the New Testament mention it plainly? They certainly were familiar with the first commandment of not having any other gods and would have definitely known about the monotheistic views of the Jewish people.

If the apostles were going to teach a contrary doctrine it would seem like they would have spent more time on it, and taught it more clearly. Why would the apostles write letters addressing topics like circumcision, the proper way to take communion, and then leave out such an important teaching as **THE VERY NATURE OF GOD?** To have faith in something you must first obtain an understanding of it. If God were a Trinity then it would seem like that would be an important concept the apostles would attempt to explain somewhere in the Bible in order for us to understand and have faith in the Trinity.

One of the main explanations I have come across in my research is that, ""*the Trinity has always existed, we as humans are just not smart enough to grasp the concept*." The problem I have with this statement is that the Trinity is not that hard of a concept to grasp; if it had been taught there is no reason to believe that people would not be able to grasp the concept. Why waste time establishing that Jesus was the Son of God when they could have spent that time convincing the world that Jesus and God were one in the same person? Why at Christ's baptism wouldn't God just say that He is now dwelling with men instead of identifying Christ as His son and saying He was pleased with Him?

If you believe in predestination then you would believe that God has known His plan since the beginning of time. If so, why would He have created contradictory statements in the Old Testament establishing a monotheistic point of view? It is ethnocentric to believe that the apostles who lived with Christ were unable to grasp or express this concept, but people several centuries later became smart enough to do so.

I don't believe that this mystery would have been hidden from the apostles, and if they knew about it why would they neglect teaching such an important concept. The Bible states that there is no hidden thing that has not been revealed. If so why would the apostles only hint around about a concept that some priest would later develop? I don't believe they would. I think that the apostles had all wisdom revealed to them as the Bible states, and that it is based on this wisdom that they warn the church of others introducing new doctrines later that THEY DID NOT TEACH (Gal 1:8-9, 2 Corth 11:4, 1 Tim 1:3, 6:3, 2 Pet 2:1). Below are the verses I am referring to that state that the mysteries have been revealed in Christ.

> **(KJV) Matthew 13:35 that it might be fulfilled which was spoken by the prophet, saying: "I will open My mouth in parables; I will utter things kept secret from the foundation of the world."**

> **(KJV) Mark 4:22 "For there is nothing hidden which will not be revealed, nor has anything been kept secret but that it should come to light.**

> **(KJV) Luke 8:17 For nothing is secret, that shall not be made manifest; neither any thing hid, that shall not be known and come abroad.**

> **(KJV) Romans 16:25-26 Now to Him who is able to establish you according to my gospel and the preaching of Jesus Christ, according to the revelation of the mystery kept secret since the world began 26 but now has been made manifest, and by the prophetic Scriptures has been made known to all nations, according to the commandment of the everlasting God, for obedience to the faith**

The above verses (Romans 16:25-26) state that the mysteries of the scriptures have been revealed in Christ, and made known to all nations. This was done by the commandment of God in order for us to gain an understanding so that we might be obedient to the faith.

(KJV) Mark 11:25 At that time Jesus answered and said, "I thank You, Father, Lord of heaven and earth, that You have hidden these things from the wise and prudent and have revealed them to babes.

(KJV) Colossians 1:26 the mystery which has been hidden from ages and from generations, but now has been revealed to His saints. 27 To them God willed to make known what are the riches of the glory of this mystery among the Gentiles: which is Christ in you, the hope of glory.

(KJV) Eph 6:19 And for me, that utterance may be given unto me, that I may open my mouth boldly, to make known the mystery of the gospel,

It is my understanding that it was the mission of the apostles to reveal the mysteries of Christ to the world. While Christ lived on the earth He spoke to the crowds in parables, but He always spoke plainly to the apostles. It was the apostle's mission to spread the teachings of Christ throughout the world. I don't think that the apostles taught in parables or left anything to be discovered later.

The Bible says that all the mysteries were revealed, so why isn't the Trinity taught in the Bible, or why can't I see it? The Bible says that the Gospel is only hidden to them that are lost (2 Co 4:3) is that me, or is that the Trinitarians? Was it the author's or God's intent to teach the Trinity, and is it taught clearly, or were some men smart enough to unravel a mystery of God that He and the apostles never intended to reveal?

The term "Trinity" is not found in the Bible. Over the years the Catholics have added many unbiblical practices to their religion. I am skeptical about the Trinity because I could see how they could have easily added it to fit into their belief systems similar to the Virgin Mary Queen of Heaven and the practice of praying to saints were added. From the research I have done the addition of "*these three are one*" in 1 John 5:7 originated in the sermon of a bishop and did not exist in any of manuscripts until around 800 A.D.

Another problem I have is that I do not trust the early Protestants either. They too were Catholic priests at one time and trained in the same traditions. From the research I have done the Biblical material created around the 1550-1620 contained added or modified verses in support of the Trinity (Catholic and Protestant), but very few before then (only 9 Bibles contain 1John 5:7 as in the KJV). I am suspicious of this era whether the Bible was influenced by the fads of that age (the Mary Mother of God was introduced into Catholic worship based on a short lived fad, and it still hasn't been corrected).

I'd like to express one other thought about the Catholic Church. I think that they could be corrupt and in error, and still be the One True Church. Whether Catholics are corrupt or not, the gates of hell have not prevailed against the Gospel of Christ. One of the main themes of the Old Testament is that the Jewish people were God's chosen people. The Jews would spend centuries in direct defiance to God, and remain His chosen people. I think it is possible that the Catholic Church could be the One True Church and can be in error the same way that the Jews existed in error for many centuries. There might not be a correct church that exists during our lifetimes, but this is just another topic.

I have found that many Trinitarians express different views on what they believe the Trinity to consist of. Some people believe there is three gods that work together in harmony, and others believe there is only one god that exists in three people beyond human comprehension. What is taught in the Bible? I believe the Bible proves authority has been vested in Christ and the pre-existence or at least the predestination of Christ, but I don't believe that Jesus is the same person as God. I believe that Jesus is God's son, which I believe the New Testament writers went through great length to prove.

(KJV) John 14:9: Jesus saith unto him, Have I been so long time with you, and yet hast thou not known me, Philip? he that hath seen me hath seen the Father; and how sayest thou then, Shew us the Father?

(KJV) John 1:18 No man hath seen God at any time; the only begotten Son, which is in the bosom of the Father, he hath declared him.

Trinitarians use the above verses to make the claim that Jesus is God's body. They then deduct that any appearance of God in the Old Testament of the Bible was Jesus in God's place, because they believe Jesus to be the physical manifestation of God. I believe Jesus was sent to earth to do the work of His father. His very job on the earth was to reveal the truth of God the Father to mankind. In the above verse I believe Jesus is telling the apostles that he has been revealing the Father to them all of the time in His teachings. I do not believe that He was saying that He was the Father and that by looking at Him they were actually seeing what God looks like.

(KJV) 1 Timothy 3:16: And without controversy great is the mystery of godliness: God was manifest in the flesh, justified in the Spirit, seen of angels, preached unto the Gentiles, believed on in the world, received up into glory.

When I researched the above verse I found that many people believe there was a typo, which changed the word HE into GOD. What was the author's intent? I believe the author is giving a quick recap of the basic belief system of a Christian (like a quick creed). In verse 15 the author talks of building up the household of God. The foundation of the church is on the gospel of Christ which 3:16 is a quick recap of. In the next verse 4:1 the author *warns of false doctrines being introduced.* <u>The author's intent in 3:16 was to spell out the doctrine of faith to prepare you to defend against the false doctrines to come, which the next verse refers to.</u> The author was recapping Christianity, and not introducing a new doctrine that God himself was manifested in the flesh, which is out of context from the other verses around it. God in the flesh is a new concept not found in the New Testament and would require more attention than to merely be included in a quick recap of the faith.

(KJV) John10:30-33 I and my Father are one. 31 Then the Jews took up stones again to stone him.32 Jesus answered them, Many good works have I shewed you from my Father; for which of those works do ye stone me?33: The Jews answered him, saying, For a good work we stone thee not; but for blasphemy; and because that thou, being a man, makest thyself God.

"I and the Father are one" does not necessarily mean that they are the same person. The Greek word for one used here is the same word used to describe a husband and wife as one flesh. Married people can act in union, agreement, or in one accord and not be the same person. We are also called one body of believers with different members, but we are not the same person. Jesus also prays that the Apostles would be one as He and the Father are one (John 17:22). Are the Apostles included in the Godhead? The word for ONE in John 10:30 is HEN meaning ONE IN ESSENSE not

NUMERICALLY (Greek Lexicon). Jesus clarifies His statement in the next few verses.

> **(KJV) John 10:34-37 Jesus answered them, Is it not written in your law, I said, Ye are gods? 35: If he called them gods, unto whom the word of God came, and the scripture cannot be broken; 36 Say ye of him, whom the Father hath sanctified, and sent into the world, Thou blasphemest; because I said, I am the Son of God? 37: If I do not the works of my Father, believe me not.38: But if I do, though ye believe not me, believe the works: that ye may know, and believe, that the Father is in me, and I in him.**

Christ states that scripture allows for someone to be called gods and not actually be the one true God. Christ then clarifies His position further and states that He was sent by His Father, and that He called Himself the Son of God. It is impossible for God to lie, (Hebrew 6:18) and there is no reason for Christ to mislead anybody; as He knew it was not yet His time.

So if Christ was really God this would have been an ideal time to say so, but He portrayed them as Father and Son, and said that He had been sent by His Father. As for the *Father is in me and I in him,* John the Baptist was full of the Holy Spirit in his mother's womb, but that did not make him the Holy Spirit. There is no doubt that the Father and Son abided in each others love and work in one accord for the same goal, but I don't see in the above context in which Christ made the statements in 31-37 clarifying that He and the Father are separate, to revert back to it and contradict himself in verse 38.

Another defense of the Trinity comes from passages that state that God (the Father) is our savior.

> **(KJV) 1Tim 2:3: For this is good and acceptable in the sight of God our Saviour;**

> **(KJV) Tim 1:3: But hath in due times manifested his word through preaching, which is committed unto me according to the commandment of God our Saviour;**

> **(KJV) Tim 2:10: Not purloining, but shewing all good fidelity; that they may adorn the doctrine of God our Saviour in all things.**

(KJV) Jude 1:25: To the only wise God our Saviour, be glory and majesty, dominion and power, both now and ever. Amen.

I agree that God the Father is our Savior as Mary stated in Luke 1:47. God has been the savior of the Hebrew people throughout the Old Testament. God retains this title, as it was ultimately God the father that saved us. He saved us through His son, which was God's predetermined plan from the beginning of time. The great mystery in Christ (spoken of earlier) which has been hidden since the beginning of creation is that Christ was to be the messiah, and was to redeem us to God due to the fall of man.

This is why Christ is called the Word of God; it is because Christ is the fulfillment of the prophesies of the Old Testament, and God has been preparing the way for Christ since the world began. Most everything that took place in the Old Testament was done as a precursor and to prepare the way for Christ to be revealed. From Abraham being willing to offer is son as a sacrifice to Moses freeing the Hebrew slaves and lifting up the bronze serpent in the desert.

Take the Bronze Serpent in Numbers 21:5-9 for example. The people were dying because they sinned against God. God had Moses create a Bronze Serpent on a pole and anyone who had faith in God's promise and looked to the Bronze Serpent would not die, but would retain their lives in spite of their sins. This is a precursor or foreshadowing of the salvation people would later receive through Christ. The serpent represents sin judged, and it was lifted up on a tree as Christ was on the cross. It was for the removal of punishment for sins and for life, and it required faith in God's promise (if the people did not believe God they wouldn't have looked to the Bronze Serpent).

This event was a major foreshadowing of what Christ would do, and is one of the mysteries the apostles revealed. There is no other reason for this event to be in the Bible other than to pave the way for Christ. It is against the commandments to make a graven image, yet God instructed Moses to do so, it doesn't make any sense without the further revelation of Christ on the cross.

I believe Christ is called God's word because God's words are all about the salvation coming to the world through Christ. Salvation came to us through Christ as God had determined before the creation of the world, but God (the father) is still our savior as stated in the verses provided above. God sent Jesus to the earth (John 3:16), and Jesus was here to do the will of His father (John 5:30). Although Jesus is the instrument through which God's salvation was to come to the world it was still God who commanded it.

Christ was God's spokesman on earth (word) just as Moses was in Egypt, but to a much greater degree as Christ was God's only begotten son, and Moses like us are only adopted children. Like Moses, Christ performed miracles for God's glory and to prove that God had sent him. Although Moses was an instrument of God, God is still the one who is credited as saving the Hebrew people, because He is the one that declared it.

(KJV) Isaiah 43:11-12 I, even I, am the LORD; and beside me there is no saviour. 12 I have declared, and have saved, and I have showed, when there was no strange god among you: therefore ye are my witnesses, saith the LORD, that I am God.

In the above verses God states that He is the only God, and as verse 12 states it is done because God has **declared** it. God sent an angel to shut the mouths of the lions to save Daniel (Daniel 6:22). God sent the angel of death for the first born of Egypt on Passover. Although God is not the actual person that performs every task, He is still credited with accomplishing them, because He is the one that has declared it.

Jesus is also credited as being our savior, which is all-apart of God's plan. Jesus is worthy of this title because He was obedient and sacrificed Himself according to God's will (Rev 5:9, 12). God had predestined this before the foundations of the earth. All power and authority has been given to Christ according to the will of God (Matt 28:18). Christ fulfilled His destiny and took His place at the right hand of His father (Mark 16:19), where he now intercedes as our High Priest to the Father on our behalf's as stated in the book of Hebrews.

I do not see the Trinity as three coequal gods, but I see that God has established a hierarchy. Christ's power and authority are given to Him by His father, and He is still subject to God (1 Cor 15:27-28). Christ didn't know everything His father knew while he was on earth (Mt 24:36). I do not see any reason to believe that Christ is anything other than the Son of God, which is what He claimed to be. As far as the Holy Ghost, I have not seen anything in the Bible to lead me to believe that He is equal to God or Christ. Nowhere does the Bible state that any authority has been given to the Holy Spirit, as is the case with Christ. I recognize that the work of the Holy Spirit is extremely important to our salvations, but I don't see that the Bible gives the Holy Spirit authority or coequal status with God and Christ.

(KJV) Mt 1:18: Now the birth of Jesus Christ was on this wise: When as his mother Mary was espoused to Joseph, before they came together, she was found with <u>ch</u>ild of the Holy Ghost.

(KJV) Mt 1:20: But while he thought on these things, behold, the angel of the Lord appeared unto him in a dream, saying, Joseph, thou son of David, fear not to take unto thee Mary thy wife: for that which is conceived in her is of the Holy Ghost.

(KJV) Mt 28:19: Go ye therefore, and teach all nations, baptizing them in the name of the Father, and of the Son, and of the Holy Ghost:

The Holy Spirit plays very significant roles in the Bible, but I don't see that the Holy Spirit as being equal to the Father and Son. I believe that the Holy Spirit played a role in the conception of Christ in the Virgin Mary. That doesn't necessarily make the Holy Spirit the father of Christ, but the agent through which God's purpose was manifested. Similar to how the angel of death was used to complete God's will during the Passover in Egypt.

(KJV) Lk 3:22 And the Holy Ghost descended in a bodily shape like a dove upon him, and a voice came from heaven, which said, Thou art my beloved Son; in thee I am well pleased.

The Holy Ghost was present at Christ's baptism in which He played the role of identifying Jesus as the Christ to John the Baptist (John 1:33). This also was a foreshadowing of receiving the gift of the Holy Ghost at baptism in the future (Acts 2:38), and the means by which we are sealed for redemption (Eph 1:13). Trinitarians use the above verse to establish a connection between the three members of the supposed Trinity. I do not deny that the three work together to bring about our salvations, I just don't believe that they are the exact same being as Trinitarians believe, nor do I believe they are three separate but coequal gods. I believe the New Testament establishes a clear hierarchy between them and specifies who does what. I understand that everyone's job is important, but that doesn't mean that each person who does a job is of equal status.

The New Testament states that we are all one body (1 Cor 12:13) and that there is no differences between Jew and Greek, free and slave, husband and wife (Gal 3:28, 1 co 11:3) and that we all have an equal opportunity *at salvation*, however there are still differences, and a hierarchy still exists. The Jews remain God's chosen people and they come before us (Romans 1:16,

2:10). The Jews will also be counted before us in the rapture (Rev 7:8-9). The twelve apostles are given authority over us, and will sit on thrones to judge the twelve tribes of Israel (Mat 19:28, Luke 22:30). The wife is to be submissive to her husband as the church is to Christ (Eph 5:22).

> **(KJV) Acts 20:28 Take heed therefore unto yourselves, and to all the flock, over the which the Holy Ghost hath made you overseers, to feed the church of God, which he hath purchased with his own blood.**

The Holy Ghost is the comforter sent by God and Christ to fulfill God's will (John 16:7-8). In the above verse I don't see the Holy Ghost as appointing people as overseers because He possesses some authority equal to God that allows Him to do so, but the men are selected as overseers based on the knowledge they have obtained from the Holy Ghost (1 Tim 3:2, Tit 1:7) as the Holy Ghost works in them to conform them into the image of Christ and seals them for the day of redemption (Romans 8:27-29, 12:2, Eph 4:30-31). The Holy Ghost is doing the job He was appointed to do by God. Moses, John the Baptist, Angels, etc... have all played their own specific roles in God's plan, that doesn't make them of equal status with God.

> **(KJV) Acts:5:3-4 But Peter said, Ananias, why hath Satan filled thine heart to lie to the Holy Ghost, and to keep back part of the price of the land? 4: Whiles it remained, was it not thine own? and after it was sold, was it not in thine own power? why hast thou conceived this thing in thine heart? thou hast not lied unto men, but unto God.**

The above verse is the main verse that Trinitarians use to claim that the Holy Ghost in God. The Holy Ghost is a messenger of God and performs God's work within us of building us into the temple of God. The Holy Ghost makes intercession for us to God (Romans 8:26), so by lying to the Holy Ghost you are lying to God in the same way that by breaking one of the Ten Commandments that Moses preached to the people on God's behalf, you are breaking a commandment of God. God knows Ananias is lying because God knows the secrets of the hearts of men, and there is nothing hidden from Him (Romans 2:16, Matt 10:26). If you want to be technical, Peter is actually the one that gets lied to, so you can just as easily claim that Peter is God as you can the Holy Ghost in the above verses.

> **(KJV) Isa:43:11: I, even I, am the LORD; and beside me there is no saviour.**

(KJV) Is 43:12 I have declared, and have saved, and I have showed, when there was no strange god among you: therefore ye are my witnesses, saith the LORD, that I am God.

In the above verses God (the father) is the one credited as the savior, because He is the one that declares the salvation.

I believe that there is only one God (the father). God has a son, which He delegated authority over us, and Heaven to. I believe Christ is the true Son of God as is taught clearly in the Bible, and that He is the true heir to His father's throne. I don't see that the Holy Ghost has been given this status. The apostles will also receive thrones, and we are considered coheirs as God's adopted children.

Many churches today teach that you must believe in the Trinity in order to be saved. Where is that in the doctrine of salvation? Shortly after the Nicene Creed other creeds were created stating that it was necessary to believe in the Trinity to be saved, but they also added that you must believe in the Holy Catholic Church in order to be saved. Joseph Smith added to his doctrines that it was essential for his wife to allow him to have plural marriage in order for her to be saved, changing her salvation so that it no longer comes from the sacrifice that Christ made, but to allowing her husband to commit adultery.

These early church leaders that attempted to add doctrines that were not found in the Bible did not seem to possess the answers. During this period for a time they even came up with a doctrine stating that Christ was not a man but a phantom in order to explain how God could exist in a sinful body. As they changed their doctrines they changed their creeds to match (you can see this in the differences between the Apostles Creed and the Nicene Creed). Even with the new doctrines that the church leaders introduced and enforced through the newly deemed state-religion, God's word was preserved and these new doctrines were not added to the Bible.

The Nicene Creed existed before the Bible was canonized and although man's doctrines demanded belief in the Trinity, support for it could to be found for it in the Bible. Even Jerome's Latin Vulgate did not include the additional words in 1 John 5:7 which didn't appear in scripture until 800 A.D. Jerome was one of the church fathers, but regardless of the beliefs of the church at the time, he did not change the Bible to match the views of the church. Only a few Bibles including the KJV differ from the other Bibles in more support of the Trinity; all this took place in the 1500s where several documents of suspect scripture emerged, which we have already discussed.

I have problems believing that the KJV is the perfectly preserved English Bible. One problem that I have found with this idea is that 1 John 5:7, 1 Tim 3:16 not only do not match other English Bibles, but they also do not match the Bibles written in other languages. I may not speak Latin or Portuguese very well, but I can recognize words like God, Father, Son, and Holy Spirit, and the other languages don't contain them in the above listed verses. So with the exception of the KJV and a few other Bibles God's word remains in agreement to this day.

As far as needing to believe in the Trinity in order to be saved I do not believe that to be true. That statement is no different than the one the Catholics make requiring you to believe in the Holy Catholic Church to be saved. In the Nicene Creed where the doctrine of the Trinity was originally documented you are instructed to <u>WORSHIP the Holy Spirit</u>. Nowhere in the scripture is this statement supported. In the same way Catholics later added the <u>Worship of Mary</u> as the Mother of God and Queen of Heaven. Most protestant churches reject the worship of Mary because such a doctrine does not exist in scripture, yet are they teaching that the Holy Spirit *should* be worshipped in the Trinity when this is also not found in scripture? If you are going to Worship the Holy Spirit, why not worship Mary? Like the Holy Spirit, God used Mary as <u>an instrument</u> to bring His son into the world.

Why do you believe that Jesus is the Son of God? Is it because the Holy Spirit conceived him, if so then Mary would actually be the Mother of God? Or do you believe that Christ is *eternally begotten* and that Christ existed as God's son even before the foundations of the world, if so then Mary and the Holy Spirit are not Christ's parents but are instruments that God used to manifest His son (who already existed) in the physical world? Consequently the Bible never states that Christ was **Eternally Begotten**. *Eternally Begotten* is also a concept that originated in the Nicene Creed.

In the Bible Jesus is presented as a humble servant living to do the will of His father. He lived this way to set an example for us to follow, so that we too would live our lives serving God. Jesus did not set the example of us making ourselves equal to God, but pointed out that *who are we to judge our neighbors* (Mt 7:1-2). After Christ's death all authority in Heaven and on Earth was <u>GIVEN</u> to Him (MT 28:18). Likewise we are told that after we die we will receive authority and will judge angels (1 Cor 6:3), but while on the earth we are to be humble and obedient.

It is not necessary for God to appear in the flesh in order for His will to be accomplished. God uses created beings throughout the entire Bible to fulfill His will. Aaron (with Moses) is the one that talked to Pharaoh, but it was God who commanded it, performed the miracles, and God is credited as freeing the Hebrew people. Christ was sent by God (John 3:16), and He performed miracles as evidence that God had sent Him, as did Moses (John 10:38). In both instances God the father is the one who commanded it, and the miracles are performed according to God's will.

God has been preparing the way for His son to fulfill His purpose since before the foundation of the world in order to transfer power to Him. Why would God do this? It is because Jesus was His beloved son in whom He was pleased. King David likewise wanted to ensure that Solomon his son would take over his kingdom at the designated time. King David's son Solomon was made of the same substance as David was and was held in higher regard in the kingdom than David's soldiers or citizens would be, but He (Solomon) was not of equal status as his father the king until he was given the authority by God (anointed as king).

I don't understand why Trinitarians believe that God himself would have to be the one to redeem us personally? God did not personally cause the Fall of Man (though He set up the events in order that it might take place), so why should He have to personally fix it. In the same way that God allowed the fall of man to come through human disobedience, He also allowed for the redemption of man to come through human obedience.

Christ is referred to as the last Adam in that through man's sin, sin entered the world, but through man's obedience the slaves of sin are freed (Romans 5:14, 1 Cor 15:22). Eve also played a role in the fall of man, and because of this woman must play a role in the redemption of man from sin. This is where Mary comes into the picture, and why Christ had to be born of a woman. Because of original sin women experience pains in childbirth, and it is through this very curse that redemption entered the world (1 Tim 2:15, Gal 4.4, Rev 12:2). All of these things come by human means, but are really accomplished by God in His will (1 Cor 11:12).

Gen 1:26-Let us make man in our own image.

According to the Jewish faith the plural form of God is used to represent God's omnipotence. Both Christian and Jewish scholars agree that in the above verses God is addressing His heavenly court of angels, as in the following verse God is spoken of *singularly as the one who creates man*

(Gen 1:1, 1:27). Regardless of who God was speaking to, I definitely believe that man was created in the *Image of God* and that *God has a body* (for Christ to sit at the right hand of God, it implies that God has a body and is sitting next to Christ on a throne).

Many modern Christians claim that Jesus is God in bodily form, and that the Holy Spirit is God in the spiritual form, and then claim that God is only a spirit. This does not make sense because either way there is either two gods with bodies, or two gods that are only spirits. Also God veiled His image in a cloud in front of the general assembly in the Old Testament, but He spoke Face-to-face with Moses (ex 33:11) meaning Moses could see God.

Trinitarians mistakenly claim that Jesus is God's body, and that all the appearances of God in the Old Testament was really Jesus. Many Trinitarians claim that the angel Jacob wrestled with in Gen 32:24-30 was really the pre-incarnate form of Christ.

Assuming that this was Christ is just speculation. In Gen 32:1 it is stated that Angels of God came to meet him, and in Hosea 12:1-4 it states that it was an angel the Jacob wrestled with. If this were not the case it would mean that Jacob was able to beat God up. According to Strong's Bible Dictionary the Hebrew word *'elohiym* used in the above verse as God can also be applied to angels as well.

(KJV) John 4:24 God is a Spirit: and they that worship him must worship him in spirit and in truth.

In the above verse John is talking about worshipping God spiritually, and not outwardly. This lesson is taught throughout the New Testament. It is not stating that God does not have a body, or else how could man be made in God's image?

Trinitarians claim that Jesus was both 100% man and 100% God. The God-man concept was created in the doctrines of man. At first the early church fathers claimed that Christ was only a phantom to attempt to explain how His divinity could exist in the form of a sinful man. They later changed their beliefs and claimed that Jesus was both man and God. This new theology is justified by saying that the concept is unexplainable because it is too deep for human understanding. The same thing is said about the Trinity (that it is a great mystery), yet the New Testament states that there are no more mysteries.

Why is it so hard for Trinitarians to take the Bible at its word, and believe that Jesus was the son of God, existed in the flesh as we do, and like us faced the same temptations we do in order to set an example for us to follow. If Jesus were really God He would have an advantage, and being sinless would prove nothing. How could we follow that example? After Jesus' death He received authority from God. Why is it necessary for Christ to have possessed all of the authority that He does now, while He was on the earth?

The fact that Jesus was conceived of the Holy Spirit does not necessarily mean that the Holy Spirit is God. Something's that needs to be considered when you make up your mind is why was Christ conceived by the Holy Spirit? Does this event play any other role than getting Mary pregnant? Was it just as simple as the Holy Spirit is God and that's why Jesus is called the Son of God, or does it play a deeper significance in God's plan?

By having Christ born through Mary, prophecies were fulfilled, Christ is tied to the line of David, the sign of the Messiah takes place (virgin birth), and redemption of original sin comes through the curse of pain in childbirth. What about the Holy Spirit? The Holy Spirit didn't need to descend on Jesus in the form of a dove if Christ possessed the Holy Spirit from His birth. So why did this happen. It happened as a sign to John the Baptist that Jesus was the one he had been waiting for, and to associate receiving the gift of the Holy Spirit with baptism (Acts 2:38). Jesus did not even need to be baptized (He was sinless). He did it for our benefit, to fulfill prophecies, and to give us an example to follow. The people that claim that it is not necessary to be baptized because they said a prayer to become a Christian have no excuse, because Jesus himself was even baptized when it was not necessary.

So why would Jesus being conceived of the Holy Spirit be done for any other reason then impregnating Mary?

Just as the Bronze Serpent in the Old Testament was erected in order to foreshadow the salvation to come through Christ, the Holy Spirit would later conceive <u>new lives within us</u>. The Holy Spirit will dwell within us, building us into the temple of the Lord (Rom 8:9, 1 Cor 3:16). We will be a NEW CREATION (2 Cor 7:15, Eph 2:15-18), and be renewed in mind and spirit (Col 3:10, Rom 12:2) through the Holy Spirit. The new creation that we become starts at our baptism where we receive the Holy Spirit of promise, and become a new creation through the Holy Spirit just as Christ did.

(KJV) Mt 7:21-23 Not every one that saith unto me, Lord, Lord, shall enter into the kingdom of heaven; but he that doeth the will of my Father which is in heaven. 22 Many will say to me in that day, Lord, Lord, have we not prophesied in thy name? and in thy name have cast out devils? and in thy name done many wonderful works? 23 And then will I profess unto them, I never knew you: depart from me, ye that work iniquity.

The people in the above verses are not non-believers, but are people that believed themselves to be Christians only to discover that they weren't when it was too late. I don't want to be in this category. I believe that it is my duty to my children to find out the truth about who God is so that we will be saved.

(KJV) Mt 15:9 But in vain they do worship me, teaching for doctrines the commandments of men.

(KJV) Mrk 7:7 Howbeit in vain do they worship me, teaching for doctrines the commandments of men.

(KJV) 1co 15:1-2 Moreover, brethren, I declare unto you the gospel which I preached unto you, which also ye have received, and wherein ye stand; 2 By which also ye are saved, if ye keep in memory what I preached unto you, unless ye have believed in vain.

(KJV) Col 2:8 Beware lest any man spoil you through philosophy and vain deceit, after the tradition of men, after the rudiments of the world, and not after Christ.

I want to make sure that I am following the Bible and not some man made doctrine. I can't say that I see the Trinity clearly documented in the Bible, but I do see where it was establish as a doctrine of man clearly, and I find several areas in the Nicene Creed unscriptural. I don't want to believe something just because others tell me, because so many times in the past I have been taught the same things by different denominations and later found them to be incorrect. I don't want to worship God in vain. I don't want to blaspheme by denying God if He is a Trinity, but at the same time I don't want to disobey the first commandment and worship other gods in direct defiance of God's commandment on the basis of the opinions of man.

Many people may be persuaded to believe in the Trinity because they can't see how so many Christians could share the same belief and all of them be wrong. But then again the Bible says that only a few will be saved, and I think that perhaps it is possible that the majority of people can be wrong (Mt 7:14, Mt 20:16, Mt 22:14, Luke 13:23-24, 1 Pet 3:20).

The sad truth is that many people can be wrong. Before I truly became a Christian I never went to church, I never read the Bible, but I believed that I was a Christian my entire life. It is only after reading the scriptures that I realized that I was lost and was not going to be saved based on the way of thinking I had been taught. This scenario is a common one. Through the years I have met several people that profess to be Christians but haven't read the Bible and don't know the first thing about God.

People raise their children telling them that God loves them for who they are and however they are. They tell them that when they die they will go to Heaven no matter what. I am speaking about people that don't worship the God of the scriptures, but believe in a God of their own creation, a figment of their own imaginations. The point is that people can be wrong. What is important to realize is that you need to follow the teachings of the Bible even if that requires you to change the beliefs that you have been enculturated to believe. I believed I knew God because of how my parents raised me, but I was wrong and was living in sin. Once I actually read the Bible and saw the errors of my ways I changed my behavior and belief system to conform to the Bible.

I don't know why the Trinitarians are so quick to call us heretics, accuse us of not being as good of Christians as they are, or call us baby Christians for not believing something that isn't taught in the Bible. Usually they will try to show us the same verses others have shown them and then not know how to explain them. Once they are unable to prove the Trinity, they tell us that we just have to believe the things in the Bible without understanding it. We then say that we would if we could be shown it in the Bible. From here they usually tell us that we are not as good of Christians as they are, as the reason that we don't see it, and then they usually write us off as lost and have nothing else to do with us.

The Trinitarians don't have any fear about making possibly blaspheming statements about the very nature of God based on a philosophy that somebody told them (that most of them don't understand, and the ones that claim to understand it say that they understand that it is un-understandable), that they can't explain, and that you just have to have faith in even though they can't find it in the Bible. To me it seems worse to claim to worship a Trinity if that is something that God didn't teach than to deny the Nicene Creed.

(KJV) Php 2:5-6 Let this mind be in you, which was also in Christ Jesus: 6 Who, being in the form of God, thought it not robbery to be equal with God:

(Standard Version) Phil 2:6 who, existing in the form of God, counted not the being on an equality with God a thing to be grasped,

(NASB) Phil 2:6 Who, although He existed in the form of God, did not regard equality with God a thing to be grasped

The different versions of the Bible express different meanings of Php 2:6. Regardless of the agreement (or lack of) between Bibles I believe that if you look at the context of the verses then the meaning of the verses are clear. Phps 2:5 states that <u>we are to think in the same way.</u> We were created in the image of God, but I certainly don't believe the Bible is telling us that we are to consider ourselves <u>Equal to God</u>. These verses contain a lesson in humility telling us to be humble. I don't think they are telling us to consider ourselves to be equal with God, but to be willingly subordinate to Him. Christ did not glorify Himself (Heb 5:5).

Another important aspect of the Trinitarian debate is the use of the term Godhead. The term Godhead as used in the New Testament did not refer to a three person triune god, but is a general term for deities used by the Greeks. This term is only used three times in the KJV of the New Testament.

Godhead is used in Acts 17:29 to address idolatry, the word Godhead is used by the Greeks as a general term for a god. The word Godhead is used in reference to the local terminology in Acts 17:28 *"as certain also of your own poets have said."* I don't see the word Godhead to be referring to a triune god in this instance of its use, but it is used as the Greek word for God while talking to the Greeks.

Rom 1:20 For the invisible things of him from the creation of the world are clearly seen, being understood by the things that are made, even his eternal power and Godhead; so that they are without excuse:

Romans 1:20 refers to our human ability to see evidence of God or God's work all around us. I don't think the word Godhead in this instance is referring to a Trinity of gods because that certainly has not been clearly visible from the beginning of creation. Different Bibles use different words in place of Godhead mostly they refer to the power of God. I believe the word Godhead was used in this instance because it is a letter to the Romans and is using terminology that they will understand as was done in Acts 17:29.

Col 2:9 contains the final mention of the word Godhead in the KJV. It is used here to mean that Christ possesses the power and authority of God. Christ possessed God's message and His message was verified through the working of miracles, as was the case with Moses. This authority was given to Christ by His Father as Jesus said himself (Mt 28:18), and can be found in scripture.

The word Godhead is not presented in the Bible to refer to a three-way share of power between three separate but co-equal gods. Col 2:9 expresses the authority Christ possesses over the principalities and powers mentioned in the next verse. Colossians was written to correct those that were falling into false teachings and worshiping angels and principalities (Col 2:18). Col 2:9 is a statement of Christ's authority over such principalities. The word Godhead can be found in the Bible, but it is not used in the way that modern Trinitarians are using it.

The term Godhead as used in the Bible is not referring to a three-way share of power as Trinitarians use it. Another problem that I have with Trinitarianism is the way that it is explained. Terms like subordinate submissive are also not from the Bible. They are man-made terms used to attempt to justify or explain the Trinitarian beliefs. Besides the Bible not stating that there are three separate but co-equal Gods, it also doesn't mention that they are subordinate submissive to each other. Of course, I understand that Jesus chose to do the will of His Father, but that is the same thing that is asked of all of us. It is obedience and not a surrender of co-equal power.

The style of kingdom that God established for King David is a model of the Heavenly kingdom. I purpose that the there are not three Gods sharing power, but One God (as in the Old Testament) who has a son, Jesus that will one day take over as king (like Solomon did). The Holy Spirit isn't in this equation, but I have found that even Trinitarians have trouble justifying the inclusion of the Holy Spirit in the Trinity (the Holy Spirit may be able to dwell inside of multiple people at the same time, but we are never told to worship of pray to him). The Temple is an earthly representation of its heavenly version

(KJV) Hebrews 8:5 Who serve unto the example and shadow of heavenly things, as Moses was admonished of God when he was about to make the tabernacle: for, See, saith he, that thou make all things according to the pattern showed to thee in the mount.

This supports the idea that some of the ordinances established by God could be a representation of their heavenly versions. The next set of scripture is included simply to state that God is the one that establishes governments and kingdoms.

(KJV) Romans 13:1 Let every soul be subject unto the higher powers. For there is no power but of God: the powers that be are ordained of God.

(KJV) John 19:11 Jesus answered, Thou couldest have no power at all against me, except it were given thee from above: therefore he that delivered me unto thee hath the greater sin.

The above verses state that God is the one that establishes authority. It is my hypothesis that God patterned at least David's kingdom after His own. While thinking about this I came to some interesting conclusions. What I came to realize is that the Jewish people are correct about the messiah. The Jews are correct in thinking that the messiah would be a king on earth, and my comparisons to David's kingdom are also not totally unfounded. Jesus is going to rule on earth at His second coming (Luke 1:32, Rev 22:3).

(KJV) 2 Samuel 7:13 "He shall build a house for My name, and I will establish the throne of his kingdom forever.

(KJV) Isaiah 9:6-7 For unto us a Child is born, Unto us a Son is given; And the government will be upon His shoulder. And His name will be called Wonderful, Counselor, Mighty God, Everlasting Father, Prince of Peace. 7 the increase of His government and peace There will be no end, Upon the throne of David and over His kingdom, To order it and establish it with judgment and justice From that time forward, even forever. The zeal of the Lord of hosts will perform this.

The Throne that Jesus will rule from is the throne of David. Christ is in the earthly bloodline of David, and is the promised heir to the kingdom. The Jews were correct that Christ will rule from the earth, but they didn't realize that He would also be the second Adam and free the world from the bondage of sin as well.

God didn't set up David's kingdom as an earthly example of Christ's heavenly kingdom, but David's kingdom is *actually the throne that was set up for Christ.* This makes sense in regards to the second coming of Christ, but does that rule out the possibility that currently three separate but co-equal Gods are sharing the throne in the mean time?

(KJV) 1 Chron 29:23 Then Solomon sat on the throne of the LORD as king instead of David his father, and prospered; and all Israel obeyed him.

(KJV) 2 Chron 6:10 The LORD therefore hath performed his word that he hath spoken: for I am risen up in the room of David my father, and am set on the throne of Israel, as the LORD promised, and have built the house for the name of the LORD God of Israel.

(KJV) Ps 9:7 But the LORD shall endure forever: he hath prepared his throne for judgment.

In the Old Testament God chose to allow the Hebrews to have an earthly king. The above verses refer to David's throne as the LORD's throne. Although David or Solomon was sitting on it, it was still considered God's throne. God did not want to share His throne, but He did at the peoples request, and ultimately He shared it with His son, which was His intention from before the earth was created.

In the above verses LORD is capitalized meaning the word LORD is not Adonai (meaning sir), but is being used in place of YHVH. All other names used for God in the Bible refer to certain events or aspects of God, but YHVH is the true name of God, and is the name you are warned not to use in vain. The name has a lot of relevance and perhaps could be compared to the unknown name of Jesus (Rev 19:12). YHVH is the personal pronoun and true name of God; it is only used to refer to God the father.

(KJV) Ps 11:4 The LORD is in his holy temple, the LORD'S throne is in heaven: his eyes behold, his eyelids try, the children of men.

The above verse could possibly be used to support my hypothesis that David's kingdom is an earthly model of the kingdom that exists in heaven. I come to this conclusion because it states that YHVH's throne is in the Holy Temple, which we do have verses that state the earthly temple is modeled after the heavenly one. I'll now move on past this hypothesis.

(KJV) Luke 1:32 He shall be great, and shall be called the Son of the Highest: and the Lord God shall give unto him the throne of his father David:

(KJV) Rev 22:3 And there shall be no more curse: but the throne of God and of the Lamb shall be in it; and his servants shall serve him:

Rev 22:3 states that both God and Christ Jesus shall have their own thrones at the second coming.

(KJV) Matt 26:64 Jesus saith unto him, Thou hast said: nevertheless I say unto you, Hereafter shall ye see the Son of man sitting on the right hand of power, and coming in the clouds of heaven

In the above verse it states that Jesus sits at the right hand of God, and Rev 22:3 states that He will also at the second coming. The point that I want to make is that the Holy Spirit does not have a throne. If the Holy Spirit equally shares in a three way rule through submissive subordination then why does the Bible never allude to the Holy Spirit sitting at the throne of God. There isn't room for a three-way rule in David's kingdom structure, and the Bible doesn't mention the Holy Spirit as having a throne in heaven. Of course there are more than God and Jesus' thrones, the apostles will have some and Rev 11:16 speaks of 24 elders having thrones. My point is merely that if God wanted us to believe that the Holy Spirit jointly ruled with Him then He did not make it clearly deductible from the scriptures.

I believe Jesus is actually God's son and not a piece of God or God's exact replica. I don't think Jesus has to be a clone of God in order to be the heir to His kingdom. I believe Jesus was born of God, and I believe that is what is taught in the scriptures. Col 1:15 says that Jesus was, *"the firstborn of every creature"*. Rev 3:14 says, *"beginning of the creation of God."* Romans 8:29 refers to Him as the firstborn of the brethren. Hebrews 1:6 says, *"brings the firstborn into the world"* (Modern KJV). Whether you believe that these verses are referring to Jesus pre-existing His birth, or that He is the first born of the resurrected, the fact remains that He is listed as a creation and not a co-eternal god.

1 John 4:9 states that God sent His son into the world. I don't see any reason not to believe this, nor do I feel that it is necessary to speculate further and reason that God sent a separate but co-equal aspect of Himself into the world that chose to be subordinately submissive in this particular area for a certain purpose. John 3:18 states that you must believe in the name of God's son. I think the Bible clearly teaches that Jesus is the Son of God. Trinitarians try to change this term (Son of God) from meaning that Jesus was actually the Son of God, to meaning that *Jesus chose to be called the Son of God merely as a term of address.*

Trinitarians find support in their beliefs through the writings of some early church fathers that first started forming the concept of the Trinity. I accept completely that writings were found that contain such doctrines, but I don't believe that simply because of this we should believe the Trinity is a true doctrine of God. Many of the books in the New Testament warn us not to follow the traditions of men. We are told to follow the scriptures and the doctrines they taught (which became scripture). The New Testament letters state that the antichrist was already on the earth and that <u>false teachings were already being introduced in the churches back in those days</u>. False teachings and incorrect practices were taking place in the churches even when the apostles were alive. It is not a hard stretch to see that false doctrines could have continued after the apostle's death and before the canon of scripture was put together.

The early churches also had debates about whether Christ actually existed in human form or if he was merely a phantom. My point is that you shouldn't believe something just because it is old. I believe that God preserved His word and kept false doctrines from being added to it. Although Trinitarian beliefs existed before the canon and were taught in some sects of Christianity this doctrine could not be found in the scriptures for several decades, and then only through suspect verses which were believed to have been footnotes of early church sermons that were mistaken for scripture.

I personally do not believe in culture, or the further revelation of prophecies after the Bible was completed. This is because I have come across many Pentecostals that feel they can make up any unscriptural practices and support it by saying that God told them it is okay. If you question them on any thing they say you are denying the work of the Holy Spirit and committing the only unforgivable sin. If you believe in the continued revelation to people other than apostles then you have no leg to stand on when denying the Pope, the Mormon President, or any insane person off the street that claims to be a prophet of God.

One lady I know is living with a guy that is a former conman and criminal that is routinely in and out of jail. She is living in sin with him and claims that they are married in God's eyes only. She works to support him, he tells her that God has commanded her to support him so that he could concentrate on God's work. He claims that he is able to be possessed by the spirit of Jesus Christ, and this lady actually gets to play with Jesus one-on-one. He gets messages directly from God and if you question anything he says even based on scripture then you are committing the only unforgivable sin. Because of people like this and all of the warnings in the New Testament about false teachings I am not inclined to believe something just because someone tells me so. If we let culture and man's wisdom within our churches then we will have gay female preachers like the Methodist do.

I believe that if something were true then it would be found in scripture, and would not require so many man-made terms to attempt to explain it. The term Trinity is a man-made term to express a belief that is only speculated to exist in the Bible. To further attempt to explain the Trinity the term Godhead is redefined and used much differently than the Apostles used it in the Bible. Other man-made terms are also needed to attempt to explain the Trinity such as subordinate submissive and incarnation. This concept of three Gods sharing power is also not found in the Bible.

The Trinity requires a lot of man-made terms to explain and man-made concept, and then when it comes down to it most Trinitarians cop-out and say that it is unexplainable or that it is beyond human comprehension. Why would God teach us something that is impossible for us to understand? Would God teach us something that we can't possibly understand, and then teach it so incompletely that nobody could figure it out in 2000 years?

Another problem is that most Trinitarians don't even believe in the same thing. Some believe in three gods and some believe in one god with three personalities. I believe that it is important to understand what God you are worshipping. The Bible says that we are always to be ready to give an answer regarding our faith (1 Peter below). Most people that I have spoken with about the Trinity are unable to give me an explanation for their faith in the Trinity. Most people say they will get back to me and then I never hear from them again. I also have people tell me that I don't understand it because God is not with me, I am not saved, and then they write me off. I believe it is our duty as Christians to be able to answer this question.

How are we supposed to evangelize to people if we can't answer the first question people will likely ask?

Have you heard about Jesus?

No who is he?

I'm sorry but that is impossible to explain.

> **(KJV) 1 Peter 3:15 But sanctify the Lord God in your hearts: and be ready always to give an answer to every man that asketh you a reason of the hope that is in you with meekness and fear**

> **(KJV) 2 Tim 3:16 All scripture is given by inspiration of God, and is profitable for doctrine, for reproof, for correction, for instruction in righteousness:**

We are to use scripture as our doctrine, and for correcting or explaining doctrine. The doctrine expressed in the Bible does not support the Trinitarian viewpoint. In the Bible it is clear that Jesus considered God (the father) **to be His God** (1 Peter 1:3, 2 Cor. 1:3, 2 Cor. 11:31, Rev 1:6, Eph 1:3, Eph 1:17, John 20:17, Matt 27:46, Rev. 3:12, Rev. 3:2). Jesus did not think of Himself as God. If Jesus was really God in the flesh then how could *He also have a God*? The Bible also makes it clear that *Jesus was a man* (Acts 2:22, Acts 10:40, Acts 17:31, 1 Timothy 2:5, 1 Corinthians 15:21, Isaiah 53:3)

References

"Scripture taken from the KING JAMES VERSION OF THE BIBLE, (KJV) Public Domain 1611"

"Scripture taken from the NEW AMERICAN STANDARD BIBLE® (NASB), Copyright© 1960, 1962, 1963,1968,1971,1972, 1973,1975,1977, 1995 by The Lockman Foundation. Used by permission."

Scripture taken from the AMERICAN STANDARD VERSION OF THE BIBLE, Public Domain

Self-Defense

This Bible study was designed with Christian homeschoolers in mind. Children in Christian families that home school often miss out on interaction with other children. They may be more sheltered than other children, or just not placed in as much of danger as children are that go to traditional schools. They may not be placed in situations where they need to deal with bullies, or be on guard against predators, but that doesn't mean they don't need to be prepared to defend themselves against them.

If you are a Christian parent it is your duty to warn your children about the dangers that exist in this world, and to prepare them to face those dangers. The Bible says that we are to be as wise as serpents, but as innocent as doves.

(KJV) Matthew 10:16 Behold, I send you forth as sheep in the midst of wolves: be ye therefore wise as serpents, and harmless as doves.

We are sheep in the midst of wolves, meaning that we are being sent into a world that is full of dangers. We are not told to hide from danger, but to face it head on and go forth into it. There is no way to avoid the fact that your world is a dangerous place. For a time parents may be able to shelter their children from the world, but eventually their children are going to face the world and all of its dangers by themselves. You are doing a huge disservice to your children if you send them into the world unprepared. Out of a loving desire to protect your children, you may wish to shelter them from the evil in the world, but the very best way to protect your children is to educate them in advance about the dangers they will face and to make them as wise as the serpents they will be facing.

Christians are to be as wise as serpents, meaning knowing and understanding what evil exists, but we are to be as harmless as doves. We need to be as wise as serpents so that we know what dangers may befall us in order for us to protect ourselves from them. The Greek word *Akeraios,* which is translated in the above verse as *Harmless,* actually means *Innocent.* We are to have an awareness of evil, but are not to partake in evil ourselves. We should possess the same cunning as the serpents, but not use our knowledge for sin as they do. This ability to be as innocent as a dove does not mean that we are not supposed to defend ourselves from danger, but rather means that we are to have an awareness of the ploys of evil yet not partake in those evil practices.

Knowing that the date rape drug exists and how it is employed will allow you to be on guard against it, and watch yourself so that you do not fall victim to it. This is being as wise as a serpent. You know what the serpent is capable of, what it may attempt to do to you, and you can guard yourself against its evil ploy. Knowing about the date rape drug gives your children the opportunity to protect themselves against it. You do not want your children to fall victim to such a ploy simply because you wanted to shelter them from the existence of such evil. Christians are as harmless as doves not because they are not supposed to protect themselves against the serpents and wolves, but because although they are aware that such things as the date rape drug exist, there is no way that they would choose to partake of such evil actions themselves.

Many liberal Christians in this day of age may be deluded into thinking that Christians are not supposed to defend themselves, and the very thought of a Christian training themselves to fight might seem outrageous to them. Many Christians believe that Christians are supposed to be pacifists, conscientious objectors, and surrender to evil unto death. They believe this is what the Bible teaches, and look at Christ as if He was Mahatma Gandhi. In order for Christians to understand what the Bible actually teaches in regards to a Christian's responsibility to defend themselves we will examine what the Bible teaches us on this subject.

(KJV) Matthew 5:38-40 Ye have heard that it hath been said, An eye for an eye, and a tooth for a tooth: 39 But I say unto you, That ye resist not evil: but whosoever shall smite thee on thy right cheek, turn to him the other also. 40 And if any man will sue thee at the law, and take away thy coat, let him have thy cloak also.

The above verse is where many Christians get the idea that they are not allowed to defend of protect themselves. In the above verses the person is not in any real danger. These verses are talking about lawsuits over material items that Christians are not supposed to place a high value on. These verses address a situation in which you are not placed in any physical danger, and they address the concept of revenge. When these verses state not to resist evil it is speaking in this limited sense about not avenging yourself or quarreling over material goods. If these verses were applied to a broader sense then they would be telling us to give into sin, not resist the devil, and would defeat the purpose of the Bible.

(KJV) Romans 12:19 Dearly beloved, avenge not yourselves, but rather give place unto wrath: for it is written, Vengeance is mine; I will repay, saith the Lord.

Christians are not supposed to avenge themselves while on the earth. This is clearly taught in the Bible, but avenging yourself is completely different than the right to defend yourself, or your Christian responsibility to protect your family. We are to live peaceful lives as much as it is in our power to do so, but we are not supposed to be overcome by evil.

(KJV) Romans 12:18-21 If it be possible, as much as lieth in you, live peaceably with all men. 19 Dearly beloved, avenge not yourselves, but rather give place unto wrath: for it is written, Vengeance is mine; I will repay, saith the Lord. 20 Therefore if thine enemy hunger, feed him; if he thirst, give him drink: for in so doing thou shalt heap coals of fire on his head. 21 Be not overcome of evil, but overcome evil with good.

Christians should be willing to overlook a transgression, and they are not to seek their own revenge. We are to live peacefully as long as it is up to us. This does not mean that we are not to defend ourselves if we are in danger. We are not to be overcome by evil, but are to be prepared to defend against it. We are to be as wise as serpents yet innocent as doves. The world is a dangerous place and the Bible warns us to be prepared for it.

(KJV) 1Peter 5:8 Be sober, be vigilant; because your adversary the devil, as a roaring lion, walketh about, seeking whom he may devour:

Christians are to be vigilant and on guard, because the devil is like a roaring lion seeking to devour us. Christians are to be prepared for danger and to defend themselves against it.

(KJV) Luke 22:36 Then He said to them, "But now, he who has a money bag, let him take it, and likewise a knapsack; and he who has no sword, let him sell his garment and buy one.

Shortly before Jesus was crucified He instructed Christians to look after themselves. We were told to bring our own moneybags with us, meaning to provide for ourselves, and we were told that if we did not have a sword then we should sell are garments and buy one. Possessing a sword was more important than clothing ourselves. Jesus instructs us to defend ourselves. We are to recognize that the world is a dangerous place, and we are to protect ourselves while we are in it.

The Christians that think of Christ as if He were Gandhi may disagree with me here, but it is only because they have a distorted view of Christ in the Bible. Living peacefully is different than opposing violence.

Being vigilant and watchful against your enemy is completely different than pacifistic non-violent resistance. God is not opposed to violence and war. The title Lord of Hosts actually means God of Armies. Jesus was not Gandhi and did not have the worldview of a hippy. He came not to bring peace on the earth but a sword, and He will tread the winepress of the fierce wrath of God.

(KJV) Matthew 10:34 "Do not think that I came to bring peace on earth. I did not come to bring peace but a sword.

(KJV) Revelations 19:13-15 And he was clothed with a vesture dipped in blood: and his name is called The Word of God. 14 And the armies which were in heaven followed him upon white horses, clothed in fine linen, white and clean. 15 And out of his mouth goeth a sharp sword, that with it he should smite the nations: and he shall rule them with a rod of iron: and he treadeth the winepress of the fierceness and wrath of Almighty God.

You may be wondering how people can become so confused as to read the above verses and think that Jesus was opposed to violence, or taught that His followers were not allowed to defend themselves. People get the wrong idea because they misinterpret other key verses in the Bible.

(KJV) Matthew 26:51-54 And suddenly, one of those who were with Jesus stretched out his hand and drew his sword, struck the servant of the high priest, and cut off his ear. 52 But Jesus said to him, "Put your sword in its place, for all who take the sword will perish by the sword. 53 "Or do you think that I cannot now pray to My Father, and He will provide Me with more than twelve legions of angels? 54 "How then could the Scriptures be fulfilled, that it must happen thus?"

(KJV) John 18:11 Then said Jesus unto Peter, Put up thy sword into the sheath: the cup which my Father hath given me, shall I not drink it?

(KJV) John 18:36 Jesus answered, My kingdom is not of this world: if my kingdom were of this world, then would my servants fight, that I should not be delivered to the Jews: but now is my kingdom not from hence.

In Matthew 26:52 (above) Jesus rebukes Peter for striking with the sword, and tells Him to return his sword to its place. Many Christians read this verse and think that it is saying that Jesus is opposed to violence, but Jesus does not say this. Jesus states that He is capable of defending Himself and could have twelve legions of angels at His side. Jesus does not rebuke Peter for attempting to defend himself, but states that it was not the appropriate time. Jesus did not resist in this situation because this was the every purpose of His birth (John 18:37). Jesus did not resist in order that prophecy would be fulfilled, and so that He could drink the cup that His father had prepared for Him. As was previously stated Jesus is going tread the winepress of the fierce wrath of God, and will fight at the appropriate time.

In the Matthew 26:52 it is stated that those who live by the sword may also die by the sword. This is a true statement and an inevitable fact of war. You need to realize that if you are involved in armed combat you can die in it. The fact that armed combat is dangerous does not make it wrong. In the New Testaments Christians are referred to as soldiers of Christ.

(KJV) Philippians 2:25 Yet I supposed it necessary to send to you Epaphroditus, my brother, and companion in labour, and fellowsoldier, but your messenger, and he that ministered to my wants.

(KJV) Philemon 1:2 And to our beloved Apphia, and Archippus our fellowsoldier, and to the church in thy house:

Christians are referred to as soldiers of Christ for many reasons in the New Testament. We are told to put on the full Armour of God, which is the garments of a soldier, and we will contend for the faith in both physical and spiritual manners. We will begin are study of the Christians role as a soldier by first examining the Armour of God.

(KJV) Ephesians 6:11-18 Put on the whole armour of God, that ye may be able to stand against the wiles of the devil. 12 For we wrestle not against flesh and blood, but against principalities, against powers, against the rulers of the darkness of this world, against spiritual wickedness in high places. 13 Wherefore take unto you the whole armour of God, that ye may be able to withstand in the evil day, and having done all, to stand. 14 Stand therefore, having your loins girt about with truth, and having on the breastplate of righteousness; 15 And your feet shod with the preparation of the gospel of peace; 16 Above all, taking the shield of faith, wherewith ye shall be able to quench all the fiery darts of the wicked. 17 And take the helmet of salvation, and the sword of the Spirit, which is the word of God:18 Praying always with all

prayer and supplication in the Spirit, and watching thereunto with all perseverance and supplication for all saints;

The purpose of the Armour of God is for us to be able to stand up against the devil. This is both a spiritual and a physical endeavor. These verses are referring to the spiritual battle that Christians fight against sin on a daily basis, but they also state that we are to be prepared to stand against the devil in his evil day (Revelations 13:7) when he will physically make war with the saints (us).

Liberal Christians will ignore the fact that the Armour of God is the battle dress of a soldier and will choose to believe that it is only symbolic of a spiritual battle against sin. To obtain a more complete understanding of what the Armour of God is, you must examine how it is used elsewhere in the Bible.

(KJV) Isaiah 59:17 For he put on righteousness as a breastplate, and an helmet of salvation upon his head; and he put on the garments of vengeance for clothing, and was clad with zeal as a cloak. 18 According to their deeds, accordingly he will repay, fury to his adversaries, recompense to his enemies; to the islands he will repay recompense. 19 So shall they fear the name of the LORD from the west, and his glory from the rising of the sun. When the enemy shall come in like a flood, the Spirit of the LORD shall lift up a standard against him.

The Armour of God are garments of vengeance and represent the judgment of God on the Day of the Lord. Christians are soldiers and will play a role in that battle. Some Christians choose to ignore this aspect of the Bible. They are happy believing that their only battle is a spiritual one against sin, and that they will not have to face any unpleasantness or physical danger in the world. They ignore all of the war and devastations that took place in the Old Testament, and believe that Christians will be spared from all unpleasantness. Some of these people have the belief that they will be raptured before any of the tribulations of the book of Revelations begin, and that any battles that take place are only symbolic.

The truth is that there are many reasons to believe that Christians will face unpleasantness. This is the reason we are warned that we are sheep in the midst of wolves, and that our adversary is a roaring lion seeking to devour us. We are also told that as Christians we can expect to suffer while we are on earth (1 Peter 2:21). We are told to be watchful and to remain vigilant. One of the points that I have heard stated against a battle of Armageddon is that Almighty God does not need an army and therefore any battle is only figurative. This belief contradicts the title of God, Lord of Hosts, which means God of Armies. There is plenty of evidence offered in the Bible that states the future wars are real and that Christians will actually fight in them.

(KJV) Exodus 15:3 The LORD is a man of war: the LORD is his name.

(KJV) Matthew 22:7 But when the king heard thereof, he was wroth: and he sent forth his armies, and destroyed those murderers, and burned up their city.

In this parable that Jesus taught the king sends his armies to avenge the death of his son by those that were left in control of the vineyard. The son in this parable represents Jesus and the armies are the armies of God.

(KJV) Revelations 19:13-14 And he was clothed with a vesture dipped in blood: and his name is called The Word of God. 14 And the armies which were in heaven followed him upon white horses, clothed in fine linen, white and clean.

The above verse is referring to the Day of the Lord, when Jesus will ride out of heaven to execute judgment on the earth. He is followed by the armies of heaven. This is the time that Jesus and His followers will fight for His kingdom (John 18:36). The armies in heaven that are clothed in fine linen white and clean are Christians.

(KJV) Revelations 19:7-8 Let us be glad and rejoice, and give honour to him: for the marriage of the Lamb is come, and his wife hath made herself ready. 8 And to her was granted that she should be arrayed in fine linen, clean and white: for the fine linen is the righteousness of saints.

(KJV) Revelations 17:14 These shall make war with the Lamb, and the Lamb shall overcome them: for he is Lord of lords, and King of kings: and they that are with him are called, and chosen, and faithful.

If you are one of the Christians that have been accepted into the wedding feast of the Lamb then you may also be apart of the army that fights in the battle of Armageddon.

(KJV) Revelations 19:19 And I saw the beast, and the kings of the earth, and their armies, gathered together to make war against him that sat on the horse, and against his army.

The above verse states that Christ (the one the sits on the horse) will be accompanied by an army.

(KJV) 2 Corinthians 10:6 And having in a readiness to revenge all disobedience, when your obedience is fulfilled.

Christians are to be ready to revenge disobedience at the allotted time, but even before the final battle of Armageddon Christians will be involved in warfare.

(KJV) Revelations 12:17 And the dragon was wroth with the woman, and went to make war with the remnant of her seed, which keep the commandments of God, and have the testimony of Jesus Christ.

(KJV) Revelations 13:7-8 And it was given unto him to make war with the saints, and to overcome them: and power was given him over all kindreds, and tongues, and nations. 8 And all that dwell upon the earth shall worship him, whose names are not written in the book of life of the Lamb slain from the foundation of the world.

The Anti-Christ will make war with the saints. These verses do not state that the Anti-Christ will go and slaughter all of the Christians that are not putting up any resistance, but that he will make war with them. War implies that the Christians will fight back, they are not going to merely be slaughtered, and they are also not going to be spared from harm. There is no reason to believe that this battle is only metaphoric as elsewhere it is stated that Christians will be beheaded for not submitting, and for holding to the testimony of Christ (Revelations 20:4).

In the above verses the Anti-Christ will make war with the saints and in this battle will overcome them (Zechariah 14:2). This is why it was a truthful warning when Jesus told Peter that those who live by the sword will die by it. Those that are captured in this war and do not deny Christ will be beheaded (Revelations 20:4). This is a real battle that is a part of an actual war. It is not a representation of people being slaughtered for their beliefs, and it is not metaphoric. As a Christian soldier you may be required to give your life for your brethren.

(KJV) John 15:12-14 This is my commandment, That ye love one another, as I have loved you. 13 Greater love hath no man than this, that a man lay down his life for his friends. 14 Ye are my friends, if ye do whatsoever I command you.

(KJV) 1 John 3:16 By this we know love, because He laid down His life for us. And we also ought to lay down our lives for the brethren.

The above verses state that you should be willing to lay down your life for your brethren. As a good Christian soldier we should be willing to die for our families, and our fellow Christians (also are family). Laying down your life for your brethren can only be done by defending them. We lay down our lives by either dying while defending our families during a battle against a predator, or by refusing to surrender their location or other information to the enemy during interrogation. We cannot die for the forgiveness of our brethren's sins as Christ did so I could think of no other interpretation of this teaching. The example that Christ gave us of being willing to die for your brethren is illustrated in the parable of the good shepherd.

(KJV) John 10:10-15 The thief cometh not, but for to steal, and to kill, and to destroy: I am come that they might have life, and that they might have it more abundantly. 11 I am the good shepherd: the good shepherd giveth his life for the sheep. 12 But he that is an hireling, and not the shepherd, whose own the sheep are not, seeth the wolf coming, and leaveth the sheep, and fleeth: and the wolf catcheth them, and scattereth the sheep. 13 The hireling fleeth, because he is an hireling, and careth not for the sheep. 14 I am the good shepherd, and know my sheep, and am known of mine. 15 As the Father knoweth me, even so know I the Father: and I lay down my life for the sheep.

The Good Shepherd looks after his own, and is willing to die defending them from whatever the threat. The thieves in the above verses wish to steal, kill, or destroy. There is nothing good in their objectives. Christians can follow Christ's example by being good shepherds of their own households, guarding and protecting their families from threats such as intruders. The above verses also ties into protecting the sheep from wolves, which we covered earlier to represent the many evils in the world that we may face. The above verses tie everything together, and state that we are to defend those in our care to the death from such dangers. There is no greater love than to be willing to lay down your life to protect those in your care. The good shepherd protects those in his care regardless of the danger.

(KJV) 1 Samuel 17:34-36 And David said unto Saul, Thy servant kept his father's sheep, and there came a lion, and a bear, and took a lamb out of the flock: 35 And I went out after him, and smote him, and delivered it out of his mouth: and when he arose against me, I caught him by his beard, and smote him, and slew him. 36 Thy servant slew both the lion and the bear: and this uncircumcised Philistine shall be as one of them, seeing he hath defied the armies of the living God.

David was a good shepherd and placed himself in danger to save his flock. David looked after his father's flock and fought is many wars for God. Jesus is the Good Shepherd; He is the descendent of David and will sit on the throne of David at His second coming.

(KJV) 1 Peter 5:2 Feed the flock of God which is among you, taking the oversight thereof, not by constraint, but willingly; not for filthy lucre, but of a ready mind;

(KJV) Acts 20:28-29 Take heed therefore unto yourselves, and to all the flock, over the which the Holy Ghost hath made you overseers, to feed the church of God, which he hath purchased with his own blood. 29 For I know this, that after my departing shall grievous wolves enter in among you, not sparing the flock.

(KJV) Luke 2:8 And there were in the same country shepherds abiding in the field, keeping watch over their flock by night.

Good shepherds keep watch, guard, and protect their flocks. As Christians we are shepherds over our families, over members of the church, and we are also soldiers keeping watch and defending them against dangers, willing to give our lives if required.

(KJV) 1Timothy 5:8 But if any provide not for his own, and specially for those of his own house, he hath denied the faith, and is worse than an infidel.

(KJV) 1 John 3:18 My little children, let us not love in word, neither in tongue; but in deed and in truth.

It is your Christian duty to watch over your household. If you fail to provide for your own then you have denied the faith and are worse than a non-believer. You need to raise your family well, prepare them for the dangers they will face, and be willing to die to defend them if required. That is love and that is the attitude the Christian Soldier is supposed to possess.

Christians not only have the right to defend themselves and their loved ones, but they are expected to. This is why the Armour of God is the clothing of a soldier. To better understand this role we will examine the behavior of soldiers in the New Testament.

(KJV) Acts 23:10 And when there arose a great dissension, the chief captain, fearing lest Paul should have been pulled in pieces of them, commanded the soldiers to go down, and to take him by force from among them, and to bring him into the castle.

(KJV) Acts 23:23-24 And he called unto him two centurions, saying, Make ready two hundred soldiers to go to Caesarea, and horsemen threescore and ten, and spearmen two hundred, at the third hour of the night; 24 And provide them beasts, that they may set Paul on, and bring him safe unto Felix the governor.

Soldiers came to Paul's aid by taking him out of the crowd by force. As much as it lies in our power Christians are to live peacefully in the world, but in certain situations force might be required to ensure our safety or the safety of others. In the Bible soldiers guarded and protected others. They use force when necessary and risk their lives to ensure the safety of others.

(KJV) 2 Timothy 2:3-5 Thou therefore endure hardness, as a good soldier of Jesus Christ. 4 No man that warreth entangleth himself with the affairs of this life; that he may please him who hath chosen him to be a soldier.5 And if a man also strive for masteries, yet is he not crowned, except he strive lawfully.

Christian soldiers are to strive lawfully, in subjection to Christ and the laws of the land that do not conflict with God's laws.

(KJV) Romans 13:1-4 Let every soul be subject unto the higher powers. For there is no power but of God: the powers that be are ordained of God. 2 Whosoever therefore resisteth the power, resisteth the ordinance of God: and they that resist shall receive to themselves damnation. 3 For rulers are not a terror to good works, but to the evil. Wilt thou then not be afraid of the power? do that which is good, and thou shalt have praise of the same: 4 For he is the minister of God to thee for good. But if thou do that which is evil, be afraid; for he beareth not the sword in vain: for he is the minister of God, a revenger to execute wrath upon him that doeth evil.

God set up the governments that are on the earth. Christians are to live in subjection to their governments, and they have nothing to fear as long as they do that which is good. However, evildoers should be afraid because the police, soldiers, judges, and government agencies do not bare the sword in vain. They are God's ministers of justice on the earth until He comes. Christians are to live peacefully and legally as long as it is within their power. Seeking your own revenge is illegal in most societies, but the right to defend yourself or your home is a legal right in many countries.

The traits of soldiers are a good accompaniment to the Christian faith. Soldiers are loyal and obey the commands (commandments) of their leader. They protect the innocent, establish justice, maintain order, and are willing to sacrifice themselves for the safety of others. The Bible has never complained against the actions of soldiers that conduct themselves honorably.

> **(KJV) Luke 13:14 And soldiers also asked him, saying, And we, what must we do? And he said unto them, Extort from no man by violence, neither accuse [any one] wrongfully; and be content with your wages.**

The soldiers in the above verse were told not use their power wrongly. The Bible has no complaints against soldiers that behave honorably. Christians are even referred to as Soldiers of Christ because these are desired traits for a Christian to have. In the Old Testament God is referred to as God of Armies (Lord of Hosts) and many times sends the Hebrew people to war. Christians are told in the New Testament that they can expect to suffer while in this world, we are told we will fight in a war against the Anti-Christ, and that some of us will be beheaded. Zechariah Chapter14 tells of other horrors (if you wish to study further) that Christians will face in the first war in which the Anti-Christ will overcome the saints.

Soldiers and Shepherds risk their lives for others. These are noble traits and are displayed throughout the Bible.

> **(KJV) Acts 7:24 And seeing one of them suffer wrong, he defended him, and avenged him that was oppressed, and smote the Egyptian:**

> **(KJV) Exodus 2:17 And the shepherds came and drove them away: but Moses stood up and helped them, and watered their flock.**

Moses protected others and tended their flock. These are actions that he performed on his own, in addition to being sent by God to stand up against Pharaoh to free the Hebrew people.

Things are not going to be easy for us while we are on the earth. We are warned that we are sheep in the midst of wolves. The world is full of dangers waiting to pounce on us. We are to be on guard and ready to defend our families and ourselves; living peacefully according to the rules of our society and in subjection to God. We can expect to face dangers and suffer while on the earth. The Bible warns us of this and tells us to be prepared to face such trials. We can have hope in the promises of God that if we are faithful through our trials then we will receive the crown of righteousness, and will be delivered from evil in the end.

> **(KJV) 1Peter 5:10 But the God of all grace, who hath called us unto his eternal glory by Christ Jesus, after that ye have suffered a while, make you perfect, stablish, strengthen, settle you.**

> **(KJV) 1Peter 2:18-21 Servants, be subject to your masters with all fear; not only to the good and gentle, but also to the froward. 19 For this is thankworthy, if a man for conscience toward God endure grief, suffering wrongfully. 20 For what glory is it, if, when ye be buffeted for your faults, ye shall take it patiently? but if, when ye do well, and suffer for it, ye take it patiently, this is acceptable with God. 21 For even hereunto were ye called: because Christ also suffered for us, leaving us an example, that ye should follow his steps:**

> **(KJV) James 1:12 Blessed is the man that endureth temptation: for when he is tried, he shall receive the crown of life, which the Lord hath promised to them that love him.**

> **(KJV) Romans 8:28 And we know that all things work together for good to them that love God, to them who are the called according to his purpose.**

We will suffer while on the earth, we will be in danger, but we have been warned about these things, we know that God is looking out for us, and watching over us. We are being tried, tested, and baptized with fire, purified and made worthy. We need to have faith in God and remember that all things work for the good of those that love Him.

One of our greatest advantages in this world is that we have been warned. God warned us of the dangers that may be fall us so that we can be prepared for them.

(KJV) Psalm 144:1 A Psalm of David. Blessed be the LORD my strength, which teacheth my hands to war, and my fingers to fight:

(KJV) 2 Samuel 22:33-36 God is my strength and power: And he maketh my way perfect. 34 He maketh my feet like hinds' feet: and setteth me upon my high places. 35 He teacheth my hands to war; so that a bow of steel is broken by mine arms. 36 Thou hast also given me the shield of thy salvation: and thy gentleness hath made me great.

References

"Scripture taken from the KING JAMES VERSION OF THE BIBLE, (KJV) Public Domain 1611"

Freewill and Predestination

God allows sin to exist in the world in order for us to have freewill, and gives us the ability to make our own decisions. Because Adam and Eve ate of the Tree of Knowledge of Good and Evil, it is now inevitable that some people will be lost. We wouldn't have freewill if people were not allowed to choose evil. God has a plan for us and controls our destinies, but at the same time He allows us to make our own choices, and gives us room to make our own mistakes. He does this so that we will be disciplined and will grow spiritually. God always gives us choices and His mercies are great.

(KJV) Ezekiel 2:3-5 And he said unto me, Son of man, I send thee to the children of Israel, to a rebellious nation that hath rebelled against me: they and their fathers have transgressed against me, even unto this very day. 4 For they are impudent children and stiffhearted. I do send thee unto them; and thou shalt say unto them, Thus saith the Lord GOD. 5 And they, whether they will hear, or whether they will forbear, (for they are a rebellious house,) yet shall know that there hath been a prophet among them.

God appeared to Ezekiel and sent him to warn the children of Israel to turn from their sins. God knows all things and knew that most of the children of Israel were beyond the point of listening to Ezekiel's message, but God sent him to warn them nonetheless. Israel will know that they had a prophet among them, and on the Day of Judgment they will not have any excuses. When the Lord spoke to Ezekiel He referred to Ezekiel as Son of Man. Ezekiel's message of salvation was a precursor to the message that Christ would later preach. Christ is also referred to with the title of Son of Man (Luke 5:24). Christ preached to the children of Israel knowing that most of them would not listen to Him, but they did have the message of salvation preached to them and will have no excuse on Judgment Day. They made their own decisions and their blood is on their own heads (Acts 18:6). It is a demonstration of God's great mercy that He would send messengers to warn those that are making themselves to be His enemies. God's mercy is displayed by the fact that the people deserve judgment, but He is patient with them and gives them every opportunity to receive mercy.

(KJV) 2 Peter 3:9 The Lord is not slack concerning His promise, as some count slackness, but is longsuffering toward us, not willing that any should perish but that all should come to repentance.

It is God's will that all people come to repentance. He does not desire for anyone to perish, but in order for us to have freewill some people will be lost. They will choose not to listen to the warnings they are given. God has a plan and purpose. One of the big questions people often pose to the idea that everything happens in accordance to God's will, is that, *"if God is in control of everything then why is there so much suffering in the world, and why does God allow bad things to happen to good people?"*

The answer is that God does not cause bad things to happen to anyone. Bad things happen as the result of sin being in the world, and without the existence of sin we would not have freewill or the ability to choose. How could we make a choice if there is only one option? God tells us what we need to do to be happy and what we need to do to receive salvation, but then He gives us the option to decide for ourselves whether or not we will follow Him.

A great deal of the time when bad things happen to people it is the result of their own actions. Of course there are times when completely innocent people fall victim to evil. How can this be? It is because evil exists in the world that we live in, and the world we live in is not fair. God is a God of justice, but He never promises us that we will receive justice on the earth, or that we will be treated fairly in this world. The Bible actually states the contrary and tells us we can expect to suffer and be persecuted in this world (2 Timothy 3:12).

(KJV) 1 Corinthians 4:11-12 To the present hour we both hunger and thirst, and we are poorly clothed, and beaten, and homeless. 12 And we labor, working with our own hands. Being reviled, we bless; being persecuted, we endure;

The objective of our lives is not to be successful in this evil and materialistic world. The objective is for us to exist in a world containing both good and evil, but for us to choose to be good and for us to choose to follow God. In this world children starve to death, people rob and kill each other, and do all manner of unspeakable evil to one another. Some people look at all of the misery in the world and wonder how God could allow it to happen. Bad things happen in this world, and the world is unjust. The thing you need to understand is that the events that take place on earth are not the things that are important in the grand scheme of things.

What is important is the decisions that you make, and whether or not you decide to follow Jesus. Once you are in Heaven it will not matter if you fell into the hands of evil men and were tortured and murdered, or if you starved to death on the street. It does not matter that sin exists in the world;

all that matters is that you do not succumb to sin, and that you make it into Heaven.

On the Day of Judgment, those that practiced evil will be judged and then you will receive justice, but while on earth, the world will not be fair. Think of the world as a testing ground where you are being tested to see whether you should be sent to Heaven or to Hell. Everyday you are given choices. God observes your choices and you will be judged according to the choices that you make. Evil and temptation are around you everyday, your goal is to endure and overcome it. Bad things happen, but you can do things about it. You don't have to allow children to starve to death; you can be there for your neighbors when they are in need, which is what you are called to do.

> **(KJV) Luke 10:30-37 Then Jesus answered and said: "A certain man went down from Jerusalem to Jericho, and fell among thieves, who stripped him of his clothing, wounded him, and departed, leaving him half dead. 31 "Now by chance a certain priest came down that road. And when he saw him, he passed by on the other side. 32 "Likewise a Levite, when he arrived at the place, came and looked, and passed by on the other side. 33 "But a certain Samaritan, as he journeyed, came where he was. And when he saw him, he had compassion. 34 "So he went to him and bandaged his wounds, pouring on oil and wine; and he set him on his own animal, brought him to an inn, and took care of him. 35 "On the next day, when he departed, he took out two denarii, gave them to the innkeeper, and said to him, 'Take care of him; and whatever more you spend, when I come again, I will repay you.'36 "So which of these three do you think was neighbor to him who fell among the thieves?" 37 And he said, "He who showed mercy on him." Then Jesus said to him, "Go and do likewise."**

Everyday we are being tested. We are given opportunities to overcome our own sins, resist temptation, and to help out our fellow man. The existence of evil in this world is what allows us to be placed in situations where we can exercise our freewill and make choices. We are able to learn from our experiences and they enable us to grow spiritually. It is not an accident that evil exists on the earth.

> **(KJV) Isaiah 45:6 That they may know from the rising of the sun to its setting That there is none besides Me. I am the Lord, and there is no other; 7 I form the light and create darkness, I make peace and create calamity; I, the Lord, do all these things.**

God is in control of all things and has a plan and purpose for everything He does. It was not an accident that God placed the Tree of Knowledge of Good and Evil in the same garden as Adam and Eve, and then left them unattended with it. Man has dominion over the animals because of his ability to use his mind. By God allowing evil to come into the world, he gave humans a way to grow both mentally and spiritually. With their minds Adam and Eve decided to defy God, resulting in choices and consequences. It is only through consequences that we seek to make the correct choices. Humans can now be observed and judged by their actions. Sin, evil, and misery came into the world with God's permission, but God does not cause anyone to sin. Evil exists in the world so that we have choices; sin exists in the world when we make the wrong ones.

Predestination vs. freewill is a subject that many people have difficulty with. If God has your destiny planned out before you are born (Romans 9:11) then how can your life be determined by the choices you make? God allows you to make your own decisions, but He already knows what decisions you will make, and how your life will turn out because of those decisions. It is difficult for us to grasps this subject, because God views our lives from a different perspective than we do. For example, we may be climbing up one side of a mountain and making plans and decisions about what we are going to do when we get to the other side. We are making our own decisions and have an idea about what we are expecting to do when we get to the other side of the mountain, but God has a different perspective than we do. From where God sits, He may see that there is an enemy army, a wild animal, or robbers waiting on the other side of the mountain to devour us. We still have freewill and are making our own decisions, but God knows our destinies, because He can see where our lives are leading us. As humans we possess this same ability, only to a lesser degree.

We can predict how our children will respond in certain situations based upon their upbringing. Our children are free to make their own decisions, but those decisions will be based on the morals and values that they have learned. We do not know exactly what our children will do in every situation and we certainly do not control their actions, but we can generally predict their behavior. Of course sometimes our children stray from their upbringing and sometimes they will make poor decisions. These are the times that they will be disciplined, and based upon whether or not they learn from their mistakes, we can predict how they will respond in similar situations in the future. This is similar to how God could allow us to make our own decisions yet still know how our lives will turn out, but God does this to a much greater degree.

It is understandable that God could predict how an individual will turn out based on the circumstances of that person's life. The area of the world the person is born in, their parents, their culture, and several other factors will come into play in shaping the destiny of each person. God has control of all of these influences giving Him the power to know what fate has in store for us, and He can influence our lives according to His will and purpose. God does not control every aspect of our lives, but he gives us room to exercise our own freewill. God controls the major events of our lives, but allows us to make our own decisions on other matters. To clarify this point we will look at the life of King David.

(KJV) Acts 13:22 And when he had removed him, he raised up unto them David to be their king; to whom also he gave testimony, and said, I have found David the son of Jesse, a man after mine own heart, which shall fulfill all my will.

God chose David because He knew David would be a good king, and because He knew David would fulfill His will. This was the major event that King David was destined for. Besides David fulfilling God's purpose of becoming King, God allowed David to use his freewill to make his own decisions, which would affect David's life but not alter his destiny. Our lives will be according to God's purpose, but we can make our lives a great deal more difficult by using our freewill to make bad decisions. We are accountable for the consequences of our sins, which may make our lives harder as was the case with King David.

(KJV) 2 Samuel 11:2-5 Then it happened one evening that David arose from his bed and walked on the roof of the king's house. And from the roof he saw a woman bathing, and the woman was very beautiful to behold. 3 So David sent and inquired about the woman. And someone said, "Is this not Bathsheba, the daughter of Eliam, the wife of Uriah the Hittite?" 4 Then David sent messengers, and took her; and she came to him, and he lay with her, for she was cleansed from her impurity; and she returned to her house. 5 And the woman conceived; so she sent and told David, and said, "I am with child."

King David was a good king and lived according to God's will. However, David also had freewill, and his life would be affected by the consequences of the decisions that he made. One night David happened to see a beautiful woman and he lusted after her. He inquired about who she was, and even though he learned that she was married he committed adultery with her and got her pregnant.

(KJV) 2 Samuel 11:6-9 Then David sent to Joab, saying, "Send me Uriah the Hittite." And Joab sent Uriah to David. 7 When Uriah had come to him, David asked how Joab was doing, and how the people were doing, and how the war prospered. 8 And David said to Uriah, "Go down to your house and wash your feet." So Uriah departed from the king's house, and a gift of food from the king followed him. 9 But Uriah slept at the door of the king's house with all the servants of his lord, and did not go down to his house.

David tried to cover up his sin by calling the woman's husband home from war in hopes that he would lay with his wife, and believe the child she was carrying was his own. However, Uriah did not go to his house and David's plan to cover up his sin failed.

(KJV) 2 Samuel 11:14-15 In the morning it happened that David wrote a letter to Joab and sent it by the hand of Uriah. 15 And he wrote in the letter, saying, "Set Uriah in the forefront of the hottest battle, and retreat from him, that he may be struck down and die."

Since David was unable to deceive Uriah into believing the child Bathsheba was carrying was his own, he decided to have Uriah killed. Uriah was one of David's most faithful and loyal soldiers, and was listed as one of David's mighty men (1 Chronicles 11:41). David betrayed Uriah and had Uriah trustingly carry the very letter that ordered his own death. David utilized his freewill to commit several sins in this matter. He coveted his neighbor's wife (Exodus 20:17), he committed adultery (Exodus 20:14), and he committed murder (Exodus 20:13), two of which are sins punishable by death under Mosaic Law (Exodus 21:14, Leviticus 20:10).

God sent the prophet Nathan to confront David with his sins.

(KJV) 2 Samuel 12:9-11 'Why have you despised the commandment of the Lord, to do evil in His sight? You have killed Uriah the Hittite with the sword; you have taken his wife to be your wife, and have killed him with the sword of the people of Ammon. 10 'Now therefore, the sword shall never depart from

your house, because you have despised Me, and have taken the wife of Uriah the Hittite to be your wife.'11 "Thus says the Lord: 'Behold, I will raise up adversity against you from your own house; and I will take your wives before your eyes and give them to your neighbor, and he shall lie with your wives in the sight of this sun.

(KJV) 2 Samuel 12:13-14 So David said to Nathan, "I have sinned against the Lord." And Nathan said to David, "The Lord also has put away your sin; you shall not die. 14 "However, because by this deed you have given great occasion to the enemies of the Lord to blaspheme, the child also who is born to you shall surely die."

David sinned against God and because of this he had to deal with the consequences of his sins. David repented and God forgave him (2 Samuel 12:13), but the consequences of his sins remained with him. The first punishment for David's sins was that the child Bathsheba was carrying would die, which happened seven days after the child's birth (2 Samuel 12:19). Other consequences were that the sword and adversity would rise from, and never depart from his house (2 Samuel 12:10,11). The adversity that followed resulted in one of David's son's raping his sister (2 Samuel 13:14), and another one of David's sons avenging the rape of his sister by murdering his brother (2 Samuel 13:28-29). Later that brother would rebel against his father and also be killed (2 Samuel 18:14-15).

So was God unjust by allowing David's daughter to be raped, and two of his sons to be killed as the result of David's sin? No! Everyone still utilized their own freewill and was responsible for their own actions. Amnon chose to rape his sister (2 Samuel 13:14, 16) and his death was the result of his own sins (Deuteronomy 22:25, 28-29, 27:22). Absalom chose to have his brother murdered (2 Samuel 13:28), and Absalom's death was also the result of his own sins (Deuteronomy 19:11-12). As for the sister Tamar she did nothing wrong (2 Samuel 13:7-14), and she certainly did not deserve the pain that was inflicted upon her. Like Uriah the Hittite (2 Samuel 11:11), Tamar was the victim of other people's sinful desires. The world is not fair and bad things do happen to good people. This is the result of sin being in the world, but if these events were not possible we would not have freewill. Although Uriah and Tamar may have endured suffering while on the earth, their reward will be great in Heaven (2 Thessalonians 1:4-7, 2 Corinthians 1:5-7).

So if the tragic events were of each individual's own making, then how is it that they were the consequences of King David's sins? King David did not cause his sons to make the choices that they did, but it is very likely that his actions could have influenced their decisions to some degree. Through David's sins he demonstrated to his children that he was willing to go against God's commandments in certain situations. This could have planted the seeds in their minds for them to do likewise when they felt it necessary or desirable.

(KJV) 1 Kings 15:4-5 Nevertheless for David's sake the Lord his God gave him a lamp in Jerusalem, by setting up his son after him and by establishing Jerusalem; 5 because David did what was right in the eyes of the Lord, and had not turned aside from anything that He commanded him all the days of his life, except in the matter of Uriah the Hittite.

David's destiny and purpose was to be king and to do the will of God. David's life turned out as God had predestined it to. David made his life harder than it had to be because he used his freewill to sin against God, but the main purpose of his life remained according to God's plan. David's sins were great, but he repented of them. He was disciplined by the consequences of his sins and he learned from his mistakes. David fulfilled God's purpose and did not lose his salvation. He dealt with the consequences of his sins, and lived out the rest of his life according to God's will. The major events of David's life were predestined by God, yet God allowed David to use his freewill to make his own choices. These choices affected David's life, but not his destiny.

God has control of our lives in that He influences them and directs them according to His will and purpose, but He does not live our lives for us. He may control some of the events of our lives, but we are given room to make our own choices, and we will be held accountable for our own actions.

(KJV) Matthew 12:36-37 "But I say to you that for every idle word men may speak, they will give account of it in the day of judgment. 37 "For by your words you will be justified, and by your words you will be condemned."

God controls our lives in that we will be put in different situations and will interact with other people according to God's plan. How we interact, and what we do in the different situations will determine how we will be judged on the day of the Lord. God does not control our actions, but influences the major events of our lives. When dealing with the topic of predestination there are three people that usually come up: Judas Iscariot, Pontius Pilate, and Pharaoh. Were these people allowed to use freewill, and if not how could God hold them accountable for their actions? Before we get into the topic of "*Some pots were made to be broken*", we will first examine whether or not these three men had a choice in the things they did. We will begin by examining the actions of Judas Iscariot. Did Judas have a choice in betraying Christ?

> **(KJV) John 5:15-18 The man departed, and told the Jews that it was Jesus, which had made him whole. 16 And therefore did the Jews persecute Jesus, and sought to slay him, because he had done these things on the sabbath day. 17 But Jesus answered them, My Father worketh hitherto, and I work. 18 Therefore the Jews sought the more to kill him, because he not only had broken the sabbath, but said also that God was his Father, making himself equal with God.**

> **(KJV) Luke 22:1-6 Now the feast of unleavened bread drew nigh, which is called the Passover. 2 And the chief priests and scribes sought how they might kill him; for they feared the people. 3 Then entered Satan into Judas surnamed Iscariot, being of the number of the twelve. 4 And he went his way, and communed with the chief priests and captains, how he might betray him unto them. 5 And they were glad, and covenanted to give him money. 6 And he promised, and sought opportunity to betray him unto them in the absence of the multitude.**

The chief priests and the Pharisees already wanted Christ dead before Judas approached them. Satan entered into Judas and Judas approached the chief priest and offered to betray Christ. What caused Judas to do this? The event that took place immediately prior to Judas approaching the chief priests to betray Christ was a dispute over costly ointment (Matthew 26:7-16).

> **(KJV) John 12:3-6 Then took Mary a pound of ointment of spikenard, very costly, and anointed the feet of Jesus, and wiped his feet with her hair: and the house was filled with the odour of the ointment. 4 Then saith one of his disciples, Judas Iscariot, Simon's son, which should betray him, 5 Why was not this ointment sold for three hundred pence, and given to the poor? 6 This he said, not that he cared for the poor; but because he was a thief, and had the bag, and bare what was put therein.**

The reason Judas got angry over the costly ointment and decided to betray Christ was because he was a thief, and he wanted the money for himself. This was the character and nature of Judas Iscariot. He was a greedy and selfish person. It is understandable that someone with those characteristics could be foreseen as a traitor. God knows the hearts of men (Roman 8:27), and could have easily determined that it was in Judas Iscariot's nature to betray Christ. God did not force Judas to betray Christ, but selected Judas knowing that it was what he would do.

> **(KJV) John 6:64-71 But there are some of you that believe not. For Jesus knew from the beginning who they were that believed not, and who should betray him. 65 And he said, Therefore said I unto you, that no man can come unto me, except it were given unto him of my Father. 66 From that time many of his disciples went back, and walked no more with him. 67 Then said Jesus unto the twelve, Will ye also go away? 68 Then Simon Peter answered him, Lord, to whom shall we go? thou hast the words of eternal life. 69 And we believe and are sure that thou art that Christ, the Son of the living God. 70 Jesus answered them, Have not I chosen you twelve, and one of you is a devil? 71 He spake of Judas Iscariot the son of Simon: for he it was that should betray him, being one of the twelve.**

Jesus knew from the beginning that Judas was going to betray him, and selected him as one of the twelve disciples so that the scriptures might be fulfilled. Jesus selected Judas as a disciple knowing that he did not believe that Jesus was the Christ. Judas was also a selfish thief that lied and pretended to be a disciple of Christ in order to steal their money. God did not make Judas betray Christ, but God did know that Judas would be the one to do so. Judas made the decision to betray Christ with his own freewill. After Judas approached the chief priests and offered to betray Christ, Judas was given a chance to change his mind and was given a final warning. This display of mercy is similar to when Ezekiel was sent to the children of Israel (Ezekiel 2:3-5). It was doubtful that Judas would listen to the warning because of his nature, but he was given the warning nonetheless so that he would not have any excuses for his actions.

> **(KJV) John 13:21 When Jesus had thus said, he was troubled in spirit, and testified, and said, Verily, verily, I say unto you, that one of you shall betray me.**

> **(KJV) Matthew 26:21-25 And as they did eat, he said, Verily I say unto you, that one of you shall betray me. 22 And they were exceedingly sorrowful, and began every one of them to say unto**

him, Lord, is it I? 23 And he answered and said, He that dippeth his hand with me in the dish, the same shall betray me. 24 The Son of man goeth as it is written of him: but woe unto that man by whom the Son of man is betrayed! it had been good for that man if he had not been born. 25 Then Judas, which betrayed him, answered and said, Master, is it I? He said unto him, Thou hast said.**

Jesus gave Judas this final warning after Judas had already made a deal with the chief priests to betray Him. God knows all things so of course He knew that Judas had approached the chief priests to betray Christ. Judas was given a chance to change his mind. Was this possible or was Judas forced to betray Christ? Judas betrayed Christ out of his own freewill. The scriptures could have been fulfilled if someone other than Judas had betrayed Christ, but Judas was selected as a disciple because God knew based on Judas' character that he would be the one to do so. Was Judas given a chance to make a different decision? Of course he was. Jesus warned him right before Judas went out the door to betray him. Judas had all the information necessary to make the correct decisions in his life. Judas lived with Christ for three years and witnessed many miracles. He was with Christ when Christ presented His teachings to the multitudes. It was predestined that Christ would be betrayed, but it through his own freewill that Judas betrayed Him.

(KJV) Psalm 41:7-9 All that hate me whisper together against me: against me do they devise my hurt.:8 An evil disease, say they, cleaveth fast unto him: and now that he lieth he shall rise up no more. 9 Yea, mine own familiar friend, in whom I trusted, which did eat of my bread, hath lifted up his heel against me.

(KJV) John 13:18-19 I speak not of you all: I know whom I have chosen: but that the scripture may be fulfilled, He that eateth bread with me hath lifted up his heel against me. 19 Now I tell you before it come, that, when it is come to pass, ye may believe that I am he.

Jesus quoted Psalm 41:9 to inform the disciples that he was going to be betrayed by someone close to Him. Jesus uses the exact words minus the words, *"friend, in whom I trusted."* Christ had to be betrayed by someone near to Him so that the scriptures might be fulfilled. God knew before hand that Judas Iscariot would use his freewill to make the decisions that he did, which were according to God's plan and purpose. God foresees events far into the future. He does not cause these events, but is able to see where mankind is going based on the choices they make. To clarify this further we will look at what God told Abraham.

God called Abraham to journey into the land of Canaan to a land that would be given to the descendants of Abraham as an inheritance (Genesis 12:1-2). Abraham did as God had instructed him, and arrived in the land that would later be given to his descendants (Genesis 12:7).

(KJV) Genesis 15:12-16 Now when the sun was going down, a deep sleep fell upon Abram; and behold, horror and great darkness fell upon him. 13 Then He said to Abram: "Know certainly that your descendants will be strangers in a land that is not theirs, and will serve them, and they will afflict them four hundred years. 14 "And also the nation whom they serve I will judge; afterward they shall come out with great possessions. 15 "Now as for you, you shall go to your fathers in peace; you shall be buried at a good old age. 16 "But in the fourth generation they shall return here, for the iniquity of the Amorites is not yet complete."

Abraham did as God directed him and moved to the land that God promised to give to his descendants. So why didn't God just give the land to Abraham at that time? It is because the time had not yet come for the land to be taken from the Amorites. At that time the Amorites' sins did not yet warrant their destruction. However, God foresaw that their sins were continually increasing and within the next four hundred years their sins would merit them being overthrown, and their land would be given to the descendants of Abraham (Genesis 15:16). In the above verses God also informed Abraham that his descendants would be taken to a different land and would be made into slaves for four hundred years. God also foretold the judgment He would inflict on Egypt to free the children of Israel from their bondage.

The life of Pharaoh is more difficult to explain than Judas, because God did harden Pharaoh's heart so that Pharaoh would continue to hold the children of Israel captive, in order for God's power to be displayed. The thing that you need to understand is that Pharaoh still had freewill, and it is because of his actions that the plagues fell upon Egypt. The plagues that fell upon Egypt were brought about by the consequences of their actions. The same way that the sword and adversity would rise from and never depart King David's house because of his sin, the people of Egypt would have to face the consequences of their sins as well.

(KJV) Exodus 3:7-8 And the Lord said: "I have surely seen the oppression of My people who are in Egypt, and have heard their cry because of their taskmasters, for I know their sorrows. 8 "So I have come down to deliver them out of the hand of the

Egyptians, and to bring them up from that land to a good and large land, to a land flowing with milk and honey, to the place of the Canaanites and the Hittites and the Amorites and the Perizzites and the Hivites and the Jebusites.

The plagues were not brought down on Egypt because Pharaoh failed to let the Hebrew people go when Moses first asked him to. God brought judgment to Egypt because He observed the oppression that was taking place there, and because He heard the cries and knew the sorrows of the Hebrew people. God foresaw these events and foretold of them to Abraham (Genesis 15:14).

(KJV) Exodus 4:21-23 And the LORD said unto Moses, When thou goest to return into Egypt, see that thou do all those wonders before Pharaoh, which I have put in thine hand: but I will harden his heart, that he shall not let the people go. 22 And thou shalt say unto Pharaoh, Thus saith the LORD, Israel is my son, even my firstborn: 23 And I say unto thee, Let my son go, that he may serve me: and if thou refuse to let him go, behold, I will slay thy son, even thy firstborn.

(KJV) Exodus 7:3-5 And I will harden Pharaoh's heart, and multiply my signs and my wonders in the land of Egypt. 4 But Pharaoh shall not hearken unto you, that I may lay my hand upon Egypt, and bring forth mine armies, and my people the children of Israel, out of the land of Egypt by great judgments. 5 And the Egyptians shall know that I am the LORD, when I stretch forth mine hand upon Egypt, and bring out the children of Israel from among them.

(KJV) Exodus 9:13 And the LORD said unto Moses, Rise up early in the morning, and stand before Pharaoh, and say unto him, Thus saith the LORD God of the Hebrews, Let my people go, that they may serve me. 14 For I will at this time send all my plagues upon thine heart, and upon thy servants, and upon thy people; that thou mayest know that there is none like me in all the earth. 15 For now I will stretch out my hand, that I may smite thee and thy people with pestilence; and thou shalt be cut off from the earth. 16 And in very deed for this cause have I raised thee up, for to show in thee my power; and that my name may be declared throughout all the earth. 17 As yet exaltest thou thyself against my people, that thou wilt not let them go?

Pharaoh's life served the purpose of God, and his freewill actions were in accordance with God's plan (Exodus 9:16). God hardening Pharaoh's heart served several purposes. Egypt was being judged because of their sins; in the same way the Amorites were about to be. By prolonging the time before Pharaoh would allow the children of Israel to be let go, God multiplied His signs and wonders, and dispensed the consequences the people of Egypt had coming to them for their sins. In doing so the people of Egypt would know that YHVH was the only true God. The plagues were a form of discipline for the Egyptian people. The Egyptian people were worshipping several other gods at that time.

God displayed His power so that the people of Egypt would know the YHVH was the only true God. Several of the plagues were targeted specifically against the gods of Egypt. For example, the plague of darkness (Exodus 10:21-29) demonstrated Ra the Egyptian sun god was powerless against Jehovah. The water of the Nile turning to blood showed that Khnum (the guardian of the Nile) could not stand against God, the death of the firstborn sons (Exodus 11:5) displayed God's sovereignty over Isis (the goddess of life), and the destruction of the crops by hail and locusts was against Osiris (god of agriculture and death). The judgments that God placed on Egypt both punished them for worshipping other gods, and corrected them by showing them whom they ought to worship. These judgments also fulfilled the prophecy that God had spoken to Abraham (Genesis 15:14) and set the stage for the Gospel of Christ by initiating the Passover and the sacrifice of an unblemished lamb so that the wrath of God would Passover the house of those that followed God's commandments (Exodus 12:11). All things worked together for the glory of God and according to His plan. God punished, saved, fulfilled prophecy, disciplined, and laid the foundation for the future death of Christ on the cross all at the same time; based on the freewill actions of several different people coming together.

So did Pharaoh have freewill? Yes, it was through Pharaoh's freewill that he kept the Hebrew people in bondage. It was through Pharaoh's freewill that he brought sorrows onto the children of Israel to the point that they cried out to God for deliverance. During the seven plagues God hardened Pharaoh's heart so that God's will would be accomplished. When Moses spoke to Pharaoh, Pharaoh was not able to prevent the afflictions that God had predestined to bring upon Egypt. The afflictions were the consequences of the sins of the people and were foretold by God many years in advance in the same way that God foresaw that the sins of the Amorites were going to increase to a point that they would likewise be judged. God did not force these people to sin so that he could afflict judgment upon them, but He foresaw that through the people's choices they would continue to increase in their sins and judgment would eventually be warranted.

As for Pontius Pilate he too was able to use his freewill to make his own decisions. It was according to God's will that Christ would be crucified, since it was the very purpose of His birth. Pilate did not want to have Christ crucified. He made a few attempts at releasing Christ, but the Jewish people would not have it. God also gave Pilate a warning, and gave him every opportunity to make the correct decision.

(KJV) Matthew 27:19 When he was set down on the judgment seat, his wife sent unto him, saying, Have thou nothing to do with that just man: for I have suffered many things this day in a dream because of him.

(KJV) John 19:12 And from thenceforth Pilate sought to release him: but the Jews cried out, saying, If thou let this man go, thou art not Caesar's friend: whosoever maketh himself a king speaketh against Caesar.

God sent a warning to Pilate through a vision that his wife received, not to have anything to do with the death of Jesus, but Pilate was too weak to standup to the people (Matthew 27:24, Mark 15:15).

(KJV) Acts 3:13 The God of Abraham, and of Isaac, and of Jacob, the God of our fathers, hath glorified his Son Jesus; whom ye delivered up, and denied him in the presence of Pilate, when he was determined to let him go.

In the above verse Paul confronts the Jewish people because they delivered Christ up and denied His release when Pilate wanted to let Him go. Pilate was warned by his wife and desired to release Christ, but he backed down to the will of the people.

(KJV) Acts 4:26-28 The kings of the earth stood up, and the rulers were gathered together against the Lord, and against his Christ. 27 For of a truth against thy holy child Jesus, whom thou hast anointed, both Herod, and Pontius Pilate, with the Gentiles, and the people of Israel, were gathered together, 28 For to do whatsoever thy hand and thy counsel determined before to be done.

Could Pilate have let Christ go and the scriptures still have been fulfilled? Of course he could of. The chief priests were determined to have Christ crucified, if Pilate did not give the order they would have taken Christ to someone else that would have. Christ had already been before Herod once; they could have easily taken Christ back to him and pressured Herod to give the order. Regardless of who gave the order, all things happen in accordance with God's will. It would not be hard for God to recognize that it was in Pilate's nature to succumb to the will of the people when placed in that situation. God influences the circumstances of our lives to ensure that His will is accomplished. He can predict how we will behave in different situations based on our behavioral patterns and character traits, but the decisions we make are still our own.

(KJV) Proverbs 16:4 The Lord has made all for Himself, Yes, even the wicked for the day of doom.

God created every one of us for a specific purpose. All of us play a particular role in God's plan, and we interact with each other according to God's purpose, in order for God's will to be accomplished. Not every person that God created will receive salvation. Some pots were made to be broken.

(KJV) Jeremiah 18: 3 Then I went down to the potter's house, and there he was, making something at the wheel. 4 And the vessel that he made of clay was marred in the hand of the potter; so he made it again into another vessel, as it seemed good to the potter to make. 5 Then the word of the Lord came to me, saying: 6 "O house of Israel, can I not do with you as this potter?" says the Lord. "Look, as the clay is in the potter's hand, so are you in My hand, O house of Israel!

We are the creation, and God can do with us as he sees fit. The potter plans out the destiny of his creation when it is still on the wheel.

(KJV) Isaiah 64:8 But now, O LORD, thou art our father; we are the clay, and thou our potter; and we all are the work of thy hand.

(KJV) Job 10:8 Thine hands have made me and fashioned me together round about; yet thou dost destroy me. 9 Remember, I beseech thee, that thou hast made me as the clay; and wilt thou bring me into dust again?

(KJV) Job 33:6 Behold, I am according to thy wish in God's stead: I also am formed out of the clay.

God is the creator and we are the creation. We are at God's mercy. Our lives and our fate are completely reliant upon the mercy of God. On this earth, our circumstances are based on God's mercy; certainly God's blessings make a big difference on the level of satisfaction we find on the earth. As for our spiritual circumstances we would not be anywhere without God's mercies. We receive salvation through the sacrifice that Christ made, and from there we begin our Christian walk, but even then we are given the Holy Spirit to guide us. Without God's mercy we would not be able to get anywhere physically or spiritually.

(KJV) Psalm 145:8-9 The Lord is gracious and full of compassion, slow to anger and great in mercy. 9 The Lord is good to all, And His tender mercies are over all His works.

God is merciful to us. He is patient with us and he is good to all. He causes the sun to rise and sends rain to both the righteous and to the wicked (Matthew 5:45). Who are we to question God's plan in our lives?

(KJV) Isaiah 29:16 Surely you have things turned around! Shall the potter be esteemed as the clay; For shall the thing made say of him who made it, "He did not make me"? Or shall the thing formed say of him who formed it, "He has no understanding"?

(KJV) Isaiah 45:9-10 "Woe to him who strives with his Maker! Let the potsherd strive with the potsherds of the earth! Shall the clay say to him who forms it, 'What are you making?' Or shall your handiwork say, 'He has no hands'? 10 Woe to him who says to his father, 'What are you begetting?' Or to the woman, 'What have you brought forth?'

We are the creation and each of us has been created according to God's purpose. What right do we have to question the plan God has for our lives? We were created to fulfill God's will and not the other way around. The events that take place in our lives take place according to God's plan, and we may not understand the reasons at the time or maybe even ever. We need to be patient and believe that God is working for our good and in our best interests. The Lord works in mysterious ways, and we are not able to comprehend the significance of the events that take place in our lives at all times. We interact with other people and influence them and vice versa in ways that we are not always aware of.

(KJV) Romans 8:28-30 And we know that all things work together for good to them that love God, to them who are the called according to his purpose. 29 For whom he did foreknow, he also did predestinate to be conformed to the image of his Son, that he might be the firstborn among many brethren. 30 Moreover whom he did predestinate, them he also called: and

whom he called, them he also justified: and whom he justified, them he also glorified.

Some pots were made to be broken and some people have been created for destruction (Proverbs 16:4). At the same time some people were predestined to receive salvation. To those who love God, all things will work together for their good (Romans 8:28). To those that do not choose to love God, God is still good to all and will be gracious and merciful to them while they are on the earth, but in the end they will be lost (Matthew 5:45).

While the clay was still on the potter's wheel God determined its destiny. Some of the clay has been predestined to be conformed to the image of Christ and will receive salvation, and other lumps of clay were created to serve their purpose on earth and then will be lost. It is not our place to question the decisions of our Creator. He assigned us each our own purposes, which are the major events of our lives. He then gave us room to use our freewill to make our own choices. God foreknows (Romans 8:29) what choices we will make, because He is the one that created us and gave us our personalities. In this way we have been predestined, but at the same time use our freewill to manifest God's plan for us.

Those that are predestined to be justified God has also called (Romans 8:30). If God did not call us we would probably be too caught up in the material world we live in to seek Him out. God calls us in many different ways. In the great commission Jesus told the disciples to make disciples of all nations (Matthew 28:19). You may also be called because God places a desire in your heart to seek Him out. God calls those He chooses to Himself and may call you several times before you hear Him. God may have placed this very book that you are reading into your hands to draw you to Him.

God uses people to serve His purpose. We interact with other people and our actions influence the lives of others and vice versa. It is true that sometimes God will appear to people in visions or dreams like He did with Abraham, Moses, Ezekiel, and so on, but most of the time God uses the lives of individuals to influence the lives of those around them (Matthew 5:16). In the Old Testament of the Bible, God spoke to the people by sending prophets to speak to them (Ezekiel 2:3). Our lives constantly influence the lives of those around us, and we must be mindful that we do not lead others astray (Romans 14:21). God knows how we will use our freewill and what our characters will be like before we are even born.

(KJV) Romans 9:10-13 And not only this; but when Rebecca also had conceived by one, even by our father Isaac; 11 (For the children being not yet born, neither having done any good or

evil, that the purpose of God according to election might stand, not of works, but of him that calleth;) 12 It was said unto her, The elder shall serve the younger. 13 As it is written, Jacob have I loved, but Esau have I hated.

God knew that He would love Jacob and hate Esau before they were even born. So if God knew He would hate Esau, then why did He create him in the first place? God created Esau and gave him freewill to serve his purpose. Esau used his freewill to become a fornicator and profane person that held nothing sacred, and he even sold his own birthright for a morsel of food (Hebrews 12:16). In contrast Jacob was a hard worker and endured fourteen years of labor for the love of Rachel (Genesis 29:18, 27-28). The interactions of these two brothers were documented so that we can learn from their triumphs and their failures. God created Esau knowing that He would hate his actions, but Esau's life served the purpose that others might be saved. We have the life of Esau as an example so that we will not repeat his mistakes.

(KJV) Romans 9:14-16 What shall we say then? Is there unrighteousness with God? God forbid. 15 For he saith to Moses, I will have mercy on whom I will have mercy, and I will have compassion on whom I will have compassion. 16 So then it is not of him that willeth, nor of him that runneth, but of God that showeth mercy.

Our fates are at the mercy of God. All of us have sinned and fall short of the glory of God (Romans 3:23). We are all deserving of judgment, but God chooses whom He chooses to have mercy on, and who are we to question God? We do not receive God's grace through our works (Ephesians 2:9), but through His mercy. By works we do not earn our way into heaven, but God shows mercy to those He chooses. That does not mean that how we live our lives will not play a role in whether or not God selects us to be shown mercy. God judges everyone according to their deeds (Revelations 2:23), and He knew whether He would love or hate Jacob and Esau before they where born based on how they would live their lives.

(KJV) Romans 9:17-23 For the scripture saith unto Pharaoh, Even for this same purpose have I raised thee up, that I might show my power in thee, and that my name might be declared throughout all the earth. 18 Therefore hath he mercy on whom he will have mercy, and whom he will he hardeneth. 19 Thou wilt say then unto me, Why doth he yet find fault? For who hath resisted his will? 20 Nay but, O man, who art thou that repliest against God? Shall the thing formed say to him that formed it,

Why hast thou made me thus? 21 Hath not the potter power over the clay, of the same lump to make one vessel unto honour, and another unto dishonour? 22 What if God, willing to show his wrath, and to make his power known, endured with much longsuffering the vessels of wrath fitted to destruction: 23 And that he might make known the riches of his glory on the vessels of mercy, which he had afore prepared unto glory,

God endured with longsuffering the evil deeds of men, that He might display His power and bring about salvation to the righteous. God did not like the actions of those that used their freewill to choose evil, but He endured it so that He might show mercy to the righteous according to His plan. If some people did not receive condemnation then to what benefit would it be to follow God and receive His mercy? Without punishment, there would be no heavenly rewards, because everyone would receive the same fate regardless of if they were good or evil. Without punishment for sin there would be no justice, and God's mercies would not be viewed as such a great gift as it is. Everyone was created for a purpose; without the vessels of destruction we would not have freewill or be able to grow spiritually.

(KJV) Revelations 6:10-11 And they cried with a loud voice, saying, How long, O Lord, holy and true, dost thou not judge and avenge our blood on them that dwell on the earth? 11 And white robes were given unto every one of them; and it was said unto them, that they should rest yet for a little season, until their fellowservants also and their brethren, that should be killed as they were, should be fulfilled.

In the above verses those who have sacrificed their lives for Christ cry out to God awaiting God to avenge their deaths on those that dwell on the earth. God tells them to be patient and to wait for the appointed time. God endures evil with longsuffering (Romans 9:22) not wanting anyone to perish, but is patient to give sinners more time to come to repentance (2 Peter 3:9). God has a plan and sticks to it. In the above verses God is withholding His judgments on the earth in order to allow more saints to be martyred and to fulfill their destinies. God has a plan and everything takes place at its appointed time according to His purpose (Ecclesiastes 3:1-8).

(KJV) Ecclesiastes 3:10-11 I have seen the travail, which God hath given to the sons of men to be exercised in it. 11 He hath made every thing beautiful in his time: also he hath set the world in their heart, so that no man can find out the work that God maketh from the beginning to the end.

God gave the travail that we experience on earth to us so that we might be exercised in it. The challenges we face on the earth will help us to grow. While we are facing challenges they may seem difficult and may cause us great sorrow, but the work will bring forth beauty in its time. Because we are born into a world containing sin, we often become too absorbed in the matters of this world to pursue the mysteries of God. That is why those that God has predestined He also calls (Romans 8:28). We are built up (exercised) by our experiences, and God directs our paths according to His purpose.

(KJV) Proverbs 21:1 The king's heart is in the hand of the Lord, Like the rivers of water; He turns it wherever He wishes.

(KJV) Proverbs 20:24 A man's steps are of the Lord; How then can a man understand his own way?

The Lord directs our paths according to His plan. We make our own decisions in this world, but God foresees and influences the directions our lives are going in, in order to manifest His will.

(KJV) Isaiah 14:24 The Lord of hosts has sworn, saying, "Surely, as I have thought, so it shall come to pass, And as I have purposed, so it shall stand:

(KJV) Isaiah 14:26-27 This is the purpose that is purposed upon the whole earth: and this is the hand that is stretched out upon all the nations. 27 For the LORD of hosts hath purposed, and who shall disannul it? And his hand is stretched out, and who shall turn it back?

The will of God will be done, His plan will be made manifest, and no one is able to resist His will. This philosophy may seem both discouraging and comforting. You may be discouraged because it seems as though you are powerless to affect your own destiny, but the opposite is actually true. If God's predominance could be affected by outside influences then how could we have faith in His promises? We can be comforted by the fact that the will of God will stand. We can be comforted because God made His will known to us, and He has shown us the path to salvation. Because God's will is unchanging we can have faith in His promises, and be assured of our salvation.

(KJV) Isaiah 46:9 Remember the former things of old: for I am God, and there is none else; I am God, and there is none like me,

10 Declaring the end from the beginning, and from ancient times the things that are not yet done, saying, My counsel shall stand, and I will do all my pleasure: 11 Calling a ravenous bird from the east, the man that executeth my counsel from a far country: yea, I have spoken it, I will also bring it to pass; I have purposed it, I will also do it.

God has declared the fate of man and the world from the beginning of time. We have a record of the things that have passed and of the things that will take place in the future. The Bible allows us to learn from the lives of those that lived before us, and foretells of the events that God has purposed for the future. The will of God is expressed in the Bible. We can have faith that what God has preordained He will also see to completion.

(KJV) Ephesians 1:9-10 Having made known unto us the mystery of his will, according to his good pleasure which he hath purposed in himself: 10 That in the dispensation of the fullness of times he might gather together in one all things in Christ, both which are in heaven, and which are on earth; even in him:

(KJV) Ephesians 1:11-12 In whom also we have obtained an inheritance, being predestinated according to the purpose of him who worketh all things after the counsel of his own will: 12 That we should be to the praise of his glory, who first trusted in Christ.

God has made His will known to us through the Bible. God preordained all of the events of the past and the events to come in the future so that we might receive salvation through His son Jesus Christ. God set the stage for the coming of Christ throughout the entire Old Testament of the Bible. The Passover in Egypt, The Bronze Serpent being lifted up in the desert, the message of the Son of Man, and the call for Abraham to follow God by faith are just some of the events that set the stage for the coming of Christ. We have been predestined according to God's plan, and all things happen according to His will (Ephesians 1:11).

(KJV) 2 Timothy 1:9-10 Who hath saved us, and called us with an holy calling, not according to our works, but according to his own purpose and grace, which was given us in Christ Jesus before the world began, 10 But is now made manifest by the appearing of our Saviour Jesus Christ, who hath abolished death, and hath brought life and immortality to light through the gospel:

(KJV) 1 John 3:8-9 He that committeth sin is of the devil; for the devil sinneth from the beginning. For this purpose the Son of God was manifested, that he might destroy the works of the devil. 9 Whosoever is born of God doth not commit sin; for his seed remaineth in him: and he cannot sin, because he is born of God.

We have been called according to God's purpose to receive salvation through Jesus Christ. God has preordained all of these events before the world was created. The Tree of Knowledge of Good and Evil was placed in the Garden of Eden so that humans may have freewill in order to grow through choices and consequences; being exercised through our experiences on the earth. Evil exists in the world in order for us to have choices. Christ came to the earth in order for us to receive salvation. Both sin and the way to overcome sin through the sacrifice of Christ were preordained before the world began. Christ came to the earth to do the will of His father, and to set an example for us to follow.

(KJV) Luke 22:42 Saying, Father, if thou be willing, remove this cup from me: nevertheless not my will, but thine, be done.

Christ prayed that God's will be done. We are instructed to do likewise.

(KJV) John 14:13-15 And whatsoever ye shall ask in my name, that will I do, that the Father may be glorified in the Son. 14 If ye shall ask any thing in my name, I will do it. 15 If ye love me, keep my commandments.

(KJV) 1 John 5:14 Now this is the confidence that we have in Him, that if we ask anything according to His will, He hears us.

If we ask anything in prayer through Christ's name it will be given to us, but there are conditions that go along with this instruction. We must keep the commandments, and the things we ask must be according to God's will. God does not want anyone to perish, but for all to come to repentance (2 Peter 3:9). If we ask God to bring one of our loved ones to repentance so that they might be saved, then we would be praying in accordance with God's will. In contrast if we pray in Christ's name for a new car or to win the lottery it is doubtful that we would receive these things; unless they just happened to coincide with God's plan for our lives. God is omnipotent and knows all. He knows the secrets of men (Romans 2:16), and He knows our needs before we even ask.

(KJV) Matthew 6:7-8 But when ye pray, use not vain repetitions, as the heathen do: for they think that they shall be heard for their much speaking. 8 Be not ye therefore like unto them: for your Father knoweth what things ye have need of, before ye ask him.

(KJV) John 3:27 John answered and said, A man can receive nothing, except it be given him from heaven.

Everything we receive and everything that we have, has been given to us by the grace of God. We need to have faith that all things will work together for our good (Romans 8:28), trust in God's plan, and pray that His will be done (Luke 22:42). We do not know what the future holds in store for us. The best that we can do is follow the commandments and have faith in God's plan for us.

(KJV) James 4:13-15 Come now, you who say, "Today or tomorrow we will go to such and such a city, spend a year there, buy and sell, and make a profit"; 14 whereas you do not know what will happen tomorrow. For what is your life? It is even a vapor that appears for a little time and then vanishes away. 15 Instead you ought to say, "If the Lord wills, we shall live and do this or that."

The will of God is going to be accomplished with or without us. We should make it a point to include God in our lives.

(KJV) Ephesians 1:4-5 According as he hath chosen us in him before the foundation of the world, that we should be holy and without blame before him in love: 5 Having predestinated us unto the adoption of children by Jesus Christ to himself, according to the good pleasure of his will,

Those that have been called by God should strive to be holy and blameless before Him out of love and respect. This is the great work and the endeavor of our lives.

(KJV) 2 Timothy 2:19-22 Nevertheless the foundation of God standeth sure, having this seal, The Lord knoweth them that are his. And, Let every one that nameth the name of Christ depart from iniquity. 20 But in a great house there are not only vessels of gold and of silver, but also of wood and of earth; and some to honour, and some to dishonour. 21 If a man therefore purge himself from these, he shall be a vessel unto honour, sanctified,

and met for the master's use, and prepared unto every good work. 22 Flee also youthful lusts: but follow righteousness, faith, charity, peace, with them that call on the Lord out of a pure heart.

God knows those that are His. The followers of Christ are called to depart from their iniquities. There are vessels of honor and of dishonor. We are to purge ourselves of our sins in order that we may be considered vessels of honor that are met for the master's use.

(KJV) Malachi 3:16 Then those who feared the Lord spoke to one another, And the Lord listened and heard them; So a book of remembrance was written before Him For those who fear the Lord And who meditate on His name.

(KJV) Revelations 20:12 And I saw the dead, small and great, stand before God; and the books were opened: and another book was opened, which is the book of life: and the dead were judged out of those things which were written in the books, according to their works.

On the Day of Judgment we will be judged based upon what is written in the books. God is our creator. Our fates have been determined before hand while on the potter's wheel. We have freewill, yet God foreknows the choices we will make, and knows whether we are vessels fit for honor or for destruction. We can be comforted by our calling, because we have been shown the path to salvation and the will of God has been made known to us. Everything works according to God's purpose. God looks down on us from Heaven and fashions each of our hearts individually. Bad things may happen to us while we are in this world, but this life is but a vapor that is here only for a while (James 4:14). We should trust in God's plan for our lives. We endure the evil in this world while we are in it, but the Kingdom of Heaven will be our home for eternity.

(KJV) Psalm 33:13-22 The Lord looks from heaven; He sees all the sons of men. 14 From the place of His dwelling He looks On all the inhabitants of the earth; 15 He fashions their hearts individually; He considers all their works. 16 No king is saved by the multitude of an army; A mighty man is not delivered by great strength. 17 A horse is a vain hope for safety; Neither shall it deliver any by its great strength. 18 Behold, the eye of the Lord is on those who fear Him, On those who hope in His mercy, 19 To deliver their soul from death, And to keep them alive in famine. 20 Our soul waits for the Lord; He is our help and our

shield. 21 For our heart shall rejoice in Him, Because we have trusted in His holy name. 22 Let Your mercy, O Lord, be upon us, Just as we hope in You.

REFERENCES

Scripture taken from the KING JAMES VERSION OF THE BIBLE, (KJV) Public Domain 1611

The Holy Spirit, Baptism, and the Temple

The Holy Spirit dwells in you after you are baptized into Christ Jesus, and acts as a conscience for you. The Holy Spirit helps you build a foundation based on Christ and works within you to help you accomplish the great work. The Holy Spirit plays an invaluable role to your salvation, and the purification of your soul. The Holy Spirit was sent by Christ as a comforter after Christ' resurrection and ascension into Heaven (John 20:17, Acts 1:2).

> **(KJV) John 15:26 But when the Comforter is come, whom I will send unto you from the Father, even the Spirit of truth, which proceedeth from the Father, he shall testify of me:**

> **(KJV) John 14:16-18 And I will pray the Father, and he shall give you another Comforter, that he may abide with you for ever; 17 Even the Spirit of truth; whom the world cannot receive, because it seeth him not, neither knoweth him: but ye know him; for he dwelleth with you, and shall be in you. 18 I will not leave you comfortless: I will come to you.**

> **(KJV) John 14:26 But the Comforter, which is the Holy Ghost, whom the Father will send in my name, he shall teach you all things, and bring all things to your remembrance, whatsoever I have said unto you.**

The Holy Spirit was sent by God at the request of His son Jesus. The Holy Spirit dwells within us, and will teach us all things. The Holy Spirit acts as a sort of conscience for us, and guides us on the rest of our path as we transcend the sin of this world and be conformed into the image of Christ.

> **(KJV) Romans 8:29 For whom he did foreknow, he also did predestinate to be conformed to the image of his Son, that he might be the firstborn among many brethren.**

The Great Work of purifying our souls and conforming them to the image of Christ begins with us receiving the gift of the Holy Spirit. We are to be followers of Christ and follow the guidelines set down before us in the Bible with Christ as our example (Matthew 16:24, Matthew 12:50).

> **(KJV) Acts 5:32 And we are his witnesses of these things; and so is also the Holy Ghost, whom God hath given to them that obey him.**

The above verse states that one of the requirements God has for us to receive the Holy Spirit is that we must obey Him.

(KJV) Luke 11:13 If ye then, being evil, know how to give good gifts unto your children: how much more shall your heavenly Father give the Holy Spirit to them that ask him?

Luke 11:13 states that we must ask God for the Holy Spirit.

(KJV) Titus 3:5 Not by works of righteousness which we have done, but according to his mercy he saved us, by the washing of regeneration, and renewing of the Holy Ghost;

(KJV) Romans 15:16 That I should be the minister of Jesus Christ to the Gentiles, ministering the gospel of God, that the offering up of the Gentiles might be acceptable, being sanctified by the Holy Ghost.

The above verses are an example of the work of the Holy Spirit. The Holy Spirit renews, sanctifies, and regenerates us. The Holy Spirit works to conform us to the image of Christ (Romans 8:28). The Holy Spirit dwells within us and acts as a conscience for us. We need to listen to our conscience after we receive the gift of the Holy Spirit, because that is how God will speak to us, and He will write his commandments in our hearts.

(KJV) Romans 9:1 I say the truth in Christ, I lie not, my conscience also bearing me witness in the Holy Ghost,

(KJV) Hebrews 10:15-17 Whereof the Holy Ghost also is a witness to us: for after that he had said before, 16 This is the covenant that I will make with them after those days, saith the Lord, I will put my laws into their hearts, and in their minds will I write them; 17 And their sins and iniquities will I remember no more.

The above verses do not say that after receiving the Holy Spirit you will not have to study the word of God.

(KJV) 2 Timothy 2:15 Study to show thyself approved unto God, a workman that needeth not to be ashamed, rightly dividing the word of truth.

We do still need to do the research ourselves, but the Holy Spirit will bring to mind the things that we have learned when we need them, and will help us to discern spiritual matters.

(KJV) 1 Corinthians 2:9-16 But as it is written, Eye hath not seen, nor ear heard, neither have entered into the heart of man, the things which God hath prepared for them that love him. 10 But God hath revealed them unto us by his Spirit: for the Spirit searcheth all things, yea, the deep things of God. 11 For what man knoweth the things of a man, save the spirit of man which is in him? even so the things of God knoweth no man, but the Spirit of God. 12 Now we have received, not the spirit of the world, but the spirit which is of God; that we might know the things that are freely given to us of God. 13 Which things also we speak, not in the words which man's wisdom teacheth, but which the Holy Ghost teacheth; comparing spiritual things with spiritual. 14 But the natural man receiveth not the things of the Spirit of God: for they are foolishness unto him: neither can he know them, because they are spiritually discerned. 15 But he that is spiritual judgeth all things, yet he himself is judged of no man. 16 For who hath known the mind of the Lord, that he may instruct him? But we have the mind of Christ.

The gift of the Holy Spirit gives us knowledge of the deeper things of God. The truths of the Bible are spiritually discerned. The interpretation of the scriptures is given to us in our hearts and minds by the Holy Spirit. To the natural man these things seem foolish, because he is incapable of understanding them without the gift of discernment that comes with the Holy Spirit.

(KJV) John 16:13-15 Howbeit when he, the Spirit of truth, is come, he will guide you into all truth: for he shall not speak of himself; but whatsoever he shall hear, that shall he speak: and he will show you things to come. 14 He shall glorify me: for he shall receive of mine, and shall show it unto you. 15 All things that the Father hath are mine: therefore said I, that he shall take of mine, and shall show it unto you.

(KJV) Matthew 13:35 That it might be fulfilled which was spoken by the prophet, saying, I will open my mouth in parables; I will utter things which have been kept secret from the foundation of the world.

The Holy Spirit will guide us into all truth, and will give us the interpretation of things that have been kept secret since the beginning of time. The Holy Spirit will also provide us with what to say when we need Him to.

> **(KJV) Mark 13:11 But when they shall lead you, and deliver you up, take no thought beforehand what ye shall speak, neither do ye premeditate: but whatsoever shall be given you in that hour, that speak ye: for it is not ye that speak, but the Holy Ghost.**

> **(KJV) Luke 12:11-12 And when they bring you unto the synagogues, and unto magistrates, and powers, take ye no thought how or what thing ye shall answer, or what ye shall say: 12 For the Holy Ghost shall teach you in the same hour what ye ought to say.**

> **(KJV) 2 Peter 1:20-21 Knowing this first, that no prophecy of the scripture is of any private interpretation. 21 For the prophecy came not in old time by the will of man: but holy men of God spake as they were moved by the Holy Ghost.**

Now that we have covered the work of the Holy Spirit, we will look into how and when you are able to receive the gift of the Holy Spirit. We will begin by examining the Baptism of Christ.

> **(KJV) Matthew 3:11 I indeed baptize you with water unto repentance: but he that cometh after me is mightier than I, whose shoes I am not worthy to bear: he shall baptize you with the Holy Ghost, and with fire:**

> **(KJV) Luke 3:21-22 Now when all the people were baptized, it came to pass, that Jesus also being baptized, and praying, the heaven was opened, 22 And the Holy Ghost descended in a bodily shape like a dove upon him, and a voice came from heaven, which said, Thou art my beloved Son; in thee I am well pleased.**

> **(KJV) John 1:32-33 And John bare record, saying, I saw the Spirit descending from heaven like a dove, and it abode upon him. 33 And I knew him not: but he that sent me to baptize with water, the same said unto me, Upon whom thou shalt see the Spirit descending, and remaining on him, the same is he which baptizeth with the Holy Ghost.**

Jesus received the Holy Spirit at his baptism. The Holy Spirit descended on him in the form of a dove. Before this John the Baptist baptized people for the forgiveness of their sins. Jesus Christ is the one whom John prophesied would baptized with the Holy Spirit.

(KJV) Matthew 28:18-20 And Jesus came and spake unto them, saying, All power is given unto me in heaven and in earth. 19 Go ye therefore, and teach all nations, baptizing them in the name of the Father, and of the Son, and of the Holy Ghost: 20 Teaching them to observe all things whatsoever I have commanded you: and, lo, I am with you always, even unto the end of the world. Amen.

After Jesus' resurrection He gave the great commission to the Apostles to baptize in the name of the Father, Son, and Holy Spirit. Many people believe that this formula of reciting the three names at baptism is a spurious Trinitarian formula added to the Bible later to support their unbiblical beliefs. This is thought because the Apostles never use this formula during any of the baptisms that they perform in the Bible. It would seem that if this were a real teaching then the Apostles would have obeyed the command at least one time. I will let you make up your own mind regarding this verse. Elsewhere in the Bible people are baptized into Jesus' name only.

The instructions in the great commission is for the Apostles to teach, which is the spreading of the Gospel informing those that might be saved of the deeds of Christ the Lord giving them the opportunity to accept salvation. After the new disciple accepts the teaching of salvation they are baptized. At this baptism the new disciple confesses Christ as their Lord and Savior (Matthew 10:31), repents and has their sins forgiven, and receives the gift of the Holy Spirit (Acts 2:38). The next step in the great commission is for the new disciple to be taught again to observe all of the things that Christ commanded. It is at this phase of the great commission that the disciple studies the word of God, with the assistance of the Holy Spirit helping them to spiritually discern the scriptures, and writes God's commandment on the tablets of their hearts.

(KJV) Ephesians 1:13 In whom ye also trusted, after that ye heard the word of truth, the gospel of your salvation: in whom also after that ye believed, ye were sealed with that holy Spirit of promise,

(KJV) Acts 2:38 Then Peter said unto them, Repent, and be baptized every one of you in the name of Jesus Christ for the remission of sins, and ye shall receive the gift of the Holy Ghost.

(KJV) Acts 9:17-18 And Ananias went his way, and entered into the house; and putting his hands on him said, Brother Saul, the Lord, even Jesus, that appeared unto thee in the way as thou camest, hath sent me, that thou mightest receive thy sight, and be filled with the Holy Ghost. 18 And immediately there fell from his eyes as it had been scales: and he received sight forthwith, and arose, and was baptized.

The above three sets of verses associate the gift of the Holy Spirit with baptism. The act of baptism is symbolic of the baptism of Christ. Like Christ when you come out of the water you will receive the gift of the Holy Spirit. You will not see (John 14:17) the Holy Spirit descend on you in the form of a dove, because this was only done for the sake of John the Baptist to know that Jesus is the one that he was waiting for (John 1:32). You will however receive the gift of the Holy Spirit, it has been promised by God (Acts 2:38). Being baptized is a requirement to get into Heaven.

(KJV) John 3:3-7 Jesus answered and said unto him, Verily, verily, I say unto thee, Except a man be born again, he cannot see the kingdom of God. 4 Nicodemus saith unto him, How can a man be born when he is old? can he enter the second time into his mother's womb, and be born? 5 Jesus answered, Verily, verily, I say unto thee, Except a man be born of water and of the Spirit, he cannot enter into the kingdom of God. 6 That which is born of the flesh is flesh; and that which is born of the Spirit is spirit. 7 Marvel not that I said unto thee, Ye must be born again.

When you are baptized you are baptized into Christ' death, so that like Christ you can be raised from the dead. When you accept Christ and are baptized, you die symbolically to your old sinful nature, and are reborn free from sin. At that time you also receive the gift of the Holy Spirit to assist you in the rest of your Christian walk.

(KJV) Colossians 2:12 Buried with him in baptism, wherein also ye are risen with him through the faith of the operation of God, who hath raised him from the dead.

John chapter 3 and Colossians chapter 2 is where the saying, *Born Again Christian* originated. Baptism is for the forgiveness of sins, and to receive the gift of the Holy Spirit. There is only one baptism and is for all people.

(KJV) 1 Corinthians 12:13 For by one Spirit are we all baptized into one body, whether we be Jews or Gentiles, whether we be bond or free; and have been all made to drink into one Spirit.

Ephesians 4:5 One Lord, one faith, one baptism,

We will examine a few more scriptures on baptism before we move on.

(KJV) Acts 8:36-38 And as they went on their way, they came unto a certain water: and the eunuch said, See, here is water; what doth hinder me to be baptized? 37 And Philip said, If thou believest with all thine heart, thou mayest. And he answered and said, I believe that Jesus Christ is the Son of God. 38 And he commanded the chariot to stand still: and they went down both into the water, both Philip and the eunuch; and he baptized him.

Acts 8:37 associates making the good confession, or confessing Christ with baptism.

(KJV) Galations 3:26-29 For ye are all the children of God by faith in Christ Jesus. 27 For as many of you as have been baptized into Christ have put on Christ. 28 There is neither Jew nor Greek, there is neither bond nor free, there is neither male nor female: for ye are all one in Christ Jesus. 29 And if ye be Christ's, then are ye Abraham's seed, and heirs according to the promise.

Once we are baptized we are all equal children of God.

(KJV) Mark 16:16 He that believeth and is baptized shall be saved; but he that believeth not shall be damned.

Once you believe and get baptized you are saved. The Holy Spirit will then assist you as you begin the great work of purifying your soul and conforming to the image of Christ. Now we will examine some other areas regarding the Holy Spirit.

(KJV) Matthew 12:31-32 Wherefore I say unto you, All manner of sin and blasphemy shall be forgiven unto men: but the blasphemy against the Holy Ghost shall not be forgiven unto men. 32 And whosoever speaketh a word against the Son of man,

it shall be forgiven him: but whosoever speaketh against the Holy Ghost, it shall not be forgiven him, neither in this world, neither in the world to come.

(KJV) Mark 3:29 But he that shall blaspheme against the Holy Ghost hath never forgiveness, but is in danger of eternal damnation:

(KJV) Luke 12:10 And whosoever shall speak a word against the Son of man, it shall be forgiven him: but unto him that blasphemeth against the Holy Ghost it shall not be forgiven.

Blaspheme against the Holy Spirit is the only unforgivable sin. But what exactly is blasphemy against the Holy Spirit? The above three sets of scripture are often used wrongly by false prophets to control Christians. These false prophets use these verses to prevent the people that fall into their trap from questioning any false statements the false prophet makes. The false prophet will claim be filled with the Holy Spirit and make any new rule or change any scripture to meet their desire, and if anyone questions them, they will immediately accuse the person of denying the Holy Spirit and threaten that if they don't rescind their objection then hellfire awaits the questioner. This is a misinterpretation of the above scriptures. The Bible tells us to test the doctrines and not to accept a doctrine that differs from the one taught in the scriptures.

(KJV) Romans 16:17-18 Now I beseech you, brethren, mark them which cause divisions and offences contrary to the doctrine which ye have learned; and avoid them. 18 For they that are such serve not our Lord Jesus Christ, but their own belly; and by good words and fair speeches deceive the hearts of the simple.

(KJV) Ephesians 4:14 That we henceforth be no more children, tossed to and fro, and carried about with every wind of doctrine, by the sleight of men, and cunning craftiness, whereby they lie in wait to deceive;

(KJV) 2 John 1:9-11 Whosoever transgresseth, and abideth not in the doctrine of Christ, hath not God. He that abideth in the doctrine of Christ, he hath both the Father and the Son. 10 If there come any unto you, and bring not this doctrine, receive him not into your house, neither bid him God speed: 11 For he that biddeth him God speed is partaker of his evil deeds.

(KJV) 1 John 4:2 Beloved, believe not every spirit, but try the spirits whether they are of God: because many false prophets are gone out into the world.

(KJV) Matthew 7:15 Beware of false prophets, which come to you in sheep's clothing, but inwardly they are ravening wolves.

The above sets of scripture makes it clear that if we are uncertain of the truth of what someone speaks, we are to test it against the scriptures. It is not blaspheming the Holy Spirit to question whether or not what somebody says conforms to the Bible. If the person's statements are not found in the Bible, then the statements are not from the Holy Spirit, because *the Holy Spirit inspired the writings in the Bible.* We are instructed in the Bible to rebuke and correct the doctrines or statements of others based on the scripture.

(KJV) 2 Timothy 3:16 All scripture is given by inspiration of God, and is profitable for doctrine, for reproof, for correction, for instruction in righteousness:

So what does constitute blaspheming the Holy Spirit? It is blaspheming the Work of the Holy Spirit. In Matthew chapter 12 and Mark chapter 3 Jesus was accused of casting out demons by the power of Satan. In Luke chapter 12 it was denying Christ. If something is based in scripture it is in accordance with the Holy Spirit. If something is not based on scripture, it is not from God (2 John 1:9). If you test the doctrines against the scriptures you will know whether or not you are blaspheming the Holy Spirit. As a Christian you are to be a follower of Christ, and to observe all the things in which you have been commanded (Matthew 28:20).

(KJV) Romans 2:22-24 Thou that sayest a man should not commit adultery, dost thou commit adultery? thou that abhorrest idols, dost thou commit sacrilege? 23 Thou that makest thy boast of the law, through breaking the law dishonourest thou God? 24 For the name of God is blasphemed among the Gentiles through you, as it is written.

Jesus Christ was conceived by the Holy Spirit; in the same way that Christ was conceived by the Spirit all Christians are also. When a person is baptized they are reborn with the Holy Spirit and our considered a new creation.

(KJV) Luke 1:35 And the angel answered and said unto her, The Holy Ghost shall come upon thee, and the power of the

Highest shall overshadow thee: therefore also that holy thing which shall be born of thee shall be called the Son of God.

John the Baptist was filled with the Holy Spirit before he was even born.

(KJV) Luke 1:15 For he shall be great in the sight of the Lord, and shall drink neither wine nor strong drink; and he shall be filled with the Holy Ghost, even from his mother's womb.

Your body is the temple of the Holy Spirit, and does not belong to you. At baptism you give yourself to the Lord. Jesus purchased you with his blood (Acts 20:28). Don't be surprised that you are not your own after baptism. Where you ever? If you build a house, does it belong to you, or do you need to wait for the thing you created to give itself to you before you own it? We have never been our own; we are the creation. Our bodies belonging to someone else is also taught in relation to marriage. Husbands and wives bodies belong to each other. This is fitting in the situation because the church is also considered Christ's bride. Being baptized into Christ is an extremely important event comparable with marriage. Baptism is a commitment that will last forever, you promise to live your life faithfully to God.

(KJV) 1 Corinthians 6:19-20 What? know ye not that your body is the temple of the Holy Ghost which is in you, which ye have of God, and ye are not your own? 20 ye are bought with a price: therefore glorify God in your body, and in your spirit, which are God's.

Your actions can grieve the Holy Spirit.

(KJV) Ephesians 4:29-30 Let no corrupt communication proceed out of your mouth, but that which is good to the use of edifying, that it may minister grace unto the hearers. 30 And grieve not the holy Spirit of God, whereby ye are sealed unto the day of redemption.

Now we will look at some verses regarding building a strong foundation in the Lord.

(KJV) 1 Corinthians 3:9-13 For we are labourers together with God: ye are God's husbandry, ye are God's building. 10 According to the grace of God which is given unto me, as a wise masterbuilder, I have laid the foundation, and another buildeth

thereon. But let every man take heed how he buildeth thereupon. 11 For other foundation can no man lay than that is laid, which is Jesus Christ. 12 Now if any man build upon this foundation gold, silver, precious stones, wood, hay, stubble; 13 Every man's work shall be made manifest: for the day shall declare it, because it shall be revealed by fire; and the fire shall try every man's work of what sort it is.

(KJV) 1 Corinthians 3:16-17 Know ye not that ye are the temple of God, and that the Spirit of God dwelleth in you? 17 If any man defile the temple of God, him shall God destroy; for the temple of God is holy, which temple ye are.

Our bodies are the Temple of God, and the Holy Spirit dwells within us to assist us in perfecting our temple. The foundation that we are to build on is a foundation based on the teachings of Christ. We will be judged based of how we build on this foundation, because we will be tried with fire.

(KJV) Luke 6:47-49 Whosoever cometh to me, and heareth my sayings, and doeth them, I will show you to whom he is like: 48 He is like a man which built an house, and digged deep, and laid the foundation on a rock: and when the flood arose, the stream beat vehemently upon that house, and could not shake it: for it was founded upon a rock. 49 But he that heareth, and doeth not, is like a man that without a foundation built an house upon the earth; against which the stream did beat vehemently, and immediately it fell; and the ruin of that house was great.

The above set of verses further elaborates on the need for us to build a strong foundation, which is one based on the principles that Christ taught.

(KJV) Ephesians 2:20-22 And are built upon the foundation of the apostles and prophets, Jesus Christ himself being the chief corner stone; 21 In whom all the building fitly framed together groweth unto an holy temple in the Lord: 22 In whom ye also are builded together for an habitation of God through the Spirit.

We are to build our temples as a holy dwelling place for the Lord through the Holy Spirit.

(KJV) 2 Timothy 2:19 Nevertheless the foundation of God standeth sure, having this seal, The Lord knoweth them that are his. And, Let every one that nameth the name of Christ depart from iniquity. 20 But in a great house there are not only vessels of gold and of silver, but also of wood and of earth; and some to honour, and some to dishonour. 21 If a man therefore purge himself from these, he shall be a vessel unto honour, sanctified, and meet for the master's use, and prepared unto every good work. 22 Flee also youthful lusts: but follow righteousness, faith, charity, peace, with them that call on the Lord out of a pure heart.

The above set of verses tell us that we need to depart from iniquity and live a righteous life, so that we are fit for the masters use. We are to make our temple holy so that we will become a vessel of honor, and be prepared for every good work.

(KJV) 1 Peter 1:19 But with the precious blood of Christ, as of a lamb without blemish and without spot: 20 Who verily was foreordained before the foundation of the world, but was manifest in these last times for you, 21 Who by him do believe in God, that raised him up from the dead, and gave him glory; that your faith and hope might be in God. 22 Seeing ye have purified your souls in obeying the truth through the Spirit unto unfeigned love of the brethren, see that ye love one another with a pure heart fervently: 23 Being born again, not of corruptible seed, but of incorruptible, by the word of God, which liveth and abideth for ever.

We purify our souls by obeying the truth given to us through the Holy Spirit. We are born again at baptism and need to keep ourselves from being corrupted; this is done by obeying the word of God.

(KJV) Matthew 16:16 And Simon Peter answered and said, Thou art the Christ, the Son of the living God.

Jesus Christ is the son of the living God. This is the good confession that accompanies baptism.

(KJV) 2 Corinthians 6:16 And what agreement hath the temple of God with idols? for ye are the temple of the living God; as God hath said, I will dwell in them, and walk in them; and I will be their God, and they shall be my people.

Before Jesus was crucified a priest would enter the Holiest of Holies to make atonement for the sins of the people (Leviticus 16:15-16). The priest would do this once a year, and not without bringing a sacrifice (Hebrews 9:7). When Christ died on the cross He was the final sacrifice obtaining eternal redemption for us all (Hebrews 9:12). Once Christ died the Veil to the Holiest of Holies was torn in two (Matthew 27:51), because man no longer needs to send a priest into the Holiest of Holies to make sacrifices for our sins. Christ is now our High Priest, which is building a perfect tabernacle in us. Not the physical temple, but the spiritual one.

(KJV) Hebrews 9:11 But Christ being come an high priest of good things to come, by a greater and more perfect tabernacle, not made with hands, that is to say, not of this building; 12 Neither by the blood of goats and calves, but by his own blood he entered in once into the holy place, having obtained eternal redemption for us.

Since the death of Christ the earthly version of the Holiest of Holies is no longer necessary. Now Jesus is our high priest and mediator, who was also the final sacrifice for our sins.

(KJV) Hebrews 9:15 And for this cause he is the mediator of the new testament, that by means of death, for the redemption of the transgressions that were under the first testament, they which are called might receive the promise of eternal inheritance.

In the Old Testament the priest would enter into the Holiest of Holies once a year. Jesus as our new high priest takes our atonement directly to God in Heaven once and for all.

(KJV) Hebrews 9:24 For Christ is not entered into the holy places made with hands, which are the figures of the true; but into heaven itself, now to appear in the presence of God for us: 25 Nor yet that he should offer himself often, as the high priest entereth into the holy place every year with blood of others; 26 For then must he often have suffered since the foundation of the world: but now once in the end of the world hath he appeared to put away sin by the sacrifice of himself. 27 And as it is appointed unto men once to die, but after this the judgment: 28 So Christ was once offered to bear the sins of many; and unto them that look for him shall he appear the second time without sin unto salvation.

Christ will come for those that look to Him, and at His second coming He will fulfill all of His promises He has made to those that confess His name. Those that take up their crosses and follow Him will be given a Crown of Life, they will be allowed to eat from the Tree of Life, drink from the River of Life, and will be given eternal life. As Christians we are to be conformed to the image of Christ (Romans 8:29). Christ's bride is the church, and the members of the Church are called to be Christ like.

(KJV) Matthew 27:51 And, behold, the veil of the temple was rent in twain from the top to the bottom; and the earth did quake, and the rocks rent;

(KJV) Mark 15:38-39 And the veil of the temple was rent in twain from the top to the bottom.

This veil was torn in two from top to bottom the moment that Jesus died on the cross. It was torn from the top to the bottom meaning that God is the one that tore it. The spiritual temple that we are being built into represents the new way of worshipping God through our spirit (John 4:23). This is the Temple made without hands the Jesus was prophesized in the Old Testament to build.

(KJV) Zechariah 6:12-15 And speak unto him, saying, Thus speaketh the LORD of hosts, saying, Behold the man whose name is The BRANCH; and he shall grow up out of his place, and he shall build the temple of the LORD: 13 Even he shall build the temple of the LORD; and he shall bear the glory, and shall sit and rule upon his throne; and he shall be a priest upon his throne: and the counsel of peace shall be between them both.

Jesus is the Branch as he was a descendant of King David. Jesus is prophesized to build the Temple of the Lord. He will sit on His throne and also be the high priest of the temple. Jesus stated when He was still alive that He would rebuild the Temple within three days.

(KJV) Mark 14:58 We heard him say, I will destroy this temple that is made with hands, and within three days I will build another made without hands.

(KJV) John 2:19- Jesus answered and said unto them, Destroy this temple, and in three days I will raise it up. 20 Then said the Jews, Forty and six years was this temple in building, and wilt thou rear it up in three days? 21 But he spake of the temple of his body. 22 When therefore he was risen from the dead, his disciples remembered that he had said this unto them; and they believed the scripture, and the word which Jesus had said.

Jesus was speaking of His crucifixion and resurrection. After Jesus died on the cross he arose on the third day. In the above verses Jesus is speaking of His body as the Temple. Our bodies are also the Temple of God and the dwelling place of the Holy Spirit (1 Corinthians 3:16).

> **(KJV) Ephesians 2:19-22** Now therefore ye are no more strangers and foreigners, but fellow citizens with the saints, and of the household of God; 20 And are built upon the foundation of the apostles and prophets, Jesus Christ himself being the chief corner stone; 21 In whom all the building fitly framed together groweth unto an holy temple in the Lord: 22 In whom ye also are builded together for an habitation of God through the Spirit.

> **(KJV) 2 Corinthians 6:16-18** And what agreement hath the temple of God with idols? for ye are the temple of the living God; as God hath said, I will dwell in them, and walk in them; and I will be their God, and they shall be my people. 17 Wherefore come out from among them, and be ye separate, saith the Lord, and touch not the unclean thing; and I will receive you, 18 And will be a Father unto you, and ye shall be my sons and daughters, saith the Lord Almighty.

We are of the household of God, and therefore are called to separate ourselves from the rest of the world. We are called to overcome the sins of the world and to live a righteous life. When Jesus died on the cross He rebuilt the temple in three days referring to His own body. We as Christians are also considered members of the body of Christ (1 Corinthians 12:12-27).

> **(KJV) Romans 7:4** Wherefore, my brethren, ye also are become dead to the law by the body of Christ; that ye should be married to another, even to him who is raised from the dead, that we should bring forth fruit unto God

The above verse refers to Christians as both of the body of Christ and as His bride. Christ rebuilt the temple in three days by His resurrection from the dead. Christ is also building the Temple of the Lord in each individual Christian that follows Him (1 Corinthians 3:16). Finally Christ will rebuild the temple physically on the earth at His second coming (Revelations 21:22-24).

> **(KJV) Revelations 3:12** Him that overcometh will I make a pillar in the temple of my God, and he shall go no more out: and I will write upon him the name of my God, and the name of the city of my God, which is new Jerusalem, which cometh down out of heaven from my God: and I will write upon him my new name.

REFERENCES

Scripture taken from the KING JAMES VERSION OF THE BIBLE, (KJV) Public Domain 1611

Christian Titles and Growth

As we grow as Christians we will go through a few different phases of growth and be referred to by different titles. These different Christian titles have to do with where we are in our relationship with God and should affect our actions.

> **(KJV) Psalm 111:10 The fear of the LORD is the beginning of wisdom: a good understanding have all they that do his commandments: his praise endureth for ever.**

> **(KJV) Proverbs 1:7 The fear of the LORD is the beginning of knowledge: but fools despise wisdom and instruction.**

> **(KJV) Proverbs 8:13 The fear of the LORD is to hate evil: pride, and arrogancy, and the evil way, and the froward mouth, do I hate.**

> **(KJV) Prverbs 14:26 In the fear of the LORD is strong confidence: and his children shall have a place of refuge. 27 The fear of the LORD is a fountain of life, to depart from the snares of death.**

> **(KJV) Proverbs 15:33 The fear of the LORD is the instruction of wisdom; and before honour is humility.**

> **(KJV) Proverbs 16:6 By mercy and truth iniquity is purged: and by the fear of the LORD men depart from evil. 7 When a man's ways please the LORD, he maketh even his enemies to be at peace with him.**

For most new Christians the first phase they will go through is the Fear of the Lord. This is where the person recognizes that they are a sinner and are deserving of punishment. At this state the person realizes that they should fear the wrath of God and respect His authority. This is the stage the person first begins working to overcome their sins, and first begins to gain wisdom.

> **(KJV) Rom 6:16 Know ye not, that to whom ye yield yourselves servants to obey, his servants ye are to whom ye obey; whether of sin unto death, or of obedience unto righteousness?**

> **(KJV) Rom 6:18 Being then made free from sin, ye became the servants of righteousness.19 I speak after the manner of men**

because of the infirmity of your flesh: for as ye have yielded your members servants to uncleanness and to iniquity unto iniquity; even so now yield your members servants to righteousness unto holiness.

(KJV) Rom 6:22 But now being made free from sin, and become servants to God, ye have your fruit unto holiness, and the end everlasting life.

(KJV) 1 Corth 7:22-23 For he that is called in the Lord, being a servant, is the Lord's freeman: likewise also he that is called, being free, is Christ's servant. **23** Ye are bought with a price; be not ye the servants of men.

The next title we will discuss is that of *Slave or Servant* (depending on which Bible translation you are reading). After receiving the Fear of the Lord and first receiving wisdom you will witness that you had previously been a slave to sin. When you first become a Christian you become a slave to Christ because you were redeemed from sin and bought at a price.

Your role as a slave is one of obedience. When you first become a Christian you do not possess the wisdom of a seasoned Christian. You have the Fear of the Lord and know that you need to follow the Bible, but you likely do not have a very good understanding of it. You are a slave because at this point you are not following the Bible because you understand the concepts in it or its beauty, but you are following it as a slave obeying it because you know that you have to in order to please your master.

(KJV) Gal 4:1 Now I say, That the heir, as long as he is a child, differeth nothing from a servant, though he be lord of all; **2** But is under tutors and governors until the time appointed of the father.

The next role that Christians take on is that of a Child. As a Child you are not that different than a servant, you follow instructions not understanding completely, but you do so to please your father. The change from servant to child is mainly in understanding God's love for you. The servant obeys out of fear or because they know that they have to fulfill their responsibilities and earn their wages. The child realizes that they are loved, and obeys because he recognizes that it is in his own best interest to do so. The child doesn't understand everything fully, but understands that he must obey and continue learning.

(KJV) Mt 18:3-4 And said, Verily I say unto you, Except ye be converted, and become as little children, ye shall not enter into the kingdom of heaven. 4 Whosoever therefore shall humble himself as this little child, the same is greatest in the kingdom of heaven.

(KJV) Ro 8:14-16 For as many as are led by the Spirit of God, they are the sons of God. 15 For ye have not received the spirit of bondage again to fear; but ye have received the Spirit of adoption, whereby we cry, Abba, Father. 16 The Spirit itself beareth witness with our spirit, that we are the children of God:

It is necessary for Christians to be born again. This is how you humble yourself as a little child in order to enter the Kingdom of Heaven. This is done at baptism when you symbolically die and are buried with Christ. You become a new creation; sealed for redemption by the Holy Spirit of promise. You receive the Holy Spirit at baptism and become a new creation conceived by the Holy Spirit just as Christ was in the womb of Mary. This is where you first begin your walk in the family of God.

As we discuss these titles some of them are going to overlap, because you actually are in several of these phases at the same time. You are child, slave, and possess the Fear of God at the beginning of your Christian walk, but we are breaking these titles down separately because they each contain slightly different characteristics that you will possess during your Christian walk.

(KJV) Php 2:25 Yet I supposed it necessary to send to you Epaphroditus, my brother, and companion in labour, and fellowsoldier, but your messenger, and he that ministered to my wants.

(KJV) 2 Tim 2:3-4 Thou therefore endure hardness, as a good soldier of Jesus Christ. 4 No man that warreth entangleth himself with the affairs of this life; that he may please him who hath chosen him to be a soldier.

(KJV) Phm 1:2 And to our beloved Apphia, and Archippus our fellowsoldier, and to the church in thy house:

As you progress out of the slave phase you move into the soldier phase. Soldiers fight for a cause. Soldiers are willing to place their lives on the line to obey orders, where slaves merely work. Soldiers not only follow orders, but are willing to endure hardship and danger to follow their leader.

(KJV) Ga 4:3-7 Even so we, when we were children, were in bondage under the elements of the world: 4 But when the fulness of the time was come, God sent forth his Son, made of a woman, made under the law, 5 To redeem them that were under the law, that we might receive the adoption of sons. 6 And because ye are sons, God hath sent forth the Spirit of his Son into your hearts, crying, Abba, Father. 7 Wherefore thou art no more a servant, but a son; and if a son, then an heir of God through Christ.

(KJV) Rom 8:17 And if children, then heirs; heirs of God, and joint-heirs with Christ; if so be that we suffer with him, that we may be also glorified together.

As you progress out of the Child phase you are also recognized as a co-heir with Christ. You are God's adopted child and Christ's brethren. You are not following orders as a soldier or a slave, nor out of fear, but you are accepted into the family of God. You are loved, and you love God in return. You trust each other and are willing to die for your family.

(KJV) Rev 21:9 And there came unto me one of the seven angels which had the seven vials full of the seven last plagues, and talked with me, saying, Come hither, I will show thee the bride, the Lamb's wife.

(KJV) Eph 5:22-33 Wives, submit yourselves unto your own husbands, as unto the Lord. 23 For the husband is the head of the wife, even as Christ is the head of the church: and he is the saviour of the body. 24 Therefore as the church is subject unto Christ, so let the wives be to their own husbands in every thing. 25 Husbands, love your wives, even as Christ also loved the church, and gave himself for it; 26 That he might sanctify and cleanse it with the washing of water by the word, 27 That he might present it to himself a glorious church, not having spot, or wrinkle, or any such thing; but that it should be holy and without blemish. 28 So ought men to love their wives as their own bodies. He that loveth his wife loveth himself. 29 For no man ever yet hated his own flesh; but nourisheth and cherisheth it, even as the Lord the church: 30 For we are members of his body, of his flesh, and of his bones. 31 For this cause shall a man leave his father and mother, and shall be joined unto his wife, and they two shall be one flesh. 32 This is a great mystery: but I speak concerning Christ and the church. 33 Nevertheless let every one of you in particular so love his wife even as himself; and the wife see that she reverence her husband.

The final title given to Christians is that of the Bride. As the Bride you have an even higher status than the child. Husbands and wives become one flesh and share everything; this is an even greater status than co-heir. As the Bride we are the female counter part and are still subject to the husband, but it is a large stretch from slave.

The different titles that Christians are referred to as possess different qualities. At first we are slaves obeying out of fear, because we first recognized our sins and saw the need to change. At this phase we are children or babies, not yet understanding the wisdom we are now being exposed to.

As we progress we stop following out of fear or service and start following because we believe in it and support it. This is the phase of the soldier. We are doing our duty and fighting for something that we believe in.

Next we are Sons of God and co-heirs. At this phase we understand what it means to be apart of the family that we are in, and we are active and accepted family members. We are obedient children living to please our father as we are being raised and growing into perfection; sealed for redemption by the Holy Spirit.

Once we are adults we become the Bride, our love and our understandings are full. We are prepared to make a life long commitment and to be faithful.

REFERENCES

Scripture taken from the KING JAMES VERSION OF THE BIBLE, (KJV) Public Domain 1611

Female Preachers and Roles

(KJV) 1 Tim 2:11-15 Let the woman learn in silence with all subjection. 12 But I suffer not a woman to teach, nor to usurp authority over the man, but to be in silence. 13 For Adam was first formed, then Eve. 14 And Adam was not deceived, but the woman being deceived was in the transgression. 15 Notwithstanding she shall be saved in childbearing, if they continue in faith and charity and holiness with sobriety.

The Bible makes it clear that women are not to be teachers in the church. Women are to be in subjection to men. In today's culture women have more rights than ever before, but it is culture that has change and not scripture. The Bible does not say that women are inferior to men. The Bible teaches that all are one with Christ (Gal 3:28). The Bible does not say that women are of less value than a man, but states that women are not supposed to exert authority over a man in regards to teaching in the church.

Many women in today's society of equal rights are offended by the role of women in the Bible, but there really is no reason to be. The Bible does not say that women are too stupid to teach nor does it teach that they are not valuable. Women are supposed to teach, it just isn't their role to teach in the worship service at church. Women have an extremely important role in the Bible; they are to teach their children and manage their households.

(KJV) 1 Tim 5:14 I will therefore that the younger women marry, bear children, guide the house, give none occasion to the adversary to speak reproachfully.

(KJV) Titus 2:2 That the aged men be sober, grave, temperate, sound in faith, in charity, in patience. 3 The aged women likewise, that they be in behaviour as becometh holiness, not false accusers, not given to much wine, teachers of good things; 4 That they may teach the young women to be sober, to love their husbands, to love their children, 5 To be discreet, chaste, keepers at home, good, obedient to their own husbands, that the word of God be not blasphemed.

Women play a huge role as teachers. Women are the ones that teach their sons, which will eventually be leading the worship services. The wisdom and values that mothers teach their children are the same values their sons will later teach to the congregation. Children are a gift from God, and their care is of far more value than a Sunday school lesson.

It is vanity and a lack of humility that offends women when they are prevented by scripture from teaching in the worship service. This is just one event in one area of life. Everyone is to be in subjection to someone else in some area of life. Just because Adam was made first and Eve was created to be his help mate, that doesn't make women any less valuable nor does it diminish the important roles they play.

(KJV) Deut 22:5 The woman shall not wear that which pertaineth unto a man, neither shall a man put on a woman's garment: for all that do so are abomination unto the LORD thy God.

The role of the preacher of a church is a man's role. Churches that allow female preachers are acting in direct defiance to the Bible. A woman does not prove herself to be a good pastor by acting in direct defiance to the word of God. In doing so she is repeating the exact same mistake that Eve made, which is the very reason she is told not to teach at church in the first place (1 Tim 2:14).

(KJV) 1Pe 3:1 Likewise, ye wives, be in subjection to your own husbands; that, if any obey not the word, they also may without the word be won by the conversation of the wives;

(KJV) 1Cor 11:3 But I would have you know, that the head of every man is Christ; and the head of the woman is the man; and the head of Christ is God.

The Bible is clear that women are to be in subjection to their husbands, but the Bible also makes it clear that husbands and wives are to be equal partners acting in unison as one flesh. Women are just not supposed to teach in the church service; this is a reasonable request. The Bible states that women are not to teach in church because they may be deceived and lead others astray. This is not an attack on women, but is learning by example. The same way that women shouldn't repeat Eve's mistake, men should not repeat the mistakes of other men in the Bible. The Bible states why women are not to teach in church and also provides us with examples.

(KJV) Re 2:20-22 Notwithstanding I have a few things against thee, because thou sufferest that woman Jezebel, which calleth herself a prophetess, to teach and to seduce my servants to

commit fornication, and to eat things sacrificed unto idols. 21 And I gave her space to repent of her fornication; and she repented not. 22 Behold, I will cast her into a bed, and them that commit adultery with her into great tribulation, except they repent of their deeds.

The woman in the above verses is an example of a woman preacher leading others astray. Being the preacher of a church is only one role; women should move beyond it and look at their more important role of raising children.

(KJV) Gal 4:4 But when the fulness of the time was come, God sent forth his Son, made of a woman, made under the law, 5 To redeem them that were under the law, that we might receive the adoption of sons.

Mary gave birth to and brought up the very Son of God. Women's roles should not be under stressed. Both men and women have their specific lots in life. Believe me, many men would choose not to work by the sweat of their brow because of Adam's mistake, but we are each given our specific roles by God and we need to be willing to drink the cup our father has prepared for us just as Christ was willing to do (John 18:11, Matt 26:42).

REFERENCES

Scripture taken from the KING JAMES VERSION OF THE BIBLE, (KJV) Public Domain 1611

Masturbation, Lust, Pornography, and Modesty

In the Bible Masturbation falls under the general category of sexual immorality. In the Old Testament there were many specific laws regarding Sexual Immorality such as; don't have sex with your father's wife or daughter-in-law (Leviticus 20:11-12), don't practice homosexuality (Leviticus 20:13), and don't have sex with animals (Leviticus 20:15-16). Masturbation is not addressed independently, but it is addressed in the New Testament in relation to lust as you will see in this study.

> **(KJV) Mt 5:27-28 Ye have heard that it was said by them of old time, Thou shalt not commit adultery: 28 But I say unto you, That whosoever looketh on a woman to lust after her hath committed adultery with her already in his heart.**

Jesus made it clear that if you lust after a woman, then you have already committed adultery with her in your heart and have sinned. The act of masturbation incorporates sexual fantasizing in most all cases. By sexually fantasizing you are committing the same sin as if you committed it physically. You are guilty of adultery and/or fornication.

> **(KJV) Mark 7:20-23 And he said, That which cometh out of the man, that defileth the man. 21 For from within, out of the heart of men, proceed evil thoughts, adulteries, fornications, murders, 22 Thefts, covetousness, wickedness, deceit, lasciviousness, an evil eye, blasphemy, pride, foolishness: 23 All these evil things come from within, and defile the man.**

> **(KJV) James 1:14-15 But each one is tempted when he is drawn away by his own desires and enticed. 15 Then, when desire has conceived, it gives birth to sin; and sin, when it is full-grown, brings forth death.**

It is your thoughts that defile you. Your thoughts are where sin begins. Sin begins in your mind. Each time you fantasize you focus on sin, and you allow your mind to become more and more corrupted. People do not accidentally become serial killers or rapists. These people's crimes start out as fantasies. The more they fantasize the more they accept these actions as legitimate possibilities. Eventually their fantasies cease to be fantasies, and turn into crimes being planned out.

Crimes do not merely have to be the earthy crimes committed by rapists and serial killers, but can also be crimes against God by breaking His commandments. If you are married and you masturbate then you are cheating on your spouse and breaking one of the Ten Commandments. You are committing a sin that in the Old Testament was punishable with death (Leviticus 20:10) and in the New Testament is punishable with hell (Galatians 5:19). If you are single and you masturbate then you are committing fornication and sexual immorality, which is deserving of hell in the New Testament (Galatians 5:19).

In this modern age we live in, condoms are distributed at schools and states are debating on whether or not children should be required to inform their parents before they have an abortion. In this day in age it is possible for you to find churches that will tell you that masturbation is okay. They are wrong! What culture teaches as politically correct is nothing other than sin. Of course children should be required to inform their parents before having an abortion. If there ever was a time when a child needed their parent's guidance, advice, and assistance it is during an unplanned pregnancy.

Some churches may tell their young people that masturbation is perfectly okay, or may even be a desirable way of controlling lust, but they are wrong. You do not overcome the sin of lust by lusting, just like you do not overcome an addition to cigarettes by smoking a cigarette. The only way to overcome temptation is to resist it. Giving into temptation will only make is easier to give in to it again the next time. The Bible makes it perfectly clear that masturbation is not an appropriate way to control your lust.

(KJV) 1 Cor 7:9 But if they cannot contain, let them marry: for it is better to marry than to burn.

In the above verse Paul states that it is better to marry than to burn with lust. Paul advises Christian's to make a lifelong commitment to another person in place of burning with lust. In the Bible once you are married your body then belongs to your spouse, and isn't even yours anymore. If lust could have been controlled by simply masturbating then Paul would not have advised such an extreme action as making a lifelong commitment to another person. If masturbation were an option for Christians then it would have been presented as the solution in the above verse.

Masturbation is not an option for Christians. Masturbation is not a way of controlling your lust. It is a way of giving into your lust. Masturbation causes you to commit adultery/fornication in your mind and it is a sin. Besides masturbation causing you to sin it will also increase your lust. If you masturbate, within fifteen minutes the semen you expelled will be replaced. Masturbation will not get rid of lust, but will cause you to lust more often, and will require your body to produce testosterone more rapidly.

If you resist your lust it will continue to decrease until it almost goes away completely. When someone first stops smoking cigarettes they have a strong desire for a cigarette. If they give into smoking they will keep this desire at the same level indefinitely. If however they fight off their urge and choose not to smoke for several weeks, their desire to smoke will be almost non-existent. The same concept applies to masturbation. If you give into lust you will maintain the same level of lust or greater. If you expel semen your body will produce more within minutes. Giving into your lust will not prevent you from lusting, but will cause you to walk around in a constant state of arousal.

Masturbation can damage many areas of your life. Besides increasing your lustfulness and temptation to sin, you also train yourself to climax very quickly, which can drastically damage your future sex life. When people masturbate they are usually ashamed (because they are able to sense in their conscience that they are sinning), they don't want to get caught so they masturbate as quickly as possible. This conditions them to climax in a matter of minutes or even seconds, which can be very damaging to the person's future sex life.

Once the person finally gets married and attempts to actually have sex with another person, they will find their performance is severally hampered. They will experience premature ejaculation or climax very quickly during sexual intercourse. They will be poor sexual performers and will find it almost impossible to meet their partner's needs or to fulfill their marital responsibilities. This can cause trouble in the marriage or if nothing else in the person's self-esteem.

Masturbators may also associate their sexual organs with shame and guilt. If this is experienced during puberty it can affect the development of their sexual organs. It can cause the person to have an under developed sexual organ. By masturbating a boy can cause himself to grow into a man that walks around consumed with lustful thoughts, possesses a low self-esteem, has a small penis, and is a poor sexual performer.

The more semen your body discharges the more it will replace. Masturbators will find themselves plagued by wet dreams when they don't masturbate. If you resist your lusts, your body may have nocturnal emissions one to three times a year, where as those that train their bodies to produce semen rapidly may find they have that many per month or week.

Masturbation and Sexual Perversion are sins because they cause you to sin in your mind, and it is what starts in a person's mind that defiles them. Even sexual relationships within a marriage can be sinful. If a married couple engages in role-playing games those too can be inappropriate fantasies. For example what does it mean to play doctor? Are you not making believe that you are a doctor or patient crossing the lines of the doctor patient relationship? If you are playing role-playing games such as this are you imagining that in the role-playing game you are actually marriage to the doctor/patient? You are more than likely fantasizing a situation in which you are having sex with somebody other than your spouse.

What role-playing sex game seems appropriate to you? Cops and robbers, master and slave, doctor and patient, realtor and client, do any of these seem appropriate to you? In every one of these role-playing scenarios you are practicing unethical professional behavior as well as cheating on your spouse. Is cheating on your spouse something that you feel is a good idea to practice? Even in a healthy marriage controlling and avoiding the lust of your mind is something that you should take into consideration.

(KJV) Gen 2:18 And the Lord God said, "It is not good that man should be alone; I will make him a helper comparable to him."

(KJV) 1 Cor 7:2 Nevertheless, to avoid fornication, let every man have his own wife, and let every woman have her own husband.

Marriage is a holy institution and is the appropriate way of handling your sexual lusts. If you are not married then you need to resist your sexual urges the same way that an ex-smoker resists the urge for a cigarette. This is the only way to lessen your lusts, and get it under control.

(KJV) 1 Tim 5:6 But she that liveth in pleasure is dead while she liveth.

(KJV) 1 Cor 9:27 But I discipline my body and bring it into subjection, lest, when I have preached to others, I myself should become disqualified.

(KJV) Romans 6:12-13 Let not sin therefore reign in your mortal body, that ye should obey it in the lusts thereof. 13 Neither yield ye your members as instruments of unrighteousness unto sin: but yield yourselves unto God, as those that are alive from the dead, and your members as instruments of righteousness unto God.

The best way to discipline your body and control your lusts is to resist your urges until they go away. Our bodies are to be instruments of righteousness. We must learn to control are members.

(KJV) James 4:1 From whence come wars and fightings among you? come they not hence, even of your lusts that war in your members?

(KJV) 1 Peter 2:11 Dearly beloved, I beseech you as strangers and pilgrims, abstain from fleshly lusts, which war against the soul;

(KJV) Col 3:5-6 Mortify therefore your members which are upon the earth; fornication, uncleanness, inordinate affection, evil concupiscence, and covetousness, which is idolatry: 6 For which things' sake the wrath of God cometh on the children of disobedience:

To gain mastery over our members we are instructed to abstain from giving into our lusts.

(KJV) 1 Cor 9:25 And every man that striveth for the mastery is temperate in all things. Now they do it to obtain a corruptible crown; but we an incorruptible. 26 I therefore so run, not as uncertainly; so fight I, not as one that beateth the air: 27 But I keep under my body, and bring it into subjection: lest that by any means, when I have preached to others, I myself should be a castaway.

(KJV) 1 Cor 6:15 Know ye not that your bodies are the members of Christ? shall I then take the members of Christ, and make them the members of an harlot? God forbid. 16 What? know ye not that he which is joined to an harlot is one body? for two, saith he, shall be one flesh. 17 But he that is joined unto the Lord is one spirit. 18 Flee fornication. Every sin that a man doeth is without the body; but he that committeth fornication sinneth against his own body. 19 What? know ye not that your body is the temple of the Holy Ghost which is in you, which ye have of God, and ye are not your own? 20 For ye are bought with a price: therefore glorify God in your body, and in your spirit, which are God's.

As Christians our bodies are members of the body of Christ. Sexual sin is a sin against our own bodies. We are told to flee fornication, obtain mastery over our members, and be temperate in all things. We are to keep our bodies in subjection, and keep ourselves holy.

> **(KJV) 1 Cor 6:9-10 Know ye not that the unrighteous shall not inherit the kingdom of God? Be not deceived: neither fornicators, nor idolaters, nor adulterers, nor effeminate, nor abusers of themselves with mankind, 10 Nor thieves, nor covetous, nor drunkards, nor revilers, nor extortioners, shall inherit the kingdom of God.**

> **(KJV) Gal 5:19-21 Now the works of the flesh are manifest, which are these; Adultery, fornication, uncleanness, lasciviousness, 20 Idolatry, witchcraft, hatred, variance, emulations, wrath, strife, seditions, heresies, 21 Envyings, murders, drunkenness, revellings, and such like: of the which I tell you before, as I have also told you in time past, that they which do such things shall not inherit the kingdom of God.**

Lust (lasciviousness), adultery, and fornication are included in the lists of things that will prevent you from entering the Kingdom of Heaven. Do not allow some liberal church to tell you that masturbation or sexual immorality is an acceptable sin. It isn't. It doesn't matter what the modern churches teach you, it matters what the scriptures say. Paul didn't consider masturbation as an alternative to burning with desire and Jesus stated that to fantasize is to commit adultery; don't allow modern churches to tell you anything different. Don't let modern liberals deceive you. It is because of these sins that the wrath of God will fall on the children of disobedience; don't be included with these people.

> **(KJV) Eph 5:3-7 But fornication, and all uncleanness, or covetousness, let it not be once named among you, as becometh saints; 4 Neither filthiness, nor foolish talking, nor jesting, which are not convenient: but rather giving of thanks. 5 For this ye know, that no whoremonger, nor unclean person, nor covetous man, who is an idolater, hath any inheritance in the kingdom of Christ and of God. 6 Let no man deceive you with vain words: for because of these things cometh the wrath of God upon the children of disobedience. 7 Be not ye therefore partakers with them.**

Many people that participate in masturbation also use pornography. Pornography exists for no other purpose than to cause people to lust. Pornography causes people to sin because it feeds their lusts and evil desires. Pornography causes people to covet and boosts people's evil or sinful desires. It doesn't matter if you are reading a magazine or watching a movie, any time spent on pornography is too much. How much time in a day do you need to spend observing situations that encourage fornication and adultery? How many times do you think you should premeditate cheating on your spouse in your mind?

In the Old Testament just having the desire to see someone naked was a sin (Leviticus CH18). Coveting is a sin of the mind, and it leads to all other sins.

(KJV) Deut 5:21 Neither shalt thou desire thy neighbour's wife, neither shalt thou covet thy neighbour's house, his field, or his manservant, or his maidservant, his ox, or his ass, or any thing that is thy neighbour's.

Before any of the other Ten Commandments are broken people first covet in their minds. Once a person lusts after another person's property then the person lies, cheats, murders, or steals in order to commit adultery or take whatever item belongs to their neighbor. Pornography reinforces a person's desire to sin. Pornography causes people to be consumed with lust and leads some people into becoming rapists, child molesters, and/or murders.

If you utilize pornography then you are supporting this kind of behavior. If you purchase pornography your money goes to pay other people to commit fornication, adultery, sodomy, and homosexuality. Your contribution ensures that runaway children and women will continue to be victimized and exploited by the porn industry. Your money actually goes to pay people for sinning and living in direct defiance to God. It is not very Christian like behavior to pay someone to break God's commandments, and my guess is that God would not approve of you doing such a thing.

By supporting pornography you become a stumbling block to your neighbor (Rom 14:21). The money you spend on pornography goes to produce more pornography, ensuring that pornographic magazines will continue to be readily available at many stores in order to tempt your neighbor into cheating on their spouses, fornicating with prostitutes, raping someone, or molesting children. These actions are not okay. How many women need to be raped or children molested before pornography is considered an unacceptable evil?

If you believe that you can handle pornography then you are deluding yourself. You are coveting and committing adultery in your mind. These are sins in both the Old and New Testaments of the Bible. Whether or not you personally are a rapist or a child molester by contributing your money to the porn industry you are contributing to such victimizations and crimes. Even if only a small percentage of those that use pornography actually commit sex crimes; any crimes at all are far too many. Would you be happy if only three or four members of your church were child molesters or rapists? Is that an acceptable number compared to the many members of your church that handle pornography acceptably?

Anyway you look at it pornography is wrong. If you support this industry then you are also paying for other sexual products to be created for homosexuals and other perverts. The pornography that you purchased you may delude yourself into believing is acceptable, but the money that you spent will also pay for butt plugs, dildos, blow-up sheep, homosexual videos, and many other types of sexual perversions and items that you more than likely would consider wrong. Regardless of how pornography causes you to personally lust and sin, by supporting it you are being a stumbling block to others. You are basically taking the money that God has provided you and donating it to the works of the Devil.

Nothing good can come from lust. When you cause your neighbor to covet, you bring disaster upon yourself. If you flaunt your blessings all that it does is cause your neighbors to covet what you have, and they will devise in their minds schemes on how they might take it for you. If you show off to your neighbors that you own a great or expensive item all you will do is cause your neighbors to covet. By showing off or boasting you cause your neighbors to resent you, they may then look for opportunities to rob you, or they may murder you for the items you boasted about.

Abraham's wife Sarah was very beautiful (Gen 12:14), and because of this, Abraham realized that as they traveled others would be willing to murder him to take Sarah as their own wife. Because of this Abraham lied to two different kings and claimed that Sarah was only his sister. After God commanded the second king to return Sarah to Abraham the king did as follows.

(KJV) Gen 20:16 And unto Sarah he said, Behold, I have given thy brother a thousand pieces of silver: behold, he is to thee a covering of the eyes, unto all that are with thee, and with all other: thus she was reproved.

The king gave Sarah 1,000 pieces of silver in order for her to purchase a covering. The king did this to rebuke Sarah for not wearing the wedding veil that was the custom of the day. If Sarah had been wearing such a veil there would not have been any problems. The king would have known Sarah was married and he would not have lusted after her. The king would not have seen Sarah's beauty behind the veil in order to begin lusting after her in the first place. If Sarah would have dressed appropriately and not gave cause for others to lust after her, then they would not have been in danger of being murdered over the covetousness of those around them.

(KJV) 1 Tim 2:9 In like manner also, that women adorn themselves in modest apparel, with shamefacedness and sobriety; not with broided hair, or gold, or pearls, or costly array;

Women are to dress modestly. This is for a good reason. If you do not cause others to covet or lust after you then you will be much better off. I understand that you might exercise and spend a great deal of time working on your body and achieving the beauty that you posses, but don't flaunt it. Don't give a rapist motivation to follow you home from the grocery store. Don't lose your job because your boss desires you more sexually than professionally. Work on your body, feel and be beautiful, but share your beauty with your husband and not with the entire world.

Presenting your beauty to everyone will only cause you problems. Other women will resent you and slander you. Your co-workers will stop looking at you as an equal, and will start looking at you like you were a piece of meat. Predators will covet you and you will be in danger of being raped, murdered, sold into slavery, or any number of other undesirable outcomes. Being cognizant of how your appearance may affect others is beneficial to your life. Causing others to lust or covet you is never a good thing. Sarah knew she was beautiful. She chose not to hide her beauty; she flaunted it, and it caused her trouble in more than one occasion. Dwell with prudence in this world, and walk circumspectly. Live cautiously and do not make yourself the target of other's sinful desires. You will be safer and more successful in this world because of it.

REFERENCES

Scripture taken from the KING JAMES VERSION OF THE BIBLE, (KJV) Public Domain 1611

Homosexuality

(KJV) Lev 18:22 Thou shalt not lie with mankind, as with womankind: it is abomination.

Homosexuality is considered an abomination before God. There is no way around that. This is clearly taught in both the Old and New Testaments of the Bible.

(KJV) Eph 5:3-7 But fornication, and all uncleanness, or covetousness, let it not be once named among you, as becometh saints; 4 Neither filthiness, nor foolish talking, nor jesting, which are not convenient: but rather giving of thanks. 5 For this ye know, that no whoremonger, nor unclean person, nor covetous man, who is an idolater, hath any inheritance in the kingdom of Christ and of God. 6 Let no man deceive you with vain words: for because of these things cometh the wrath of God upon the children of disobedience. 7 Be not ye therefore partakers with them. 8 For ye were sometimes darkness, but now are ye light in the Lord: walk as children of light:

(KJV) Col 3:5-6 Mortify therefore your members which are upon the earth; fornication, uncleanness, inordinate affection, evil concupiscence, and covetousness, which is idolatry: 6 For which things' sake the wrath of God cometh on the children of disobedience:

(KJV) Hebrews 13:4 Marriage is honourable in all, and the bed undefiled: but whoremongers and adulterers God will judge.

(MKJV) 1 Cor 6:9-10 Do you not know that the unrighteous will not inherit the kingdom of God? Do not be deceived. Neither fornicators, nor idolaters, nor adulterers, nor homosexuals, nor sodomites, 10 nor thieves, nor covetous, nor drunkards, nor revilers, nor extortioners will inherit the kingdom of God.

The word used for *fornication* in the in the above verses is the Greek word *Porneia,* which describes illicit sexual intercourse such as adultery, fornication, homosexuality, or intercourse with animals. The word *whoremonger* is the Greek word *Pornos,* also refers to homosexuals or male prostitutes. The above verses state that theses types of practices provoke God to wrath. These verses make it clear that homosexuals will not enter the Kingdom of Heaven.

Some modern churches attempt to diminish the sin of homosexuality, and make it seem as though it were only a minor sin because it is included in a list of sins with sins like *foolish talk*. Make no mistake about it, God considers homosexuality an abomination, and in the Old Testament it was a sin worthy of death.

(KJV) Deut 23:17 There shall be no whore of the daughters of Israel, nor a sodomite of the sons of Israel.

(KJV) 1 Kings 14:24 And there were also sodomites in the land: and they did according to all the abominations of the nations which the LORD cast out before the children of Israel.

(KJV) Lev 20:13 If a man also lie with mankind, as he lieth with a woman, both of them have committed an abomination: they shall surely be put to death; their blood shall be upon them.

In the Torah (Leviticus 20:13) the punishment for homosexuality was death. It was also due to the sin of homosexuality that cities of Sodom and Gomorrah were destroyed.

(KJV) Gen 19:5-7 And they called unto Lot, and said unto him, Where are the men which came in to thee this night? bring them out unto us, that we may know them. 6 And Lot went out at the door unto them, and shut the door after him, 7 And said, I pray you, brethren, do not so wickedly.

(KJV) Gen 19:24 Then the LORD rained upon Sodom and upon Gomorrah brimstone and fire from the LORD out of heaven; 25 And he overthrew those cities, and all the plain, and all the inhabitants of the cities, and that which grew upon the ground.

Christians do not follow the Law of Moses in the same way as the Hebrew people and because of this Homosexuality is not punishable by death in this modern world, but that does not alter the fact that God considers it a sin deserving of death. The New Testament reaffirms that those who practice such behavior will be condemned to hell.

Gays have been receiving more and more rights in the past few decades, and it has become politically correct to accept homosexuals as possessing an alterative lifestyle. Because of the changes in modern culture some liberal churches have even begun allowing homosexuals to be the pastors of their churches. Churches that condone such practices may claim to be Christian, but in reality they are severally confused in their basic definitions of Christianity.

Jesus taught to love your neighbor and not to judge them wrongly, but He never taught to allow or ever condone sin. Christians are supposed to obey the scriptures, and are to teach, reprove, and rebuke (1 Tim 4:2, Eph 5:11) sinners, especially among the brethren. Some modern day Christians mistake being politically correct with being a Christian. If you are a Christian then you must follow the teachings of Christ, which are opposed to homosexuality.

I understand that some homosexuals either believe or were enculturated to believe that they were born gay. I also understand that some gay couples are monogamous and love each other very much. As Christians we are not to judge anybody based on if we feel their lifestyle is right or wrong, but we are to follow the teachings in the Bible. Regardless of whether homosexuals are in love or not, or how natural they believe their lifestyle to be, it doesn't change the fact that they are living in perversion, and clearly in defiance to the Bible.

> **(KJV) 1Cor 5:9-13 I wrote to you in my epistle not to keep company with sexually immoral people. 10 Yet I certainly did not mean with the sexually immoral people of this world, or with the covetous, or extortioners, or idolaters, since then you would need to go out of the world. 11 But now I have written to you not to keep company with anyone named a brother, who is sexually immoral, or covetous, or an idolater, or a reviler, or a drunkard, or an extortioner-not even to eat with such a person. 12 For what have I to do with judging those also who are outside? Do you not judge those who are inside? 13 But those who are outside God judges. Therefore "put away from yourselves the evil person."**

As Christians it is not our duty to cast our pearls before swine and attempt to correct every sinner, but if there is a homosexual that is claiming to be a Christian then we are doing them a huge disservice if we allow them to believe that their lifestyle is okay.

It doesn't matter how natural it feels to them, their lifestyle is sinful, and they need to overcome their sins if they wish to follow Christ. Child molesters, necrophiliacs, and those who practice beastiality also don't see anything wrong with their behavior. As humans we must draw a line somewhere, and for Christians that line has been drawn for us in the Bible. If you have a homosexual in your church it is your duty to correct them using the scriptures. Show them the need for them to overcome their sins so that they might begin working towards doing so.

Culture may have changed, but the Bible hasn't. Homosexuality is still a sin. Everyone has sins in their lives that they must overcome. It doesn't make you into a prejudiced bigot for pointing out that someone is living a sinful lifestyle and needs to work at changing it if they wish to be a follower of Christ.

> **(KJV) Deut 22:5 The woman shall not wear that which pertaineth unto a man, neither shall a man put on a woman's garment: for all that do so are abomination unto the LORD thy God.**

The Bible also forbids cross-dressing and the practices of transvestites.

> **(KJV) Rom 1: 26 For this cause God gave them up unto vile affections: for even their women did change the natural use into that which is against nature: 27 And likewise also the men, leaving the natural use of the woman, burned in their lust one toward another; men with men working that which is unseemly, and receiving in themselves that recompense of their error which was meet.**

> **(KJV) Rom 1: 32 Who knowing the judgment of God, that they which commit such things are worthy of death, not only do the same, but have pleasure in them that do them.**

The Bible makes it clear that it is not only male prostitutes that are sinners, but also any person that has sexual relations with a member of the same sex. As Christians we are not to judge anybody based on our own opinions, but we are to follow the Bible. In the matter of homosexuality, we are not told to correct all homosexuals because of their lifestyles, but we are told to correct those in the church. We are also told that we are to know the judgments of God, and not condone behavior that we know contradicts the scriptures in our churches.

REFERENCES

Scripture taken from the KING JAMES VERSION OF THE BIBLE, (KJV) Public Domain 1611

Marriage and Divorce

Marriage is a holy union that was instituted by God. Marriage provides us with a unique opportunity to know and understand God's love as well as fulfilling our human needs.

> **(KJV) Gen 2:18 And the Lord God said, "It is not good that man should be alone; I will make him a helper comparable to him."**

> **(KJV) Gen 2:23-24 And Adam said, This is now bone of my bones, and flesh of my flesh: she shall be called Woman, because she was taken out of Man. 24 Therefore shall a man leave his father and his mother, and shall cleave unto his wife: and they shall be one flesh.**

Women were created to be helpers to men. It was not good that man should be alone. Man and woman are to be married and become one flesh. They are to be partners, work together in unison, and complement each other. They are to raise their children and face the world together. This is what God intended.

> **(KJV) Ecclesiastes 4:9-12 Two are better than one; because they have a good reward for their labour. 10 For if they fall, the one will lift up his fellow: but woe to him that is alone when he falleth; for he hath not another to help him up. 11 Again, if two lie together, then they have heat: but how can one be warm alone? 12 And if one prevail against him, two shall withstand him; and a threefold cord is not quickly broken.**

The partnership between a husband and wife allows them to be more successful in each of their specific roles this world. Men and women may perform different jobs or fulfill different roles in life, but the support they offer each other is invaluable. They offer each other courage and comfort, they pick each other up when they fall, and two heads are better than one in regards to problem solving and making decisions in this life.

> **(KJV) 1 Tim 5:14 I will therefore that the younger women marry, bear children, guide the house, give none occasion to the adversary to speak reproachfully.**

Men are to work and provide for their families. Men are to protect their families and provide for their food and shelter. Women are charged with managing their households. They are to guide the house and raise their children. Husbands and wives are to be one flesh with each other, and work together in unison in regards to raises their families.

> **(KJV) Eph 5:22-24 Wives, submit yourselves unto your own husbands, as unto the Lord. 23 For the husband is the head of the wife, even as Christ is the head of the church: and he is the saviour of the body. 24 Therefore as the church is subject unto Christ, so let the wives be to their own husbands in every thing. 25 Husbands, love your wives, even as Christ also loved the church, and gave himself for it;**

Wives are to submit to their husbands as unto the Lord. Many modern women who are living in this age of women's rights might find the above verses offensive, but there is no reason to be offended. Women are to be subject to their husbands, as the church is to Christ. This does not mean that women are not equal partners in the relationship nor does it diminish their status as one flesh. All that has taken place is that men have been given the responsibility of guiding and overseeing their partner's actions. The church is one body of believers in Christ (Rom 12:5), but Christ is the head of the church. Christ was willing to sacrifice His life for the church; in the same way men need to be prepared to lay down their lives in defense of their household. Christ is not a dictator, who desires to control the church, but wishes the church to share the same goals and desires as Him and His father. Husbands are to listen to their wives and support them in their ideas. Christ likewise said that if we ask anything in prayer in His name He will do it. The same way that Christ will grant the church (Christ's bride) its requests that are in accordance to God's will, husbands should do the same for their wives.

If a wife asks her husband to do something that is contradictory to the Bible then this is where the husband is to use his authority to correct his wife in her error. If the wife sets a goal for herself or desires something that does not contradict the Bible, then her husband should be willing to support her in her endeavors. Marriage is about supporting each other and each other's ideas. Husbands and wives are partners and are to work together in one accord.

> **(KJV) Eph 22:28-33 So ought men to love their wives as their own bodies. He that loveth his wife loveth himself. 29 For no man ever yet hated his own flesh; but nourisheth and cherisheth it, even as the Lord the church: 30 For we are members of his body, of his flesh, and of his bones. 31 For this cause shall a man leave his father and mother, and shall be joined unto his wife, and they two shall be one flesh. 32 This is a great mystery: but I speak concerning Christ and the church. 33 Nevertheless let every one**

of you in particular so love his wife even as himself; and the wife see that she reverence her husband.

Spouses are to love the their partners as they love themselves. They are not to be selfish, but are to support and make sacrifices for each other.

(KJV) 1Cor 7: 2-5 Nevertheless, to avoid fornication, let every man have his own wife, and let every woman have her own husband. 3 Let the husband render unto the wife due benevolence: and likewise also the wife unto the husband. 4 The wife hath not power of her own body, but the husband: and likewise also the husband hath not power of his own body, but the wife. 5 Defraud ye not one the other, except it be with consent for a time, that ye may give yourselves to fasting and prayer; and come together again, that Satan tempt you not for your incontinency.

Another important aspect of marriage is the sexual relationship. When you get married your body no longer belongs to you, but belongs to your spouse. You no longer have the freedom to control your own body. Your body belongs to your spouse. This does not mean that husbands own their wives, but that both husbands and wives do not have permission to use their bodies for fornication. Once you are married you are not authorized to have sexual relationships with anyone other than your spouse without their permission. Of course they cannot give you permission, to do so would be in violation of God's commandments. Husbands and wives are to have sexual relations with each other to prevent them from be tempted into fornicating and committing adultery.

Both husbands and wives are entitled to sexual satisfaction. If the wife is not equally satisfied with the sexual relationship then the husband failed to provide his wife with the means to avoid fornication specified in the Bible. Of course if a husband fails to satisfy his wife one time that does not give her liberty to commit adultery, but the husband should make every effort to fulfill his responsibilities in the marriage. To do this husbands and wives need to have open communication in regards to their sexual needs. Husbands and wives are partners and should work together at all of their goals, including each other's sexual satisfaction.

(KJV) Proverbs 5:18-19 Let thy fountain be blessed: and rejoice with the wife of thy youth. 19 Let her be as the loving hind and pleasant roe; let her breasts satisfy thee at all times; and be thou ravished always with her love.

Husbands are to be satisfied with their wives and are to remain faithful to them. Adultery is a sin discussed throughout the entire Bible. It is included in the Ten Commandments, and in the Old Testament was punishable by death.

(KJV) Hebrews 13:4 Marriage is honourable in all, and the bed undefiled: but whoremongers and adulterers God will judge.

(KJV) Lev 20: 10 And the man that committeth adultery with another man's wife, even he that committeth adultery with his neighbour's wife, the adulterer and the adulteress shall surely be put to death.

(KJV) Deut 22:22 If a man be found lying with a woman married to an husband, then they shall both of them die, both the man that lay with the woman, and the woman: so shalt thou put away evil from Israel.

Marriage is a serious commitment. Adultery is not punishable by death in the New Testament, but God's intention for it to remain a holy and undefiled union has not diminished. It is clear throughout the Bible that adultery is one of the biggest betrayals and worst sins that you can engage in. Husbands and wives are to be one flesh and their bodies actually belong to the other person. Adultery is one of the worse betrayals possible. By committing adultery you are betraying your own flesh, you are destroying a holy bond, and you will devastate the person that loves and trusts you the most in this world. If you have children then you betray them as well, and take away many opportunities from them. You will set a poor example for your children and damage their future relationships. If adultery leads to divorce then your children will also miss out on a great deal of guidance. Their parents won't be acting as one team in the best interest of their families, but will be living selfish and sinful lives, fulfilling their own needs and making their children suffer the consequences of their actions.

(KJV) Mt 5:31-32 It hath been said, Whosoever shall put away his wife, let him give her a writing of divorcement: 32 But I say unto you, That whosoever shall put away his wife, saving for the cause of fornication, causeth her to commit adultery: and whosoever shall marry her that is divorced committeth adultery.

(KJV) Mt 19:3-9 The Pharisees also came unto him, tempting him, and saying unto him, Is it lawful for a man to put away his wife for every cause? 4 And he answered and said unto them, Have ye not read, that he which made them at the beginning

made them male and female, 5 And said, For this cause shall a man leave father and mother, and shall cleave to his wife: and they twain shall be one flesh? 6 Wherefore they are no more twain, but one flesh. What therefore God hath joined together, let not man put asunder. 7 They say unto him, Why did Moses then command to give a writing of divorcement, and to put her away? 8 He saith unto them, Moses because of the hardness of your hearts suffered you to put away your wives: but from the beginning it was not so. 9 And I say unto you, Whosoever shall put away his wife, except it be for fornication, and shall marry another, committeth adultery: and whoso marrieth her which is put away doth commit adultery.

Jesus stated that the only acceptable reason to get divorced is in cases of fornication. Christians are not allowed to get divorced simply because they do not like each other anymore, or because they have different goals. The truth is that husbands and wives are to be one flesh; they should have the same goals and be working in one accord. Christians should not get divorced for any other reason than fornication. Any other reason that Christians are contemplating getting divorced over should be handled through communication. The couple should work out their differences. Both partners need to be willing to compromise. Marriage is a cooperation between two people, it is not the time or place to be selfish. Women need to be humble and submit to the authority of their husbands, and husbands need to be willing to sacrifice themselves for the well being of their wives. Both partners are required to compromise. They need to work out their differences and work together as a team.

(KJV) 1 Cor 7:10-14 And unto the married I command, yet not I, but the Lord, Let not the wife depart from her husband: 11 But and if she depart, let her remain unmarried, or be reconciled to her husband: and let not the husband put away his wife. 12 But to the rest speak I, not the Lord: If any brother hath a wife that believeth not, and she be pleased to dwell with him, let him not put her away. 13 And the woman which hath an husband that believeth not, and if he be pleased to dwell with her, let her not leave him. 14 For the unbelieving husband is sanctified by the wife, and the unbelieving wife is sanctified by the husband: else were your children unclean; but now are they holy.

Christians are not supposed to get divorced, but if they do then they are to remain unmarried. If a Christian is married to a non-believer and the non-believer wants to stay with them then the Christian is obligated to stay in the marriage.

(KJV) 1 Cor 7:15-17 But if the unbelieving depart, let him depart. A brother or a sister is not under bondage in such cases: but God hath called us to peace. 16 For what knowest thou, O wife, whether thou shalt save thy husband? or how knowest thou, O man, whether thou shalt save thy wife?

If a Christian is married to a non-believer and the non-believer wants out of the marriage then a Christian is allowed to get divorced for a reason other than fornication.

(KJV) 1 Cor 7:39 The wife is bound by the law as long as her husband liveth; but if her husband be dead, she is at liberty to be married to whom she will; only in the Lord.

When a Christian is married they are married for as long as they both shall live. Once one of the spouses dies the other spouse in free to remarry, but only if they marry another Christian. This is because the earlier scenarios are assuming the person became saved after they were already married to a non-believer. Christians are not to marry someone that worships a different God than they do. This is just common sense. How do you expect to be one flesh and share the same goals as another person if you don't even have the same God in common?

(KJV) Deut 24:1-4 When a man hath taken a wife, and married her, and it come to pass that she find no favour in his eyes, because he hath found some uncleanness in her: then let him write her a bill of divorcement, and give it in her hand, and send her out of his house. 2 And when she is departed out of his house, she may go and be another man's wife. 3 And if the latter husband hate her, and write her a bill of divorcement, and giveth it in her hand, and sendeth her out of his house; or if the latter husband die, which took her to be his wife; 4 Her former husband, which sent her away, may not take her again to be his wife, after that she is defiled; for that is abomination before the LORD: and thou shalt not cause the land to sin, which the LORD thy God giveth thee for an inheritance.

There is no going back. If you chose to get divorced and your ex-spouse marries another then you are never allowed to be together again. If Christians get divorced then they are to remain unmarried unless they return to each other (1 Cor 7:11). If their ex-spouse marries someone else then the union is over forever.

REFERENCES

Scripture taken from the KING JAMES VERSION OF THE BIBLE, (KJV) Public Domain 1611

About The Author

Daniel E. Loeb is a non-denominational Christian. He has studied Hypnosis, Leadership, and the Bible for over a decade. He completed his hypnosis training at the Hypnosis Training Institute of Central California in 1992. He has since worked as a Hypnotherapist in private practice, performed hypnosis stage shows, and taught hypnosis and Behavioral Modification internationally. He possesses a Bachelors degree in Psychology, and is currently a graduate student in Homeland Security and Emergency and Disaster Management. He served in Operation Iraqi Freedom as an NCO in 2004. He is happily married and the father of three. Daniel Loeb is a Christian, a Father, a Scholar, a Teacher, and a Patriot. For more information go to;

www.danloeb.com

Dwell With Prudence Publishing

Dwell with Prudence is dedicated to providing fellow Christians with information that will either allow them to live wisely or cautiously. The goal of Dwell With Prudence Publishing is not to make money, but is to provide Christians with information/resources to protect their families, assist them in serving God, or to give them every advantage in navigating the challenges they may face in this world.

Dwell with Prudence is not aimed at saving souls. We believe there are many good Christians working at saving the lost. Dwell with Prudence wishes to help those who are already Christians by providing additional resources that they can use to be successful in this world as they raise and protect their children. As Christians it is our duty to guard and protect our families while raising our children to be followers of the Lord. It is an evil world that we live in, and it is full of dangers. Our children are going to have to face these dangers by themselves, and later teach their own children to do the same. Dwell with Prudence wishes to assist Christian families in acquiring life skills in order to give them every possible advantage in this world until our Lord returns for us.

We do not spend a lot of money on advertising because our goal is not to become rich, but to provide information. We do however need to charge enough money for our products, to allow for their creation and distribution. We make our books available to everyone, but we are not concerned about advertising to reach everybody. If God wants someone to have the information we provide then He will lead them here, or prompt others to share this website or book with their loved ones. You are not reading this by accident. If God has led you to this site or placed this book in your hands, then it probably contains something valuable to you in your particular Christian walk.

For more information on Dwell With Prudence or to see a list of available products go to;

www.dwellwithprudence.com

Be Ye Transformed:

Christianity, Hypnosis, and Behavioral Modification - So, you have decided become a Christian. Now what do you do? When you become a Christian you become a new creation, and the entire Christian faith is judged by your actions. The Bible provides specific standards that Christians are to live by. Behavioral Modification is of key importance to both new and mature Christians. This book explores behavioral modification, willpower, and leadership from a Biblical perspective, and also covers the techniques used by man. This book teaches how to use hypnosis in conjunction with other techniques to assist you in modifying your behavior. This is a comprehensive study of techniques of motivation and mental influence. Some topics covered are: Hypnosis, Spirit vs. Flesh, Leadership, Classical and Operant Conditioning, Aversion Therapy, Systematic Desensitization, Implosion Therapy, Motivation, Conflict Resolution, Weight loss, Smoking Cessation, Power Learning, Subliminal Messages, Propaganda, Logical Fallacies, Brainwashing, Mind Control, and a study of the Trinity.

This book is the Companion Manual to Be Ye Transformed: Christianity, Hypnosis, and Behavioral Modification. This book provides instructions for using the Behavior Modification Software associated with this book, which can be installed from the Internet using the link provided with in. This software provides multiple applications than can be used towards your behavioral modification goals. The program contains multiple dieting resources used to calculate your weight loss progress. It includes a Calorie Counter, and a counter based on the Food Pyramid. The Weight loss section calculates your Percentage of Body Fat, Body Mass Index, and projects the date you will reach your goal weight. The program also allows you to set audible alarms, and can be used to track an exercise program or other behavioral modification goal. Strategies are provided for using Aversion Therapy to stop smoking, and for creating and administering a Behavior Contract to be used with troubled teens. The program uses a Text-to-Speech engine to read the resulting data out loud. The CD-ROM version of the software (sold separately) also contains five hypnotic inductions or audio recordings, and contains both this book and the book "Be Ye Transformed" in electronic format.